FROM PASTA TO PAVLOVA

Studies in Society and Culture

General Editors:

Jeremy Beckett
and
Grant Harmon

FROM PASTA TO PAVLOVA

A Comparative Study of Italian Settlers in Sydney and Griffith

BY RINA HUBER

University of Queensland Press

© University of Queensland Press,
St. Lucia, Queensland, 1977

Set by Academy Press Pty. Ltd., Brisbane
Printed and bound by Silex Enterprise & Co.,
Hong Kong

Distributed in the United Kingdom, Europe, the
Middle East, Africa, and the Caribbean by Prentice-
Hall International, International Book Distributors
Ltd., 66 Wood Lane End, Hemel Hempstead, Herts.,
England

National Library of Australia
Cataloguing-in-publication data

Huber, Rina.
    From pasta to pavlova.

    (Studies in society and culture series).
    Index.
    Bibliography.
    ISBN 0 7022 1410 8.

    1. Italians in Australia. 2. Australia —
    Foreign population — Social aspects. I. Title.
    (Series).

    301.45150944

For
FELIX,
JULIE, DAVID, and ANNE

CONTENTS

INTRODUCTION

An inner suburb of Sydney called Leichhardt is sometimes
referred to as "Little Italy". To the outsider it might appear
that most people who live there share sentiments, attitudes,
and beliefs; in other words, that it is a community. The place
was once an old Australian suburb, but since the war many
changes have taken place. Italian immigrants began to
regard it as a stepping-stone in their new environment. They
did so because industry was close at hand and houses cheap.
In the 1960s Italians bought almost every dwelling that came
on the market in the area.

Initially, I had hoped to conduct a study of women in a
community but soon discovered that Leichhardt, after all,
did not constitute a community in the sociological sense of
the word. There were virtually no second-generation Italians
other than young children. Priests, real estate agents,
lawyers, and many others agreed that few families remained
for longer than five to ten years. Most of them moved to
more prestigious suburbs. Because the population is made
up of transients, therefore, all I could say was that Leichhardt housed many immigrants, a large proportion of whom
were Italian. The exact number, however, was unknown.
Electoral rolls were of little use as many of the people were
not naturalized. Furthermore, household heads were also
reluctant to disclose the correct number of people living in
the dwelling, and the census was, as a result, equally unhelp-
ful. A lawyer, a real estate agent, and a priest each gave me
10,000 as a rough estimate of the number of Italians living
there. An official of the municipality told me that whereas
on paper it would appear that Leichhardt had fewer residents than before, in fact the number was much greater.[1]

Italian shopkeepers, lawyers, doctors, dentists, pharmacists, and real estate and travel agents, who generally
lived elsewhere, worked in the area. They took advantage of
the fact that most Italian immigrants, because of difficulty in
communicating in English, preferred to transact affairs in
their native tongue.

In the early stages of my research I lumped together all
who came from Italy under a blanket term. I was aware of
the sense of separation that exists between Northerners and
Southerners but not of the extent of the animosity. Nor did I
have any inkling of the intra-regional jealousies: Piemontesi
versus Veneti, Calabresi versus Siciliani, and so on. Such op-
positions were contextual: a number of Southerners faced
with a Northerner closed ranks, but if the Northerner left,
then the divisions reappeared. These immigrants felt most at
ease with people they could call *paesani*, those who had come
from the same small region or village.[2] Some Northerners
assumed an air of benevolent condescension to others, and
some wanted to dissociate themselves, saying, "They are
not really Italians!"[3] Southerners, on the other hand, tended
to be touchy about their origin. When I asked a real estate
agent where he came from he said, "Just a few miles south of
Rome." It turned out, in fact, that his village was near the tip
of Calabria.

Although a number of professionals and real estate agents
were helpful with general background information, they
were not hopeful about my chances of entering the homes of
Italian women, let alone establishing a rapport with them.
They admitted, however, that my speaking Italian would be
of immense value. The greatest help came from a priest. He
gave me detailed information about a number of families
and paved the way by first telling the women about me and
asking their permission to bring me to see them. No doubt
he chose carefully for he had no refusals. He was almost
always present during the first interview, and told the
women that I was from the university and that I wanted to
write a book about Italian women.[4]

I started visiting these women during the day when they

were either alone or with their small children. They welcomed me and seemed happy to have someone to talk to, though at first some of them could not make me out. One asked the priest whether my husband was a pensioner, another whether he was so bad at his work that he needed to send me out to earn extra money. Only after a few visits did they accept me as a sympathetic listener. At the home of a woman who came from Rome I frequently met a Polish girl who was married to a labourer from Treviso, which is part of the Veneto, a region in Northern Italy. Through her I established contact with several Trevisan families who then introduced me to some of their friends.

We started most interviews with generalities that invariably led to the women's problems: loneliness, inability to communicate in English, and nostalgia. Why, I asked, did they feel so lonely and isolated with so many Italians around? It became clear that although they had Italians living next door, or one floor above or below, they talked only when it was essential to do so. The main reason was that where people came from different regions old prejudices were as rife as they had been back home. On the whole, social interaction was restricted where possible to *paesani*, and even here nuclear families tended to build a protective wall around themselves and view outsiders with suspicion.

Gradually I realized that indiscriminate meetings with women unrelated to each other who came from all parts of Italy were not producing fruitful results. I decided, therefore, to curtail the size of my universe, and to study one specific group in depth, choosing respondents who had some interaction with each other. I concentrated on a group of Trevisani who had come from the same socioeconomic background, migrated to Australia at about the same time, and settled into an urban industrial environment. Some lived in Leichhardt, others not far from there. In this way I hoped it would be possible to study patterns and attitudes more clearly.

Occasionally these Trevisani talked with obvious envy about *paesani* who were farmers in Griffith.[5] This aroused my curiosity. If life was so wonderful in Griffith, why did they not go there? This opened up a completely new avenue in my work—a possible comparison between Trevisan migrants living in an urban and a rural environment. I decided, therefore, that on completion of my study of a small number of Trevisan families in Sydney I would visit others in Griffith, about 650 kilometres[6] away, and investigate any differences between the two groups. From this then the study evolved.

From Pasta to Pavlova reports my study of two groups: Trevisani in Griffith and in Sydney. In it I hope to show, first of all, the significance of social and economic factors in the development of patterns of settlement of these immigrants, and secondly, to suggest that people find it easier to settle in a new country if traditional customs and institutions can be adapted or reconstructed to dovetail with new ones.

Migration loosens traditional bonds and constraints, and many institutions are either abandoned or changed. In a new country the choices are not only more numerous but also different from those offered in the place of origin. It is important, therefore, that we look at the core institutions in Treviso in depth and then see whether these were abandoned, reconstituted, or modified in rural and in urban Australia. Having done this we can then compare and contrast the social patterns that evolved in Sydney and in Griffith with each other and also with those conditions which existed in Treviso.[7]

In comparing the settlement of Trevisani in Griffith and Sydney I will not be directly concerned, therefore, with answering such question as, how do these Italians interact with Australians? How quickly are they absorbed? At what stage do they become indistinguishable from the indigenous population? Adaptation is obviously a two-way process between the migrants and the host society, and ideally I should also discuss the latter. I have not done so because I did not carry out systematic fieldwork among Australians who lived nearby or worked with my Trevisan respondents.

To understand the total situation of immigrants we must

first look into their background and the reasons for their migration. An immigrant who leaves his native land because of political or religious persecution ranks his priorities differently from one who migrates to improve his economic status. The former is likely to plan a lengthy or permanent stay, the latter may view the move as temporary—say ten or fifteen years—during which he hopes to work hard and save in preparation for a return. With the person who comes primarily for financial reasons, it is important for us to be aware of the conditions and opportunities prevailing in both his country of origin and in the country to which he migrates. The economic situation of the region from which he emigrates will in part dictate whether he is likely to contemplate going back. This in turn affects his attitudes to the old and new social, cultural, and economic institutions. A new view of himself and of the world around him evolves.[8]

The traditional agricultural organization in the Italian region of the Veneto, of which Treviso is a part, resembled most closely what anthropologists and sociologists call a peasant economy. People who participate in this kind of life-style are generally referred to and regard themselves as peasants. I have refrained from using the term as freely as I would have liked because to many it has pejorative connotations.[9] Most of the time I shall speak of the people of Treviso as rural workers, labourers, agriculturalists, villagers, or small farmers.

Most villagers from this region had only between one and five years schooling. The regularity of attendance as well as the standard of education was poor, so that for all practical purposes many were virtually illiterate even after a few years at school. Children of wealthier small farmers, however, who attended several years of high school, no longer belonged to the category of their elders, as, for example, boys who became priests.

Modern communication and the mass media have accelerated the breakdown of traditional life and stimulated aspirations to a life-style moulded by urban values. Post-war industrialization and later the European Common Market improved communications, and the greater facilities for travelling in Europe and overseas stimulated the economy. For the first time the material goods displayed on the television and movie screens were brought within the people's grasp. As the cultural generation gap among villagers widened, so the rural-urban gap closed. Core institutions were modified but did not disappear.

Most of these rural labourers however, were either unaware of, or unable to claim their rights. Indeed, patronage systems of various kinds rely and thrive on the inability of these people to fend for themselves. Neither education nor wealth necessarily give power, but power is easier to wield with one or both of these attributes.[10] Most peasants have neither, and thus face numerous difficulties when migrating to an urban centre, be it within their own country or outside it. Innumerable problems arise from their inability to use, understand, or cope with the governmental and public institutions of an industrial society. I refer in particular to agencies such as banks, insurance offices, lending societies, social welfare institutions, health funds, workers' compensation, pensions, taxation departments, and trade unions. This difficulty can be related, I think, to lack of formal education. When migrating outside their country, however, they face the additional handicap of coping with a new language.

In Treviso, it had been customary for men who were not needed in the extended household to cross the Alps for seasonal work. Many travelled back and forth further afield, to the Americas, Africa, and Australia. Some remained abroad, sent for their wives and children and so frequently started a chain migration. Such was the beginning of the Italian settlement in Griffith in the early 1920s.

Throughout my fieldwork in Griffith I concentrated primarily on the Trevisani, or Veneti as they sometimes call themselves. In this study I will be discussing other Italians or Australians only in so far as these impinged on this group. As we shall see, the patterns of settlement and of interaction among the Trevisan families in this area were unlike those of rural communities in Italy. These differences resulted from a number of factors, many of which were conducive to the establishment of institutions similar to, but not the same as, those of Treviso before World War II. The main factor, however, was the land-tenure system of the Murrumbidgee Irrigation Area.[11]

In the 1920s and 1930s jobs were difficult to find in Australian cities, and the majority of immigrants were forced to seek work on the land. The original handful of Trevisani who settled in Griffith sent for their families and friends, and so started chain migrations. In spite of the animosity they encountered, the majority, surrounded by kin and fellow countrymen, planned to stay. Starting as labourers on farms owned primarily by Australians, they soon aspired to become commercial farmers. The first step was to lease land and grow vegetables.

The land-tenure system in the irrigation area limited the size of a farm a man could own, to what was considered adequate to support an average nuclear family under normal conditions. This size was called a Home Maintenance Area (H.M.A.). An additional stipulation of the Water Conservation and Irrigation Commission (W.C. & I.C.) which controlled the area was that only one nuclear family could live in the homestead. This was to prevent an extended household from settling on a farm too small for its support. Land was not partible and on the death of the owner the property went to one heir only. If there were several claimants it had to be sold and the money divided. The restriction generally meant that when a man accumulated sufficient surplus to contemplate enlarging the holding, he bought another farm in the name of a son, starting with the eldest. Ideally then, if he had two sons he aimed to buy three farms, one for himself and one each for them. If he had only daughters he was content to have just one place. The result was that most sons stayed on the land and technically owned their own establishments at an early age, often before they married. Here is the probable reason why so few Trevisani entered the professions. The usual tensions between father and adult sons were reduced, and the relationship resembled that of a partnership more than of a hierarchy. Sons did not have to wait until the father died to acquire a share in the farm but needed his financial support to buy one.[12] This, of course, would not have been possible had Australians been unwilling to sell their farms.

For Veneti who came from extended families, with the endemic inter- and intra-generational friction, Griffith offered the best of both worlds. They became commercial farmers, had their own farms, and lived in nuclear households. Telephones and cars enabled them to be in close touch with their near relatives.

With the continuous influx of Trevisani, their percentage of the total population increased as well as their concentration on horticultural farms close to the centre of the town. Although the average distance between farms was often less than a kilometre, communication improved with the years, and gatherings of relatives presented few problems.

Socially there was little communication between Australians and Italians. Before the 1950s it was difficult for them to join Australian clubs. In the late 1930s, therefore, they started a centre where they could meet at weekends, an adaptation of the Italian *osteria* or *trattoria*.[13] This was the beginning of the proliferation of clubs and of the lively social scene so unlike other country towns in New South Wales.

The manner in which Trevisani in Griffith established themselves contrasts sharply with the behaviour of the group who settled in Sydney. Unlike the depression years before the Second World War, when there was little work in the cities and men were forced to go onto the land, the post-war years ushered in an era of high employment. On disembarking men were able to find work almost immediately, collect pay after a few days, and so avoid the uncertainties of farming life. Many came as assisted immigrants but had no firm intention of staying; indeed their attitude was like that of north Italian seasonal workers who each year crossed the Alps. There was little or no chain migration, and nobody had more than a couple of relatives living nearby.

Although I met many Trevisani in Sydney, I restricted my intensive study to eight families, all in the early stages of settlement. The original aim of most was to work hard for a number of years, save, and then go back home where they hoped to build and furnish a house, buy a car, and take a job that would enable them to live in comfort. Letters kept them in touch with the latest news and developments, and they were well aware of the new industries that had opened up job opportunities in Treviso, the industrial regions of northern Italy, and the Common Market countries.

Difficulties in Sydney resulted not only from the strange environment but also from the immigrants' background, which did not equip them to cope with the institutions of a metropolis. The loneliness of the women, their inability to communicate in English and dearth of friends and relatives within easy reach, aggravated the nostalgia, and increased their sense of uncertainty and marginality. Inevitably there was little role segregation in the home, and the husband and wife assumed what Goffman called "a conspiratorial aura" vis-à-vis the outside world. They became more dependent on each other and discussed their plans with little outside help; certainly, they rarely admitted that they had sought or taken anyone else's advice. Their goals altered with each stage of settlement, and accompanying these changes were shifts in dominant reference groups, that is, both the group to which they belonged as well as the group to which they aspired.

When they returned to Treviso after the initial stay in Australia, the close husband-wife relationship, now established over a number of years, made family interference intolerable. None wished to establish or live in an extended household. Once the honeymoon of the family reunion, the presents, and the conspicuous consumption was over, disillusionment accompanied the realization that as unskilled workers in Treviso they could not earn enough to live in the manner to which they had become accustomed in Australia. Their standard of living would have been lower than that of their skilled compatriots in Italy. It was at this stage that they re-migrated, now with a positive attitude, to a country they already knew. The trip to Treviso and the return to Australia assumed the importance of a *rite-de-passage*. The urban setting in Sydney, however, did not encourage the reconstituting of old traditional institutions as in Griffith.

From the studies in Sydney and Griffith, we can see the influence of social and economic factors on patterns of settlement, and on the likelihood of reconstituting core institutions resembling those of Treviso. This in turn affected other facets of life of the immigrants.

NOTES

1. Statistical information given in the Department of National Development's publication *Atlas of Australian Resources: Immigration*, p.18, indicates that 9.3 per cent of the 53,520 Italians in metropolitan Sydney in 1966 lived in Leichhardt. This would give an approximate figure of 5,000 or half the number suggested above.
2. *Paesano* comes from the Italian word *paese*, a term that can be used for village and country. It is used to refer to someone who comes from the same town or region.
3. See Oswald Bonutto's *A Migrant's Story*, especially p. 64.
4. This priest was of Lebanese descent and spoke Italian. He was extremely kind to the women who came to him for help, generally concerning immediate problems such as illness or death in the family. He was not, however, regarded as a regular confidant. None of the women I met through him came from Treviso.
   For details of fieldwork methods see appendices 2 and 5.
5. Griffith is a town in the Murrumbidgee Irrigation Area which is part of a region known as the Riverina, in south-western New South Wales.
6. All measures (weights, areas, distances) have been converted into metric notation, even where these occurred in the reported conversation of the respondents.
7. As S. Eisenstadt points out in *The Absorption of Immigrants*, p. 18:
   " ... usually a transformation of such customs and values takes place. Instead of their being universal and binding, as in the country of origin, they become, in the absorbing country only alternatives or specialities and have to be readjusted and redefined ... "
8. Again quoting from Eisenstadt, ibid., p.4:
   " ... the analysis of the immigrant's motives for migration and his consequent 'image' of the new country is not of historical interest

alone, but is also of crucial importance for understanding his attitudes and behaviour in his new setting."

9. There is little agreement among anthropologists on the definition of peasants. To date writers have agreed on two points only: a peasant society is a part society of a wider whole, and agriculture is the main occupation. R. Redfield (*Peasant Society and Culture*, p.20), G.M. Foster ("Interpersonal Relations in Peasant Society", p. 174 and "What is a Peasant? ", p.6), and E. Friedl ("Lagging Emulation in Post-Peasant Society", p.57) stressed the cultural aspect; E. Wolf (*Peasants*, p.10) and R. Firth (*Elements of Social Organization*, p.87) the economic or political. Redfield (p.20) and Wolf (p.13) excluded landless labourers, J. Lopreato (*Peasants No More*, p.40) included them. O. Lewis ("Some of My Best Friends are Peasants", p.180) excluded craftsmen, Foster (p.183) included them but unlike Firth (p.87) not fishermen.

10. Friedl, writing about Greece ["Lagging Emulation in Post-Peasant Society", *American Anthropologist* 66, no.3 (June 1964):572] said, "Commerce and trade are viewed with ambivalence; merchants and traders have low prestige but it is recognised that if they are wealthy they have power. White collar jobs and the professions, however, are unquestionably highly valued, with teaching, law, medicine, and the higher ranks of the priesthood in the forefront. Jobs in the government bureaucracy are considered very good indeed, and villagers whose sons have attained such positions are much respected."

11. I shall follow the argument Silverman used in her article on agricultural organization and social structure ("Agricultural Organization, Social Structure, and Values in Italy: Amoral Familism Reconsidered") in which she compared central and southern Italy. One of the main points was the importance of the land-tenure system in influencing social relationships. In his study of an Italian village, Pitkin also stressed the effect of the land-tenure system on family organization. (See D.S. Pitkin, "Land Tenure and Family Organization in an Italian Village", p.60.)

12. This differed from situations where young men moved out to claim frontier or virgin land. For a discussion of this see E. Wolf, *Peasants*, p.74 and H. Miner, *St. Denis: A French Canadian Parish*, p.86.

13. An *osteria* is an inn or tavern, or the local pub. A *trattoria* is also an inn but with an attached restaurant or eating house.

PART I
ITALY

AGRICULTURE IN ITALY

Over the past 100 years agricultural properties in Italy have been characterized by two extremes: large estates (*latifondi*), frequently owned by absentee landlords, and excessively fragmented small plots.[1]

Before the land reforms of 1950 as much as 17 per cent of the area under private ownership consisted of properties of two hectares or less, 31 per cent of properties of five hectares or less.[2] By 1955 the proportion of properties of the latter size had increased at the expense of the large estates. Nevertheless, very small holdings still prevailed. Thus although the reforms of 1950 increased the proportion of farms of less than twenty hectares as against those of 200 hectares and over, few were in the middle range of 50–200 hectares.

The Italian National Institute of Agrarian Economics distinguished five main types of farm enterprise: the first is the independent working farmer who owns his land, manages the farm, and contributes his own manual labour and that of his family; the second is basically the same as the first, but here the farmer does not own his land: he is a tenant paying fixed rent either in cash or in kind; the third is a share-tenancy (*mezzadria*) where the farmer and his family work the mixed farm as a unit and the size of the holding is adjusted by the entrepreneur (who generally owns but sometimes rents the property) to the size of the family labour force. The larger the work force the family can offer, the larger the property they are given to sharecrop. Until recently the entrepreneur and the share-farmer or *mezzadro* shared the produce equally. The fourth type is also a form of share-tenancy, but the arrangements are looser than the third; the contract covers only one or two plots and relates only to the sharecropper himself, not to the family. The fifth or last type is the loosest form of sharecropping arrangement. Here the sharecropper attends either to certain tasks connected with specialized tree cultivation, or to all the work connected with single field crop. In return he receives anything from one-quarter to one-half of the crop concerned. The duration of the contract is usually for less than one year. Wage labourers frequently fall into this category of sharecropping.

In an analysis of the distribution of arable and productive land according to the type of farm enterprise carried out in 1956, it appeared that the small farmer or peasant who depended primarily on his family for help was the most widespread. Forty per cent of all arable land in Italy was farmed by owner-peasants. Proprietary and tenant farmers together worked about 60 per cent of the arable land. If we include the *mezzadri*, then about 80 per cent was made up of family farms. Wage labour worked about one-eighth.

My concern here, as I have mentioned, is with the province of Treviso in the Veneto, a zone with family farms lying on the fertile slopes of the Alps and plains. Following the classification of the National Institute of Agrarian Economics of the different types of farm enterprises, types one, two and three are the ones most commonly found in this region.

THE VENETO

The Veneto is a region in the north-eastern part of Italy bounded by Venezia Giulia, Austria, the Trentino (or Alto Adige), Lombardia, and Emilia. Lake Garda forms part of the boundary with Lombardia. Venice, the capital, is situated on the eastern coast.

The Veneto may be divided roughly into four geographic zones: the littoral, the plains, the foothills (or pre-Alps), and the Alps. About 34 per cent of the province is mountainous, 17 per cent foothills, and 49 per cent plains. Apart from Venice, the principal towns are Verona, Vicenza, Padua, Rovigo, and Treviso, all situated on the plains.

The foothills rise towards the Alps along a line from the south-west to the north-east, reaching their peak in the Dolomites, at the northern sector of the Veneto. The plains extend from the south-west to the north-east section, from the Po to the Livenza River in the north. The Po, Italy's largest river, spills into the Adriatic. The other most important rivers are the Adige, Bacchiglione, Brenta, Sile, Piave, Livenza, and Tagliamento.

ILLUSTRATIONS AND TABLES

MAPS

FIGURES

TABLES

PREFACE

Between 1947 and 1974 just over 2,562,000 people migrated to Australia, of whom about 271,000 were Italians. They make up the largest single non-English-speaking group to have settled in this country.

Although a number of general works have been written on Italian immigrants, I was anxious to carry out research dealing more directly with the women. I felt that as a woman I was in a better position to establish rapport with housewives and thus shed light on some hitherto unconsidered aspects of migration.

I hope, therefore, that the results of my investigations will be of interest to social and child guidance workers, teachers, hospital staff, and others concerned with immigrants. With such people in mind, I have concentrated in this book more on the ethnography than on the theoretical implications of my findings.

ACKNOWLEDGMENTS

This study is a revised version of my M.A. (Honours) thesis presented to the Department of Anthropology, University of Sydney, in 1972. The fieldwork was carried out in the years 1968–70. I have, however, added two postscripts, one written in 1972 and one in 1974, to round off the stories of two families, one of whom returned to Italy.

I wish to thank my supervisor, Dr. Jeremy Beckett for his encouragement and advice, Professor Chandra Jayawardena for his suggestions and penetrating criticisms, and Dr. Arnold Goldman and Mr. Greg Woodburne for their help in redrafting sections of the manuscript. My deepest gratitude, however, is to Professor Ian Hogbin who first stimulated my interest in anthropology, and who has at all times been a friend, guide and mentor. His tireless efforts editing this work and teaching me to write clearly have been invaluable, and for this I thank him.

My work would not have been possible without the trust of the people about whom I write. They permitted my intrusion, confided in me, and gave me much of their time. To the families in Griffith with whom I lived, I am grateful for allowing me to share in the warmth of their homes and experience some of the joys and frustrations of rural life. My promise to these friends in Sydney and Griffith that they would remain anonymous prevents my acknowledging them individually.

I also wish to thank Don Erasmo Pilla of Fonte Alto, who helped me contact many relatives of Trevisani I knew in Sydney. During my two brief stays in Treviso, both he and the people I visited showered me with kindness.

My special thanks go to the Hon. A.J. Grassby, whose dedication and concern for immigrants dates back very many years. I shall always be extremely grateful for the advice and friendship he so generously gave me.

Finally, I wish to thank my family for their infinite patience.

Sydney April, 1975   R.H.

Province of Treviso

In 1931 the total population was 4,123,267, 58 per cent of whom lived mainly in villages and towns and 42 per cent in dispersed homesteads in the countryside. Thirteen per cent lived in the three largest centres, Venice, Verona, and Padua, each of which had a total of over 100,000 inhabitants.[3]

There are eight provinces in the Veneto, but I am concerned with only one of them, Treviso.

Treviso had been part of the Republic of Venice for over four hundred years when Napoleon forced the Doge to abdicate in 1797. From 1814 until the unification with the rest of Italy in 1866 Venice was part of Austria.

Treviso is situated in the midst of the fertile plains, covers an area of 2,477 square kilometres, and is divided into 95 communes. Its capital, the town of Treviso, is thirty kilometres from Venice and has today a population of approximately 75,000. Other centres are: Vittorio Veneto (population 26,000), Castelfranco Veneto (22,000), Conegliano (22,000), Montebelluna (17,000) Oderzo (13,000), and Asolo (7,000). In 1931 the population of the province was about 560,000; thirty years later it had risen to 608,000.[4]

IDENTIFYING CORE FEATURES

What are the core features of this traditional society? What are the elements which, if altered, would bring about major changes throughout the rest of the social structure? To facilitate comparison between the Italian and the Australian experiences of the Trevisani, it is essential that these features be isolated. Furthermore, we must look closely at the question of whether a change in feature A is likely to produce significant changes in features B,C,D, and E and also whether a change in B, C, D, and E is likely to effect radically or only superficially changes in A.[5]

In Treviso, for example, a change in the agricultural organization radically altered the use of leisure time. The gradual move from a peasant-type economy towards an industrial one gave young people employment alternatives that made them less dependent on their elders. Social and geographic mobility increased; many newlywed couples were able to establish nuclear households and to buy cars. The new wealth affected, among other things, traditional patterns of recreation such as church *feste* and the social circles centred on the *osteria*. Although these forms of pastime by no means disappeared, they became less important and competed with such activities as driving to the mountains or the seaside, or visiting friends further afield. It is unlikely, however, that a modification in *feste* or facilities in the *osteria* would have radically affected farm organization. For this reason farm organization must be seen as a core feature while *feste* or the *osteria* are not.

Similarly in Griffith the prevailing form of agriculture, and the manner of distribution of the farms in a circle around the centre of town, created an environment that encouraged clubs. Yet it is unlikely that a change in the clubs would have radically altered the form of farming. In other words it is this particular type of agricultural economy and not the club which must be seen as a core feature of the society.

I shall compare the core institutions of Trevisani in Griffith and in Sydney with those of Treviso before and after the war in order to demonstrate the nature of the changes.

Analysing the changes will enable us to understand the new patterns of settlement and distinguish between conditions that favoured or discouraged the adaptation, reconstitution, or shedding of old institutions. Although it may be tempting for us to call some of the adaptations assimilation, we should do this with caution because they must also be related "to the metamorphosis which immigrants' lives undergo by the very fact that they migrate and settle with fellow countrymen who have not recreated a community to receive them, like that from which they came".[6]

The complexes in which traditional institutions were embedded in Treviso existed in a new way in Griffith. Both the economy and the type of residence encouraged the reconstitution and adaptation of some of the institutions. These conditions did not prevail in Sydney.

CORE INSTITUTIONS OF PRE-WORLD WAR II TREVISO

In the introduction I stated that the aim of this study was to look at the core institutions that formed the framework of the social structure of the small farmers' and agricultural labourers' life in Treviso and to examine whether, or to what extent, these have persisted, been shed, or adapted in a rural and an urban setting in Australia.

To do this it is essential to describe first the core features of Treviso as they had been for many generations before World War II. This entails a description of the economic system based on agriculture, and of the peasants or small farmers, pointing out those aspects that directly affected their lives. These features, as we shall see, were principally the extended household, the lack of formal schooling, the strong church influence, the primary associations, the dispersed settlement of homesteads and villages, and the influence of seasonal and overseas migration on the social structure. Having looked closely at these we can then move on to examine the changes that have occurred in each of these features since World War II.

The economic system

Treviso was primarily a zone of small-farmer or peasant holdings, with the extended family as the working unit, until after World War II. There were a number of big estates and villas, however, and relationships between some large landlords and peasant families continued over several generations. I have not been able to discover from the literature the part played by the wealthy landowners, but, from the impressions of respondents from *mezzadrie* who had had contact with landlords or heard stories about them from their parents, I would judge that they were not as important here as in other parts of Italy.[7]

Customary rules of inheritance required that the land be equally divided among sons, and with each generation the farms became more fragmented. The girls did not inherit real estate or cash. The 1930 census of the Veneto revealed that there were 433,974 farms in an area of 1,106,300 hectares. More than half were owned directly, the rest rented or leased. One-third of the properties ranged from five to twenty hectares. The largest farms tended to be in the hilly grazing region.[8]

The people engaged in the production of maize, wheat, grapes and other fruit, silk, and pigs, and on the slopes above they grazed cattle and sheep. Work routines changed with the seasons. The hardest periods were at sowing and harvest. The men laboured as a team under the direction of the head of the household. Those in employment in the vicinity helped with the farm when they returned home in the evening. Whatever these men earned went into the family purse. It was the women's duty to look after the vegetable garden and farmyard animals, but during the sowing and harvesting they joined the men in the fields and frequently toiled from dawn until midnight. Although this system of agriculture resembled that of a self-sufficient economy, the proximity to larger centres stimulated trading in the surplus.

To make a living a family could simultaneously own, rent, and sharecrop plots and also send out some of the men as labourers to other people's properties. In spite of the fragmentation the extended household worked the land as a unit. If there was not enough to feed everyone, the family structure enabled some of the men to migrate for several months of the year across the Alps secure in the knowledge that their wives and children would be adequately cared for. They returned home during the winter months when their employment came to an end. Earnings went into the communal purse held by the head of the household, the oldest married male. Some men migrated for long periods to North or South America, North Africa, or Australia; others sold their share of the land to those left behind and departed for good.

Thus the push and pull of the land-tenure, kinship, and seasonal-migration systems dovetailed, ensuring the viability of the total structure.

Small farmers and agricultural labourers

These people referred to themselves and were regarded by the rest of society as peasants (*contadini*). The extended household in which they lived, the extent of formal education they had had, their associations, and the church dictated their way of life.

i] *The extended household* People lived in patrilineal extended families, in one or more long stone buildings facing a courtyard enclosed by sheds. The latter were used as stalls and stores for equipment and fodder. The entire establishment was known by the family name. The houses were generally divided into several identical sections not unlike a terrace, each occupied by an extended family closely related to the

21

one next door. A woman told me that when she was a teenager about sixty relatives lived in three buildings around the courtyard. The interior of each family apartment consisted of a large kitchen that served as the communal room. In the middle stood a table and a number of benches. A fuel stove occupied one wall, and there was no electricity or running water. Drinking water came from the village fountain, sometimes up to two kilometres away, and washing water either from a well on the land or a running stream nearby. The women washed the laundry in the river.

Ideally each nuclear family had a room of its own. Several people slept in one bed, but if there were more children than the room could accommodate, the girls shared a room with female cousins and the boys went into the loft. Many men complained about how cold it was and how they tried to seal the cracks with paper. Privacy was virtually unknown, and there was also much gossip. One respondent told me she had fourteen female cousins of about her age who were constantly quarrelling, usually about boys.

Courting started at about twelve or thirteen, and girls were frequently pregnant before marriage, but this did not carry the same stigma as in the South. Although they were supposed to be chaperoned, in fact they had greater freedom than in many other parts of Italy.[9] Many were engaged several times before marriage. Before an engagement the girl's father visited the priest in the boy's village to find out about his reputation, and generally the priests were truthful. The bride and groom were usually about the same age; one of my respondents hesitated before marrying her husband because he was eight years older.

Marriages were occasions for festivity. The number of guests depended on the financial position of the family, and it was not unusual to have as many as eighty present. The ceremony took place in the morning and was followed by a meal and dancing. The most popular season was after the harvest, when the worst of the year's work was over, and money was there to spend. The girl did not have a dowry but was expected to have a trousseau (*corredo*) consisting of underwear, bedlinen, an eiderdown, a mattress, and a dressing table. Men preferred to wait for marriage until the trousseau was ready. Although fashion goods such as frocks were seldom part of it, clothing supposed to last for many years was included. One of my respondents had accumulated forty-two brassieres, twenty-eight nightdresses, and thirty-six pairs of underpants. After her first baby, when she had put on several stone, she stored the garments in a big trunk, much to the chagrin of her friend whom they would have fitted.

After marriage the women went to live with the husband's family (patri-virilocal), and, as one woman remarked, the life of slavery then began (*vita di schiavitu*). Within the family the eldest male dominated and controlled the financial arrangements, but the eldest wife was in charge of the daughters-in-law and, above all, of the food and kitchen. There was a strict hierarchy, and the eldest son had authority over the younger and was also the first to marry. Ideally the eldest daughter was supposed to be the first girl to marry, but things did not always work out this way. It was the exception rather than the rule for girls to get on well with their mothers-in-law. A man who showed his wife affection was ridiculed, but he was expected to demonstrate love for his mother. Within the household and kitchen the eldest wife reigned supreme. Men never helped with the children or lent a hand in the kitchen. If the wife was ill, other women took over her duties.

Life in the village and at home was fraught with quarrels, arguments, tensions and gossip. One woman recalled how her grandmother locked up all the food in order to control its distribution. She kept the bread to make crumbs, which she mixed with water for the babies. A younger child had preference over an older when it came to food. The older children lived on a slice or two of *polenta* (a kind of maize pudding) and a hard boiled egg. When it was a question of food, the needs of the very young and of the very old were considered before all else. Only here then, was there no strict hierarchy. Wives frequently fought over the way their

Fig. 1. Typical countryside in Treviso province.

Fig. 2. Vineyard in Treviso.

Fig. 3. An old courtyard house where extended households lived. Old people live here now. Young people move out when they marry.

Fig. 4. An old *trattoria* where people met, played cards, and enjoyed a drink.

Fig. 5. A loft where men used to sleep when it was too crowded inside the house.

Fig. 6. A kitchen which has been used for many generations of extended households. Now only an old couple use
.

mother-in-law allocated the food, arguing that their child was unfairly treated. Many were hungry for a good deal of the time. Husbands did their best to avoid taking sides when their wives and mothers quarrelled but when forced to do so generally sided with the wife "otherwise they would have had to pay for it in bed".

Children turned to their mother rather than father for help and affection. The ties binding mother and son were particularly strong and lasting. Adult males, young and old, often shed tears in front of me when talking about the sacrifices their mothers had made for them.

The poverty or relative wellbeing of extended families depended on such factors as whether they owned the land, rented it, sharecropped it, or had none at all; and on how many children there were. If a man had only daughters, then on his death the land was sold and the money divided among them. No man worked his wife's family land; he would have been ridiculed and called someone whose wife wears the trousers (*cappellano*). Obviously an only son was better off than one with several brothers. When men worked as labourers they gave their earnings to the father or head, who then returned them pocket money. If they wanted to buy something expensive the father or grandfather went with them. As soon as there were more men than could be usefully occupied at home, some migrated. Where food became really short the daughters went into service, preferably nearby, but if this was not possible then further afield, and sent all their earnings home, visiting the family once a year. Such girls returned with a knowledge of a more refined way of life (*una vita più fine*). Generally, however, an older girl's experience of the outside world was limited, and her courting and relationships with boys were different from those of her younger sisters. One young woman said, "I did anything I liked because I was the youngest; my parents were too old and sick to chaperon me. I went out to work and had plenty to eat. My eldest sister is twenty-four years older than I and went to school for just a year. I went for five. My sister used to tell me that it'd be impossible for me to imagine what life

was like when she was little, it was so terrible. My grandmother ruled everybody with an iron fist. I don't remember
her well. By the time I was ten both grandparents had died,
and my parents were head of the house. My older brothers
and sisters were working and giving their earnings to my
father, so I was never hungry, and life wasn't bad. They all
spoiled me, especially when my parents sent me to chaperon
my sisters and their boy friends. The boys bought me sweets,
and I'd run off.''

The extended family acted as a haven in times of need, but
relations were fraught with tensions, mainly because of the
virtual total overlap of home and work situations. The code
of behaviour was rigid, imposing such strongly enforced
constraints, that there were almost no alternatives for the
dissenting other than permanent migration. It was an
egalitarian peasant society where each family was interested
in maintaining or improving its economic status. There was
little social or economic mobility.[10]

When the father died and sons inherited the land they
often stayed and worked together for a number of years
under the direction of the eldest. As children grew up and
there was not enough land or money to feed them adequately the quarrelling became more bitter, and one or more
nuclear families split away from the extended household.
Sometimes one brother bought out another and started his
own extended household, or perhaps he migrated permanently overseas.

Unlike conditions in the south of Italy, where godparent
or patron-client ties were extremely important, in the
Veneto they were insignificant. None of my informants
could recall having heard of children of peasant farmers or
rural workers becoming professionals, apart from the few
who entered the priesthood.

ii] *Education* The kind of life a child led and the education
he received depended on order of birth and number of
brothers and sisters. The eldest of a large family was likely to
have the worst time. An eldest girl who had to look after the

0747538

younger children, wash the nappies, and attend to other household chores shouldered a burden almost as heavy as her mother's. She did not attend school for more than one or two years. An eldest son also had a minimum of formal education. He joined his father in the fields as soon as possible or went with him across the Alps for seasonal work.

Before World War II few people completed five years of primary school. Most attended for one to three years and learned to read and write, but what they learned was frequently soon forgotten. Even when they understood the implications, they disliked filling in forms, negotiating contracts, borrowing from banks, or dealing with institutions that required even a minimum of sophistication on their part. They were not only ill-at-ease and suspicious, but, a point that cannot be overstressed, they also avoided situations where they could lose face. They preferred transacting deals orally with someone they knew.

iii] The church The church had an all-embracing hold on the people's lives; it influenced every sphere. The priest was the most powerful man in the commune, and his word was law.[11] He told people how much of their crop they had to donate to the local parish, how to vote, and when to marry. Some priests were stricter than others, and people frequently chose to confess to one who was less exacting or reputed to have a "wide sleeve" (*di manica larga*).

Each commune had a church, and on the day of the patron saint the congregation organized a festival (*festa*). Every family attended ten or twelve each year, taking the opportunity to visit friends and relatives in neighbouring places. Young people looked forward to these occasions and planned for them especially during the summer months when they could dress in finery, meet young people from other villages, and flirt.

iv] Associations From my respondents I gathered that there were few voluntary associations as we know them, although Macdonald wrote, "The Pre-Alps had collective economic organisations like its neighbour in the High Alps, but its economy relied more heavily on the family as a production unit."[12] Everyone knew everyone else. People met as relatives, neighbours, age and sex mates, drinking and card-playing partners, and so on. These made up the primary groups. There was overlap of roles, and the emotional content of the relationships resembled more closely those of primary rather than secondary groups. The primary group was widely spread.

Church festivals, religious holidays, and *rites-de-passage* were the only occasions when the husband, wife, and children went out as a family. Men met regularly on Sunday afternoon at the inn (*osteria* or *trattoria*), played cards, Italian type bowls (*bocce*), and drank. The women stayed at home or visited their mothers, daughters, sisters, and cousins.

The winter was the quiet period and the time when most seasonal workers were at home. During the long evenings young people congregated in the barns, which were warm and, therefore, the most comfortable of their surroundings. They pushed the cows and other animals to one side, cleared the dung, and sat on stools, boxes, or the hay, and talked and sang by the light of a kerosene lamp or a candle.

It is to this kind of intimate association and to summer *feste* that people refer with pangs of nostalgia when they are a long way from home.

The settlement

Villages were dispersed. In the centre of each there was little more than a shop or two, a church, a school, and an inn. The homesteads were built on farms surrounding the centre of the village. Some were within a few minutes' walk of each other and the centre, others may have been half an hour's walk away. The close-density living of unrelated people, a feature of the southern agrotowns, was unknown.

In 1931 about half the population of the province of Treviso lived in scattered homesteads throughout the ninety-five communes. Four hundred and thirty-eight centres were situated in the plains, 188 scattered in the hills nearby. Of the 438, only 153 (about one-third) had a population totalling more than 500.[13]

Fields separated villages, but young people walked or cycled to visit each other. By "my village" a person meant the one in which he was born, and it was to this that he felt sentimentally attached; it formed the core of his *campanilismo*.[14]

Migration

i] *Seasonal migration* For the past 80–100 years and perhaps even longer seasonal migration has been an accepted means of subsidizing the family economy. The yearly move across the Alps to France, Germany, and Switzerland acted as an in-built safety valve that was turned on or off and adjusted to the needs of each individual extended family.

According to Alberoni:

> For the most part it was a question of temporary emigration of agricultural workers from Piedmont and Venetia, going to carry out certain agricultural work in France or Germany, and to these were added the masons and builders bound for France, Germany, and Switzerland. The emigrants were predominantly male. The Venetian and Piedmontese peasants went abroad for a certain period of time, leaving their parents or their wife and children behind in Italy. In general they already knew where they were going, what work they were to do, and also how much they would earn and could expect to save. Sometimes they were away only at certain periods of the year when they would otherwise have been unemployed, returning when there was a demand for labour. Even small-holders sometimes went away at certain seasons, leaving the household and the women to do the small amount of work required. They could not have been said to be "looking for work"—even less "seeking their fortune". There is little or nothing in this type of emigration of the idea of risking one's livelihood: the level of expectations was never exaggeratedly high, and the financial calculations, although rough and ready, always formed the basis of the decision. Thus separation from the family since it was temporary, did not have the dramatic overtones which we shall see making their appearance in overseas emigration.[15]

ii] Overseas migration Overseas migration was different in kind and expectation. There were broadly two types: those who left with the intention of settling permanently, preferably in rural or new frontier areas—they either took their families or sent for them in due course—and those who intended to spend a number of years away, return, and perhaps repeat the performance before finally settling at home. Some of the latter did in fact settle permanently overseas and start off chain migrations.[16]

Macdonald quoted emigration figures for the period 1902–13 for various parts of Italy, differentiating between transoceanic and total emigration rates.[17] Table 1 shows figures for the Veneto. Seasonal migration was a crucial variable in the social structure, affecting and affected by the other core features.

Table 1. Emigration from the Veneto, 1902–13

	Transoceanic emigration rates, 1902–13	Total emigration rates, 1902–13
Veneto	4.5	35.4

Note: As Macdonald points out (p. 455), "Transoceanic rates are the percentage of the population . . . which emigrated to transoceanic countries over this period. Total emigration rates are the percentage of the population . . . which emigrated to European, Mediterranean and transoceanic countries over this period."

SOURCE: J. S. Macdonald, "Italy's Rural Social Structure and Emigration", *Occidente* 12 (1956): 455.

ITALY: THE POST-WAR RECOVERY

For Italy the post-war years proved to be a watershed socially, economically, and politically. True, in no country in Western Europe was life the same after the war as before; but there was in Italy an accelerated rate of change. The most important, immediate, and dramatic effect was the replacement of a dictatorship by democratic government.

The economic growth rate, the movement from

agricultural to industrial occupations, and the rise in the per capita income were all factors that could be evaluated quantitatively. The social changes occurred more slowly and were harder to pin down. Certainly the level of consumption and rise in standard of living could be measured, but on the whole the changes were qualitative. These followed on new methods of production, increase in opportunity, and a general broadening of the sphere of interaction.

Most statistics that recorded changes in post-war Italy used figures for the early 1950s and the early 1960s to demonstrate the contrast, and it is to these that I shall refer. As I am concerned primarily with continuous trends the fact that I have but few figures for the immediate pre- and post-war years is not of crucial importance.[18]

As a result of demobilization, the return of prisoners, and reduced economic activity unemployment was increasing alarmingly. According to 1946 statistics, over two million were registered as out of work.[19] Between 1901 and 1950 Italy's economic progress showed a per capita income increase of 62 per cent, and in the ten years 1950–60 the figure was 47 per cent.[20]

The most obvious change was the movement from agriculture to industry. As table 2 indicates, in 1952 the highest percentage of the working population was engaged in agriculture, but by 1962 those in industry and other occupations had outnumbered those engaged in rural labour. This was the result of a massive exodus from the land to the industrial triangle of Torino, Genova, and Milano. Many enterprises, handicapped by a shortage of skilled workers, tried to induce those who had emigrated abroad to. return. (See table 3.) Table 4 shows that spending on consumer goods such as food, beverages, tobacco, clothing, housing, health, transportation, communication, culture, and recreation almost doubled between 1953 and 1961.

This economic change had profound effects on the social and political life of the country. Many who would have preferred to stay on the land did not have the money to buy stock or equipment to start producing again. The return of

Table 2. Italy: movement from agriculture to industry, 1952–62

	Agriculture	Industry	Tertiary
1952	7,663,000	5,728,000	4,681,000
1962	5,430,000	7,991,000	6,368,000

SOURCE: G. Mammarella, *Italy after Fascism: 1943–65*, p. 346.

Table 3. Italy: emigration and return of workers

	Emigration of workers to foreign countries	Return of workers to Italy
1957	341,733	163,277
1958	255,459	139,038
1959	268,490	156,121
1960	383,908	192,235
1961	371,611	207,132

SOURCE: G. Mammarella, *Italy after Fascism*, p. 347.

Table 4. Italy: consumer spending, 1953–61 (in billion lire)

1953	8,532
1958	11,294
1959	11,810
1960	12,777
1961	13,800

SOURCE: G. Mammarella, *Italy after Fascism*, p. 347.

men who had been away during the war and the high birthrate swelled the rural population. Shortage of food gave added impetus to the exodus from the land and disrupted the traditional agricultural system, affecting in particular the large estates that had previously relied on the agricultural labourers and sharecroppers.

With constant expansion in the industrial complexes, men with technical skills found little difficulty in securing jobs, but for former rural workers who had no other training it was not easy to find suitable occupations under reasonable conditions. For these men emigration offered many attractions and was an answer to post-war poverty and their inability to compete with skilled workers.

CORE INSTITUTIONS OF POST-WORLD WAR II TREVISO

During World War II Treviso suffered badly. Many of the men were called up, and others who were eligible fled to the hills. The villages and fields were left in the hands of old men, women, and young children. Much of the land was untended, and communities that at best lived close to the breadline now had to adjust to semi-starvation.

Those who were old enough remembered the terror of those years. Bombardment and atrocities were commonplace. Fascists and Germans shot and hung anyone suspected of being communist or anti-fascist, but towards the end of the war the tables were turned, and partisans executed the collaborators. Many of the big landowners were also killed.

Although the cessation of hostilities in 1945 brought an end to the massacres, the late 1940s and early 1950s were years of hardship and re-adjustment.

Changes in the traditional structure, the shift from the peasant or small farming society, prised individuals loose from their families and communities, and the core institutions had to accommodate new circumstances. Let us now turn to these changes.

The economic system

After years of neglect, the land could not support all the people returning from the army and the prisoner-of-war camps or from hiding. Money and patience were required to tide families over till the first harvest. Young men began to leave in vast numbers to seek work elsewhere. To start the economy moving, the government and its agencies undertook such projects as road-building and water and electricity schemes for the bigger centres.

Landlords who survived the war, realizing that the labourers, tenants, and *mezzadri* were no longer willing to tolerate the demands and conditions imposed on them, were keen to sell. Thus, new opportunities and a widening of horizons also spelt the beginning of the end of the *mezzadria* system. The 1950s saw the introduction of industry into Treviso, particularly to those regions with good communications. The European Common Market opened up further avenues for work in the mid 1950s.

Table 5 demonstrates the shift from agriculture to industrial and other non-agricultural work in the years 1951–61. It shows a decrease of 20.87 per cent of people engaged in agriculture and increases of 15.14 per cent of those engaged in industry and 5.73 per cent of those engaged in service occupations such as hotels, garages, and restaurants.

Table 5. Province of Treviso: shift from agriculture to industry

	Total active population	% in agriculture	% in industry	% in other occupations
1951	273,166	49.63	30.87	19.50
1961	248,249	28.76	46.01	25.23
		- 20.87	+15.14	+5.73

SOURCE: Province of Treviso, *Dati Sommari,* pp. 21 and 23.

Whoever could do so purchased land, some with remittances from relatives abroad, others with money accumulated doing seasonal or construction work. They bought as fast as areas became available, and the prices soared. Some wished to continue as agriculturalists; others just wanted to build a house, keep a few chickens, and grow vegetables on an area that the wife could tend while the husband was employed in industry nearby. Here he worked fixed hours for a secure wage without investment in land or dependence on a landlord.

Inheritance practices remained unchanged, but the custom of brothers working the land together as a unit after the father's death altered. Although before the war units such as these ultimately broke up, after the war the fission occurred much sooner. Where possible the elder bought out the younger, who either migrated or shifted into a non-

33

agricultural occupation. Sometimes a man sharecropped the land belonging to a brother who worked elsewhere.

After the war most households were no longer the basic peasant-type multi-purpose social units. Whereas before most aimed to produce as many of their needs as possible, with a lesser emphasis on production for the market, those who wished to remain on the land now started crop specialization. Thus a definite shift occurred from a peasant or small farming economy to one stressing commercial farming.

Small farmers and agricultural labourers

Improved communication and contact with the world beyond the village environs altered the traditional culture. New opportunities and incentives for training and earning encouraged greater social mobility than ever before. Many tenants and sharecroppers who had accumulated enough, either through remittances from migrant members of the family or through their own efforts, bought land and became owner-cultivators. Some who already had a little land increased their holdings. Sons of those who remained on the land expected to become commercial farmers (certainly not *mezzadri*), or to continue with their education. Those who had acquired some technical training joined the socially mobile, but men who had neither land nor skill became rural or urban labourers.

i] *The extended household* Although we might still find a few extended households that included two or more married sons utilizing their land as a group, they were the exception. These existed most frequently in regions far removed from the larger centres. I refer particularly to the north-west, to such places as Cavaso del Tomba, Possagno, Castelcucco, Fonte, San Zanone, Monfumo, Paderno del Grappa, and Crespano from whence many of my respondents came.

Where previously acceptance of the extended family, and the hierarchy within it, was unquestioned, industry and the facilities for migration now offered new alternatives, especially to young people. Even where men would have preferred to remain on the land, there was not enough to go round.

Within each family more and more combined working at a job during the day with helping on the farm after hours. Wages earned outside went to the head of the household, who then, as before, gave each member pocket money; now, however, the young men expressed resentment. With the change in occupation came a move to nuclear households. Although most young people in the 1950s and 1960s lived in an extended household while still single, it gradually became usual for only one or at most two married sons to stay on in the paternal home. The rest at marriage moved into their own nuclear establishment. Earnings from steady employment, coupled with the possibility of girls working in factories, shops, and restaurants, enabled young couples to plan for a home and material comforts away from the criticism of the husband's mother and other relatives.

The extended household tended to persist in special circumstances, as, for example, when there were only two sons to inherit an economically viable property. Again, some men who left for seasonal work liked to feel that their children or whoever was left behind would be well looked after in the large household.

A few married women left home temporarily and worked in hotels and restaurants during holiday periods. Such employment had not been readily available before the days of the European Common Market and newly found affluence.

Dependence on the older generation lessened. Girls no longer worked for years accumulating a trousseau. Earnings from the factory or hotel enabled them to buy garments that previously took months to sew and embroider. A change also occurred in the husband-wife relationship. Although, to use Elizabeth Bott's terminology, the two were not as "joint" as they were found to be among immigrants in Sydney, they were not as "segregated" as they had been in the extended household.[21] The young wife demanded greater freedom of action at the expense of her mother-in-law. Limitation on the number of children and increased earning capacity altered the expectation of the younger generation.

ii] Education A significant factor, one that is impossible to overemphasize, is the importance of the increase in quality and duration of schooling. Even though education was compulsory before World War II, the law was not only difficult to implement, but villagers were unwilling to allow a child to stay at school when he could be useful at home. Today, people realize that education is the key to improved life-style.

I have no figures for earlier years, but looking at the differences between 1951 and 1961 we find the following: the illiteracy rate of those over the age of six fell from 5.4 per cent to 3.2 per cent and the number of university graduates increased by approximately 50 per cent. But most significant is the approximate 85 per cent rise in the number of students who completed eight years' schooling and attained a Junior Certificate. Tables 6 and 7 indicate the shift in greater detail.

An example of the concern shown by one priest for the education of young people and indirectly for the church was that of Don Erasmo Pilla of Fonte. In the mid-1950s he realized that something had to be done to ensure that the boys moving off the land were equipped with a trade—to prevent them from becoming labourers and, as he put it, communists. He started a technical school for mechanics, electricians, plumbers, and other tradesmen. After a number of years, and in the face of much opposition from the parents, he introduced courses for girls at the same school. They trained as secretaries, machinists, and so on. Today the school is highly regarded, and both parents and children are grateful. In Don Erasmo Pilla's opinion only through progressive and positive action such as this, rather than repressive threats of hell, could the church retain its influence and prevent the spread of communism.

iii] The church The widening horizons, increased mobility, and greater range of alternatives changed the relationship of the local church to its parishioners. The priests no longer

Table 6. Province of Treviso: formal education and illiteracy distribution graph, 6 years of age and over (1951–61)

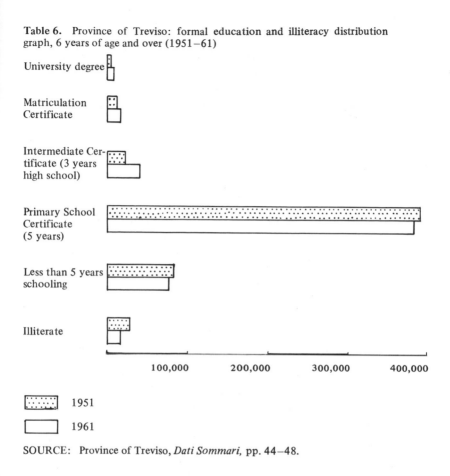

SOURCE: Province of Treviso, *Dati Sommari,* pp. 44–48.

dictated without being questioned. Doubtless there were others besides Don Erasmo Pilla who had sufficient insight and understanding to conclude that the church must alter its approach to meet the new challenge if it was to retain some degree of authority. Today, in spite of the fact that the church has less influence than before, the Veneto is still a stronghold of the Christian Democratic Party.

37

Table 7. Province of Treviso: distribution of educational standards, 6 years and over (1951 and 1961)

	University graduates		Matriculation Certificate		Intermediate Certificate (3 years high school)		Primary School Certificate		Total		Less than 5 years school		Illiterate	
	M F	M	M F	M	M F	M	M F	M	M F	M	M F	M	M F	M
1951	2,741	2,315	12,475	6,919	21,141	13,178	395,520	193,337	431,877	215,749	82,890	38,988	29,120	11,7:
1961	4,069	3,302	15,825	8,518	38,503	24,122	391,158	187,309	449,555	223,251	79,943	37,316	17,749	7,3:
	+1,328		+3,350		+17,362		-4,362		+17,678		-2,947		-11,371	

SOURCE: Province of Treviso, *Dati Sommari*, pp. 44–48.

iv] Associations Cars, scooters, and relative affluence improved communication and allowed greater freedom of choice not only in work but also in the enjoyment of free time. Many industrial workers in particular, now took their wives and children to the seaside, the mountains, or to visit friends and relations in other villages. Church *feste* and local inns were not as all-important for social interaction as they used to be.

The definition of who was a neighbour or *paesano* widened. Greater segregation of home and work roles took place, and with this came a narrowing of the primary and a widening of the secondary groups. Those who lived in the village but travelled to jobs in industry straddled two worlds and experienced the advantages and disadvantages of both. The younger adjusted, but the old were baffled by the changes and disintegration of so much that they knew.

The settlement

With increasing demand for nuclear family housing, fields were broken up into small blocks. Where previously it had been easy to see where one village ended and another began, today the built-up areas along a main road are continuous. Many migrants revisiting their homes find difficulty in recognizing familiar places. There are now more shops, restaurants, inns, cinemas, schools, garages, and other facilities associated with modern living. Distances that were once measured in walking time are now referred to as so many minutes' drive.

Migration

i] Seasonal and permanent European migration The advantages offered by industry in Italy and Common Market countries were so great that fewer and fewer Trevisani migrated overseas. Men and women still availed themselves of the opportunities for seasonal employment, but where work was permanent, many nuclear families moved for good and returned to their native village only for holidays. These migrations, unlike the old seasonal movement, were outward looking and hastened social change.

ii] Overseas migration Before the war, overseas migration meant heavy expense and being a long way from home in terms of distance, time, and money. Since the early 1950s, with assisted passages, availability of work, and the possibility of saving large sums of money quickly, travel to another continent no longer connoted a virtual separation from family for very many years. It was possible to return home even from Australia after two years without refunding the fare. In other words, a man could come to Sydney with a similar attitude to that of his father migrating seasonally across the Alps. Tables 8 and 9 show the population trends in Treviso.

Table 8. Province of Treviso: shift in population (breakdown of age groups)

	0–6 years	6–14 years	14–21 years	21–25 years	25–35 years	35–45 years	45–55 years	55–65 years	Over 65	Total Resident Population	Average Age
1951	68,913	91,179	76,925	44,468	86,079	83,794	66,921	47,278	47,243	612,800	31.82
1961	60,369	80,739	71,425	40,495	85,978	75,706	77,633	59,217	56,054	607,616	34.29

SOURCE: Province of Treviso, *Dati Sommari*, pp. 7 and 9.

Table 9. Province of Treviso: increase in population, 1962–66

1962	612,878
1963	623,079
1964	631,156
1965	636,890
1966	642,136

SOURCE: Province of Treviso, *Dati Sommari*, pp. 18–19.

The break-up of traditional groupings, which, of course, often accompanies poverty, war, and famine, stimulated emigration, especially overseas.

THE WORLDS OF ANTONIETTA AND GRAZIA

The following two short biographies of the early lives of two women now living in Sydney highlight material discussed earlier. Antonietta's story approximates more closely to life before the war, Grazia's to life afterwards.

Antonietta: "I was born in Fonte, a village close to Treviso, in 1933. I was the third of seven children, three boys and four girls. Although it was compulsory to go to school, my elder sister and I went for only two years because my parents couldn't afford to pay for the books. My younger sister went for five years and the youngest for eleven years.

My family was very poor. We were *mezzadri* who paid monthly rent and also gave half the produce to the landlord. There were three houses around our yard (*cortile*). Each was inhabited by one of the three sons of great-grandfather and their sons, unmarried daughters, daughters-in-law, and grandchildren.

In our house we had three main bedrooms, and each married couple and their children occupied one; but we partitioned part of the kitchen to accommodate the overflow. Some slept in the granary. Although there was a corridor in the house we avoided using it. Each room had a door direct to the outside. The women took turns at cleaning the corridor. Each of the daughters-in-law had to scrub part of the kitchen floor. When things were really bad you could see dirt lines dividing the sections that each one had to keep clean.

At one stage sixty people, including fourteen girls of approximately the same age, lived in the three houses around the yard. There was a great deal of friction, jealousy, and fighting. We girls argued about boys and courting. Everybody was always gossiping about the rest. In the early days it was difficult to avoid all this. You couldn't get away as you can now.

My grandmother handed out the food, and the young

mothers always fought over it. Apart from working on the land, my father was employed at an ammunition factory nearby. Then the factory was shifted because there was so much bombardment during the war, and he lost his job. Although we grew all our food, we had to pay the landlord 30,000 lire a month and give him half the produce.[22] Money was very short. I didn't have a pair of shoes until I was fourteen. At twelve I was sent to look after the station-master's children each afternoon till nine in the evening. I also milked the cows and washed the dishes there. At fourteen I went into service full-time. My eldest sister also worked as a maid from seven in the morning until one in the afternoon, and my younger sister Silvia went to Verona as a live-in maid. She only came home once a year for three weeks although Verona was not far away. At sixteen I was sent to Venice and was a maid in an admiral's household. There were no days off, no regular hours, and just two weeks a year holiday. I became ill and went home after one year there. When I was twelve I earned 60 lire a month, at fourteen 120 lire, and at sixteen 4,500 lire. All the money went home to help pay the rent. When I was seventeen my aunt and I left for France, where I had a job as a cook in a convent. I had half a day a week off and came home for Easter. I stayed there for three years and earned 7,000 lire a month. At this stage I started saving for my trousseau (corredo) and didn't send all the money home. I had to collect at least a minimum for it. If I hadn't I'm sure my husband, even if he denied that he wanted it, would at the first opportunity after marriage have said to me: 'You didn't even have a minimum corredo.' I collected eight sheets, eight towels, three bedspreads, one blanket (my mother wanted me to buy a cheap one for 13,000 lire, but I insisted on getting the best quality for 25,000; she was furious and called me bastarda, but she did get it for me in the end), sixteen pillowcases, eight petticoats, two dozen menstruation pads (the washable kind), six pairs of socks, two dozen handkerchiefs, one bridal frock (a long white one) and veil, one coat, six dresses, two pairs of shoes, two tablecloths, four tea towels, eight underpants, six brassieres, and three nightdresses.

My mother told me that a woman should delay marriage for as long as possible because living with a mother-in-law is hell. She'd lived like a slave with hers for sixteen years, and she's right. My two sisters live with their mother-in-law and families, and they really are no better off than slaves. I get letters from them full of their dreadful treatment. One of them got into terrible trouble for buying her child a banana without asking the mother-in-law. There was a terrible row about it when the greengrocer came to collect the money and told her mother-in-law that my sister had bought a banana.

A lot of men were away for long periods, sometimes months, sometimes years, doing seasonal work and sending money home. If the grandfather was dead or away the grandmother was boss. The mother is the most important person in anybody's life.

Apart from the hard and cruel work, people who couldn't read or write had to be especially careful because the landlords or officials often tried to trick them.

My parents-in-law were not happy when Paolo wanted to marry me because my family was very very poor, but he didn't mind, so we became engaged when I returned from France at twenty-one. Two years later, in 1956, Paolo left Italy as an assisted migrant to Australia. He paid for my passage when I followed him to Sydney in 1958. We were married three days later.

In Italy we looked forward to *feste* and to visiting friends and relatives on Sunday and sometimes sitting at the inn and drinking a *liquore*, although on the whole men only took out their wives and children on special occasions. But it was never lonely. Here in Sydney I have many worries, especially because of the language, and I don't like living in a city. I would love to have a farm. But in spite of that I feel freer than my sister. I am my own boss in the house, there isn't the gossip and the fighting that we had in the *cortile*; I can please myself about what I do and whether or not I get the children ice cream. I only ask Paolo. I would love to have one more child even though I already have three, but I don't want them to be labourers like my husband. I would like them to work in an office. I don't mind how hard I have to work or what sacrifices I need to make for this."

Grazia: "I was born in Paese in 1946 and am the youngest of seven children, five girls and two boys. The age difference between my oldest brother and myself is twenty-six years.

Before the war my father was a peasant on the land, but during the war he was sent to work in a factory in Germany. He was away for four years, and my mother was left with six children. But they lived in a house with many relatives. My big brother told me that they were hungry most of the time and had only bread and *polenta* when they could get hold of any. They used to get the water from a well in the woods, and mother also went out to the woods to collect firewood for the kitchen. When my older brother and sister started to work they did so just for their food, not money. When later they earned wages they gave all the money to the parents.

By the time I was born my grandparents had died, so my father was boss in the house. He inherited some land and bought some as well so he was lucky and didn't need to rent any. I was never hungry because everybody was working and they all spoiled me. I went to school for five years, then I stayed home for three and helped my father and mother and brother who lives with his wife and children. My father died two years ago. When I was fifteen I went to work in a clothing factory in Paese. I worked there for two years and then moved to a factory making shirts. There are lots of new factories in the area. My last job was hairdressing. I really liked that. But I always helped on the farm when I came home after work. In the summer I used to be employed in hotels or restaurants at the seaside. The proprietors supplied the summer workers with quarters, and sometimes twenty or more of us girls slept in a dormitory and worked during the day. It was fun working in these holiday resorts. I used to earn about 150,000 lire a summer and sent it home to my father. I've seen a lot more of Italy than my other sister. I've been to Venezia, Roma, Napoli, Verona, Torino, Trieste, San Remo, and Genova.

My sister, who's fourteen years older than I, went to live with her in-laws when she married. My mother told me it was terrible because there were five families living together. In the large kitchen there were five tables. Every family ate at its own table, and each woman only washed the floor under her own table, so the kitchen floor had many shades depending on how clean each woman happened to be. I just couldn't stand that sort of life. This sister then went to America with her husband and children. They stayed there for eight years. When the husband inherited some land three years ago they came back to Paese.

I had many boy friends, and sometimes three or four visited me in one evening. My big brother always went mad at me and wanted me to go to church, but I didn't like it and only went every couple of weeks. When I went to confession I made sure I went to the priest who was the most lenient. But my parents never said much to me or tried to stop me going out because I was a good worker, and anyway they were much too old and tired. Some people called me '*canietta*' (the bitch), because I had so many boy friends, but the only one I ever slept with was my husband, and that was when I was thirteen and he was nineteen, and he was just leaving for Australia to avoid military service. We were unofficially engaged, but after he left I got engaged to three other boys. His parents wrote to him and told him that I had lots of boy friends, so the engagement was broken, and we stopped corresponding.

I didn't see him for about six years. Then one day he just turned up in front of our house with a new car. I couldn't believe it! In fact he still wanted me to marry him, so I had to choose between him and the current fiancé who was working for Olivetti in Milano. I decided there and then, and within two weeks we were married. He'd come to Italy just for a four-week visit. My two brothers didn't want me to go because I was helping them as an unpaid labourer with the two houses they were building for themselves. There are so many new houses where there used to be just fields!

My father spent a whole week going around with me buy-

ing my trousseau (*corredo*). In most families it was the father
who did the shopping. He tried to spend the same amount
on each girl when she married. I had eighteen dresses made
(they are all too tight for me now, and that was only three
years ago), six slips, twenty underpants, thirty-five brassieres, twelve skirts, sixteen blouses, six pairs of shoes, seven
pairs of stockings, three cardigans, six jumpers, thirty
handkerchiefs, two coats, one raincoat, three handbags,
three pairs of gloves, eighteen singlets, twenty-nine
menstruation pads (father insisted on these although I used
disposable ones, so I gave them to my mother-in-law), three
pairs of slacks, twelve sheets, three blankets, three
bedspreads, three suitcases (this was instead of the dressing
table a woman usually brings with her *corredo*), six pillowcases, seven tablecloths, sixteen nighties, two dressing
gowns, six aprons.

We had seventy guests at the wedding. My father paid for
our friends and family and my husband for his. I had a
beautiful white wedding dress. We married in the morning.
For lunch I changed into a pink dress and in the evening for
the dancing into a long black frock. We then spent two weeks
at my mother-in-law's place before leaving for Australia.
That was in 1965.

I wish I had some relatives I liked here, but I wouldn't
want as many as I had in Treviso, because this always causes
trouble. These days, though, people live with their husbands
and children in their own home if it is at all possible, especially if the husband doesn't work on the land. Most couples don't want to have more than two or three children so
they can educate them better and live better. Most of my
nieces and nephews are trying to get on. One works in a
bank and another is a typist in an office. But even in Paese if
a wife and husband have a fight, the woman runs straight to
her mother and cries there for a few hours. My biggest
problem here is that I don't speak English, and if I go to
hospital or to a doctor I need an interpreter. The first
English words I learned were from my brother-in-law when
he came back from America. Most of the things he taught

me were swear words. I never had any proper English lessons. When I talk to Australian neighbours I manage somehow, but it isn't easy. I'd like to have a second child, a girl, because I already have a boy, but my husband doesn't want to, certainly not until we have had our trip back home. I'd like my children to go to university and become important people."

From the two biographies we can see that the experiences and aspirations of people belonging to the same generation can be quite dissimilar. The extent depends on the age difference and position in the family. A comparative analysis of the attitudes and expectations of Antonietta and Grazia would reveal similarities between the two sets of older sisters on the one hand, and the two sets of younger sisters on the other.

ITALIAN MIGRATIONS

For the purpose of analysis writers have found it useful to divide migrations into the categories "voluntary" and "involuntary". The most extreme form of involuntary migration is slavery; other forms are those where people are compelled, generally on political, religious, or ethnic grounds, to leave. These people we know as refugees, displaced persons, émigrés, or resettled persons.

Apart from a few individuals who migrated on political grounds, almost all Italian migrations have been voluntary. Most were for economic reasons, although the migrants at various periods had different aims, ambitions, and expectations. Macdonald pointed out that "Italian emigration rates have not been inversely correlated with level of income, as is generally presumed. Rather they have been directly related to the nature of Italy's various social systems."[23] In other words, economic factors became activated in certain social contexts, not in others.

Leaving aside those who migrated at the end of the last century with the intention of becoming farmers in South America, the migrants traditionally planned to return and were nearly always emotionally tied to their place of origin.

This contrasted with the rejection of the old community that often accompanied internal migration since the mid-1950s. Alberoni suggested that this was "a cultural transformation characterised by the appearance of new prospects, need, and requirements, new hopes and a new intolerance".[24]

Although Italian immigrants had come to Australia as early as 1850, by 1921 there were still only about 8,000 Italian-born here, the majority from the north. Impetus to greater migration came in 1924 when the United States imposed restrictions; a number of families in Griffith would originally have preferred the States, and many had siblings or other close relatives already settled in America.[25] In 1947 48.3 per cent of persons born in Italy and settled in Australia were living in urban areas and 51.61 per cent in rural regions. In 1966 87.5 per cent were living in urban and 12 per cent in rural areas.[26] Which group of Trevisani settled in Griffith and which in Sydney?

TREVISAN MIGRATIONS TO GRIFFITH AND SYDNEY

The settlement in Griffith was made up chiefly of immigrants who intended to settle there for good.[27] The men came out first, and when they decided to stay sent for their wives, children, relatives, and friends, thus starting chain migrations. By the early 1950s farms were too expensive for new arrivals to buy without capital or relatives to help them.

Trevisani started settling in Sydney in the late 1940s and early 1950s where, apart from one short period of economic recession, there were good opportunities for employment as unskilled labourers. Numerous men came out on assisted passages with the idea of staying for a limited period, making money, and returning home to live. Some of these did not go to join friends or relatives necessarily but were often instrumental in giving newcomers information and advice.

The men maintained their ties, sometimes returned to Italy for a short period, married, and returned to Australia; sometimes they arranged for a fiancée to come out. The change in intention from temporary to permanent settlement did not take place until the man, his young wife, and children had been back to Treviso, where they became disenchanted with their family or felt they no longer fitted. They then returned to Australia with the new intention of staying permanently.

The following oversimplified diagram gives some notion of which group of Trevisani settled in Griffith and which in Sydney.

Treviso before World War II	Treviso after World War II	Griffith rural	Sydney urban
agricultural workers: landless, or with small holdings aiming primarily at self-sufficiency	(a) small farmers and agricultural workers (b) landless labourers (c) skilled workers	commercial farmers	unskilled urban labourers

Virtually no skilled workers came to Australia (Category C); it was common for tradesmen who did migrate, to go temporarily to Canada. Those who migrated to Griffith were the small farmers and agricultural workers who left Treviso before and immediately after the war. Immigrants to Sydney came principally from categories A and B.

NOTES

1. For the most part, the information in this section comes from V. Lutz, *Italy: A Study in Economic Development*, especially chapter 8, pp. 155–89.
2. 1 hectare = 2.471 acres.
3. *Enciclopedia Italiana di Scienza, Lettere, ed Arti*, vol. 35, p.81.
4. *Enciclopedia Italiana*, vol. 35, p.81; Province of Treviso, *Dati Somari sui Comuni della Provincia di Treviso*, p.9.
5. See P. Cohen, *Modern Social Theory*, p.174–178.
6. J. S. Macdonald, "Migration from Italy to Australia", p.393.
7. J. S. Macdonald, "Institutional Economics and Rural Development", p.117, wrote that in this region property was vested in "collective bodies and individuals" and operations and management in "self-employed individuals and their associations".
8. *Enciclopedia Italiana*, vol. 35, p.82.

9. My respondents' stories approximated closely to Silverman's description of courtship and early years of marriage of girls who married *mezzadri* and moved into patrilocal extended families in central Italy. See S. Silverman, "The Life Crisis as a Clue to Social Functions", pp.132–35.
10. As Macdonald has pointed out ("Migration Versus Non-Migration: Regional Migration Differentials in Rural Italy", p.6): "The Alpine cooperatives and communal bodies, unlike those of the Centre and Apulia, were not revolutionary. Both in ideals and practices, they were compatible with private property and aimed at bolstering the status quo, not overthrowing it. This egalitarian-associative economy was not conducive to a class struggle."
11. After the priest the most influential person was the mayor (*sindaco*), generally a well-to-do small farmer who was literate, and whom the people elected. During Mussolini's times, however, the government appointed him, and he was mostly feared.
12. J.S. Macdonald, "Migration from Italy to Australia: Conflict between Manifest Functions of Bureaucracy Versus Latent Functions of Informal Networks", p.265.
13. *Enciclopedia Italiana*, vol. 35, p.81.
14. *Campanilismo* comes from the word *campanile*, a bell tower. It is the term used for the sentimental attachment to one's home, or place of birth. Those who come from the same village or *paese* regard themselves as *paesani* and share the sentimental attachment or *campanilismo* for that village or small region.
15. F. Alberoni, "Aspects of Internal Migration Related to Other Types of Italian Migration", pp.287–88.
16. One respondent in Griffith told me that his father had migrated to South America at sixteen years of age, stayed there for a few years, returned to Italy, migrated again, this time to North America, and returned home after a few more years. When Mussolini came to power he felt he could not stay home any longer, so he migrated to Australia because he could not now enter America. After a number of years in Griffith he sent for his wife and two sons. Out of forty years of married life he had spent only twelve with his wife.
17. J.S. Macdonald, "Italy's Rural Social Structure and Emigration", p.455.
18. The statistics for losses in agriculture and industry as a result of the war are:
    Agriculture: "Production in 1945 compared to that of 1938 showed a decrease of 60%; livestock were reduced by 75%: The total damage was estimated at approximately 550 billion lire, but in addition to the losses that could be directly assessed, there was also incalculable damage resulting from the diminishing productivity of the soil caused by the lack of fertilizer and manpower during the entire course of the war. The yield per hectare of cultivated grain which in

1938 was 56 bushels on the average had in 1945 been reduced to 45 bushels."

Industry: " ... at the end of 1945 the level of industrial production was reduced to 25% of pre-war output ... electric energy, for the most part of hydraulic origin, had diminished to 35% of its highest output (in 1941)".

See G. Mammarella, *Italy after Fascism: 1943–63*, pp.121–22.

19. Ibid., p.124.

20. Ibid., p.344.

21. As E. Bott pointed out (*Family and Social Networks*, pp.53–54):
"The phrase *segregated conjugal role-relationship* is here used for a relationship in which complementary and independent types of organisation predominate. Husband and wife have a clear differentiation of tasks and considerable number of separate interests and activities. They have a clearly defined division of labour into male tasks and female tasks. They expect to have different leisure pursuits, and the husband has his friends outside the home and the wife has hers. The phrase *joint conjugal role-relationship* is here used for a relationship in which joint organisation is relatively predominant. Husband and wife expect to carry out many activities together with a minimum of task differentiation and separation of interests. They not only plan the affairs of the family together but also exchange many household tasks and spend much of their leisure time together."

22. The exchange rate in 1972 was about 685 lire = A$1.00. In late 1976 it is 1,037 lire = A$1.00.

23. J.S. Macdonald, "Italy's Rural Social Structure", p.437. F. Alberoni, in his "Aspects of Internal Migration", outlined a typology of Italian migrations. Although one kind did not necessarily succeed another in time, each was more fully realized at certain periods. He divided them as follows:
Type 1: This started round about the middle of the nineteenth century when male agricultural workers from Piemonte and the Veneto left for seasonal work in other parts of Europe.
Type 2: This consisted of emigrants from the north migrating permanently to settle in rural areas. This wave took place around the 1890s and was directed to Argentina and Brazil. Whole families moved with the intention of building up their own farms.
Type 3: After the 1890s a new kind of temporary migration of men to the U.S.A. commenced. The idea was to make a fortune and return rich. The migration was curtailed after World War I.
Type 4: This consisted of internal migration that has assumed vast proportions since the mid 1950s.

24. F. Alberoni, "Aspects of Internal Migration", p.293. See also J. Lopreato, *Peasants No More*, pp. 88–89.

25. For a summary of administrative conditions and volume of migration to Australia see J. S. Macdonald, "Migration from Italy to Australia", appendix 2.

26. Department of National Development, *Atlas of Australian Resources: Immigration*, p.11.
27. For detailed demographic information on immigrants from Treviso to Australia up to 1939, see C.A. Price, "The Method and Statistics of Southern Europeans in Australia". For Trevisani in Griffith see C.A. Price, "Italian Population of Griffith".

PART 2
GRIFFITH

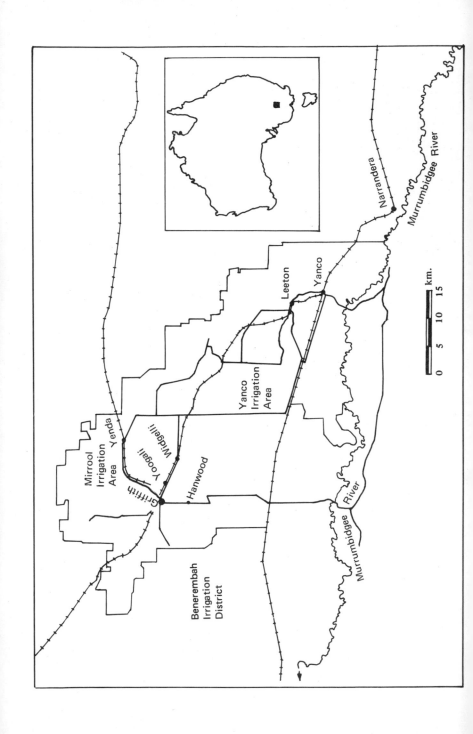

INTRODUCTION

In this section we will look at the economic conditions in the Murrumbidgee Irrigation Area in the 1920s and 1930s which encouraged Trevisani to settle there, and also indicate how the land-tenure system influenced family interaction and social life. Furthermore, as will become obvious, the economic opportunities and the land-tenure rule created a favourable environment not only for the adaptation, but, in the settlers' own opinions, for an improvement in their traditional institutions.

Trevisani, while retaining their occupations as agriculturalists, moved from a peasant-type economy that was primarily concerned with growing food to ensure self-sufficiency, to commercial farming that entailed greater specialization and partaking in the wider national economy. There was a shift from living in an extended household to a nuclear one. The church wielded less power than in Treviso, and priests now persuaded rather than dominated. Numerous clubs replaced the old inns and encouraged a degree of social interaction, particularly among people who came from the same region, that has given Griffith the reputation of being "the liveliest country town in Australia". Additionally, a charismatic political leader who straddled the ethnic groups led to the emergence of a new sense of *campanilismo*.[1]

THE MURRUMBIDGEE IRRIGATION AREA (M.I.A.)

The Murrumbidgee Irrigation Area, 640 kilometres south-west of Sydney, is located where the Murrumbidgee River flows into the great riverine plain of south-eastern Australia.[2] It is made up of two parts, Yanco and Mirrool. Leeton in Yanco and Griffith in Mirrool, sixty kilometres apart, are the two principal centres. The population has reached approximately 30,000. The main crops are fruit, rice, wheat, and vegetables; fat lambs and wool are also important in the economy.

The plan to irrigate the plains of the Murrumbidgee River

was conceived toward the end of the last century, and by 1912 many pastoral holdings had been resumed and subdivided into small farm blocks. Twelve months later 441 applicants had been allotted farms, although many of them had had no experience in agriculture.

Land settlement was regarded as one solution to urban unemployment, and many viewed the project as a socialist experiment, an attempt to encourage families with meagre means to become farmers. The administration took precautions against landlordism by limiting the size of the property a person could hold.

Plans were drawn up for the Yanco and Mirrool areas around the town sites of Leeton and Griffith. At first farms of approximately one, two, four, and ten hectares surrounded each town, but later the geometrical pattern was amended. Two and ten hectare farms were dropped, and properties were divided into one, four and twenty hectare farms. The one hectare blocks were for men who worked as labourers on larger farms but could utilize their land to grow vegetables and fruit. Farms of four hectares were for horticulture only and those of twenty hectares for mixed farming.

The early history of the M.I.A. abounds in stories of fighting among politicians, bureaucrats, and settlers, and even within political parties. At times vested interests were the cause of troubles; more often problems resulted from lack of adequate planning, financial assistance, and sound scientific knowledge and advice.

Information about the M.I.A. disseminated by official bodies among miners in Broken Hill brought a flood of applicants, and by 1913 these made up about 20 per cent of the farmers. Many were invalids before they came, and it was almost a foregone conclusion that they would fail. In 1919 returned soldiers, most of whom had no previous farming experience, moved into the area. The peak year of soldier settlement was 1923, when 878 held almost half the farms, but discontent grew, and a number of commissions and round-table conferences were called to offset the growing disenchantment.

ITALIAN MIGRATION TO THE M.I.A.

There were at least two Italians working in the M.I.A. as early as 1913–14. A number of Veneto miners from Broken Hill soon joined them. Each in turn wrote to friends and relatives asking them to come, so that by 1921 there were thirty-three Italians—sixteen men, five women, and twelve children—in the area. The Treviso group was particularly active in sending for relatives and started a chain migration from the communes of Cavaso del Tomba and Possagno.[3] A number from other communes also joined the stream, and by 1925 there were seventy-four males and ten females from Treviso, of whom seventy-five had come direct from Italy to relatives or friends. In this same year there arrived also nine from Calabria, some from Friuli and some from Abruzzi, Piemonte, Lombardia, Campania, and Sicilia. By 1933, 747 people in Griffith were either Italian-born or of Italian descent. This number had increased to 1,889 in 1947. By this time, largely as a result of the war, when migration stopped, "nearly half the Italian population of Griffith had received or were receiving part or all of their upbringing in Australia".[4]

The early to middle 1940s were thus years of consolidation. Seventy-five per cent of Italians came from the north, and the rest were immigrants from Calabria, Abruzzi-Molise, and Sicilia. Sixty-five per cent were from the Veneto.

In 1947 Italians owned 163 horticultural farms (about 27 per cent of the total). Of these Veneti had 126, Friulani 8, Piemontesi 7, Abruzzesi 3, Calabresi 17, and Siciliani 2.

Large-scale immigration started once more in 1947, and by 1954 the number of Italians had increased from 1,889 to 4,185. The number who had received either part or all of their education in Griffith declined. The proportion of Northerners also declined to 58 per cent. Calabresi accounted for 22 per cent and Abruzzesi for 6.8 per cent. Veneti, Calabresi, and Abruzzesi who settled in Griffith almost always came direct from Italy as a result of chain migration. In 1954 60 per cent of migrants in Griffith were from thirteen principal Italian communes. The few from the

Piemonte and Sicilia came as a rule via Queensland, the sugar cane area primarily, where large settlements of Piemontesi and Siciliani had existed since the end of the nineteenth and the beginning of the present centuries.

The common pattern of migration to Griffith was for the father to come out alone or with an elder son and work as a labourer on an Australian farm. After he had saved or borrowed money for fares, his wife and the rest of the children joined him. The family then leased a few hectares to grow vegetables, saved, and paid a deposit on a horticultural farm, which during the depression years of the 1930s and the early 1940s would have been cheap.

During the early 1940s Australia supplied food to the Allied forces in the south-west Pacific, and vegetable growing, hitherto a minor industry in the M.I.A., boomed. People grew vegetables either on their own farms, frequently in rows between fruit trees, or on leased land. No farm was wholly devoted to vegetable growing. Soon after the war Australian farmers gave up this industry, and growing vegetables became an exclusively Italian occupation. The new wave of Italian settlers in the second half of the 1940s was eager to take advantage of the opportunity offered. Vegetable growing required little capital and needed labour-intensive methods that suited family units. Italians, who were willing to work hard under poor conditions, saw this as a chance to save money to buy or put a deposit on a farm.

The women worked side by side with the men in the fields, and the children joined them as soon as they were old enough. Australians were shocked to see Italian men allowing their wives to perform tasks regarded as strictly for males. Their success aroused much animosity, suspicion, and friction.

After World War II many Australians, returned soldiers in particular, expressed alarm at the rate of Italianization of the area, and as late as 1947 the Full Court of the state of New South Wales heard a test case over the refusal of the Water Conservation and Irrigation Commission (W.C. & I.C.) to permit the transfer of farms to persons of Italian origin whether they were naturalized or not. The W.C. & I.C. argued that Italians generally did not make good irrigation farmers. The judgement of the court ruled that the W.C. & I.C. had no right to discriminate on grounds of national origin. The W.C. & I.C. then appealed successfully to the High Court of Australia which conceded that under the provisions of the relevant acts the Commission could use its discretion in granting irrigation holdings. The morality of the decision, the High Court pointed out, was not a matter for legal jurisdiction.[5]

In the early 1950s a number of Australians formed a branch of the Good Neighbour Council, an organization that had government support, and a small group of Australians and Italians started the Continental Music Club in an endeavour to bring the two ethnic groups together. By the late 1950s and early 1960s the efforts bore fruit and encouraged a gradual change in attitude, a conscious attempt on the part of both groups to accommodate, co-operate, and restrain ill-feeling. An important point was that those Australians who did not like irrigation farming or living among Italians could obtain good prices for their farms and move out. Those who remained in the area were thus a select group who either did not mind being in a community a large proportion of which was Italian, or else thought the benefits were worth putting up with what they viewed as possible disadvantages.

GRIFFITH

In what follows we will be looking at Griffith as it was when I began my fieldwork in mid-1969 and, unless otherwise stated, when speaking of Italians I am referring to Trevisani. For the purposes of this study I included within the area of Griffith the immediate environs of Wade Shire—in all an area of approximately 1,600 square kilometres with a population of 18,500. The town of Griffith itself has about 2,700 households and a population of 12,000.

To the newcomer the striking features of Griffith are its flatness and its symmetry. The small town-centre, surrounded on one side by concentric rings of houses and small farms, emphasizes that settlement was not haphazard but part of a master plan. Griffith, like Canberra, was designed by Walter Burley Griffin.

The shopping centre as well as most offices, banks, and government buildings are situated in the main street, one parallel to it, and three that cross it. There is a co-operative store, supermarket, newsagent, numerous clothing shops, delicatessens, pharmacies, garages, hairdressers, hardware and electrical goods stores, a cinema, four modern motels, and car and agricultural machinery showrooms—in fact, all the goods and services associated with modern living are readily available.

Few people live in the centre. Those not on farms have houses located a few minutes' drive away. Most of the horticultural farms that surround the town are situated from about three to ten kilometres out in such places as Hanwood, Yoogali, Bilbul, and Beelbangera. The average distance between neighbouring farmhouses is just under one kilometre, and to drive from a farm in Bilbul on the one side to Hanwood on the other takes no more than ten to fifteen minutes. Every family has at least one vehicle and virtually everyone a telephone. Roads are generally good, but after heavy rains it is sometimes difficult to drive into some farms.

The seasons offer striking contrasts. The summers are hot and dry, the winters cold with heavy morning frosts. Spring and autumn are visually the most beautiful times. In the spring the orchards are a blaze of pink, red, and white blossoms; in the autumn the leaves turn from gold to brown and form a splendid carpet of crisp leaves. Each season is accompanied by changes in the work rhythm and social life.

The population

I shall refer to all those with an Italian name as Italian even though they may be Australian citizens or born here. Almost all the foreign-born in the area were naturalized (one reason was that until a few years ago everyone was required to be naturalized within three years of acquiring a farm).

The population was made up almost entirely of two large ethnic groups, on the one hand Italians, on the other British, Irish, etc.[6] Of the Italians a rough estimate was 50 per cent Northerners, primarily from Treviso, 40 per cent Calabresi, and 10 per cent Abruzzesi. About 53 per cent of the population was Roman Catholic.[7]

Calabresi settled in Griffith some years after the Veneti, the peak years of southern immigration were the late 1940s and early 1950s. The majority were sponsored by relatives or friends and came mainly from Plati and Catanzaro. By the time these newcomers arrived a large proportion of the Veneti already owned farms. In 1969 the Veneti as a group were wealthier than most Calabresi, many of whom were vegetable growers.

That Northerners look down on Southerners is well known.[8] Some did not even consider them Italian. A Veneto woman discussing the clubs said, "Only Italians go to the Catholic Club at Yoogali; Calabresi have their own place." I asked an important Veneto businessman with connections among Calabresi to introduce me to some of the poor farmers. He replied, "Every tree has its good and its bad apples. You have tasted the good apples in Griffith, so why do you want to taste the bad?" Yet none of the people would dream of openly or deliberately insulting or harming a Southerner.[9]

Northerners and Southerners agreed that, unlike Veneti, Calabresi clung together and acted and voted as a block. Almost always they accepted the guidance of Frisina, a kind and intelligent man in his fifties who had been in the area about twenty years. All respected and trusted him, and he was known as "the father of the Calabresi". His shop, or rather the footpath in front of it, was a meeting place where Calabresi stood and talked during the day. At night they often met in his house. Although he was not the only important Calabrese in Griffith, his influence was different from the others in that he was consciously Calabrese and concerned primarily with Calabrese welfare. Whether a person wanted to sell insurance or secure votes, to be successful with

Fig. 7 Aerial view of Griffith

Fig. 8. Sunday evening dining at the Catholic Club, Yoogali. Women come only on special occasions.

Fig. 9. The Hanwood Catholic Club.

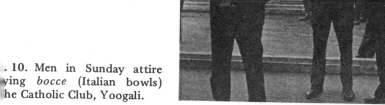

Fig. 10. Men in Sunday attire playing *bocce* (Italian bowls) at the Catholic Club, Yoogali.

Fig. 11. A modern kitchen in a house built recently on a horticultural farm owned by a second generation Italian family. The owner's parents bought the farm for him when he was sixteen (about twenty years ago).

Calabresi he first had to have Frisina's support. This contrasted with the Veneti where, despite a number of prominent people, no one was regarded as spokesman for the group.

The majority of Italians were engaged in agriculture. Price, writing about the Veneti in Griffith, stated, "... whereas less than one-tenth of the first generation were engaged in occupations other than farming about one-quarter of the second generation were engaged in non-farming activities". He contrasted this with Greeks in New South Wales: "Whereas 10 per cent or less of first generation settlers entered the skilled trades, the higher branches of business, the professions, very nearly half the second generation have done so."[10] The desire and ability of families to buy farms for sons partially explained the dearth of Italian professionals.

The price of farms had been rising steadily and by the mid-1950s and early 1960s was too high for most newcomers and for many who would have liked to buy for their sons. The peak was reached in 1969 when a Calabrese paid $81,000 for a horticultural farm and a Trevisano $115,000 for a large area farm. Newcomers were forced to become waiters, carpenters, bricklayers, blacksmiths, garage attendants, or other semi-skilled artisans. Some who wanted a farm in spite of the high prices started, as many did in earlier years, by leasing a few hectares to grow vegetables. The men frequently had additional jobs outside to increase their income.

Boys who a few years earlier would have hoped for a farm entered the Technical College to learn a trade or continued at the High School in the hope of a tertiary education or becoming white-collar workers. According to the High School headmaster, who would not give me the exact figures, in the past four years "about ten or fifteen" Italian pupils continued on to tertiary education. During the same period, according to the headmaster, eight to ten times as many Australians did so.

Of the fourteen doctors in the area not one was Italian or

spoke Italian, and there was no Italian dentist, bank manager, engineer, architect, veterinary surgeon, or schoolteacher. But there were four accountants and two lawyers. Of the lawyers one grew up in Griffith and started in practice in 1965. Of the two Italian pharmacists, one has been in the town a number of years, was successful, highly regarded, and interested in local civic affairs. The other started business in 1968. The Italian consular representative told me that people felt there was a need for an Italian doctor, or at least one who spoke Italian. "The man could make a fortune," he said. Italian professionals, shopkeepers, and businessmen could rely on attracting Italian customers. One Australian woman told me that since her husband took in an Italian partner business improved, and they now had many more Italian customers.

The high price of farms and the lack of industry meant that little movement into the area had taken place in the late 1960s. As far as the Italians were concerned there was also almost no movement out. The community was thus relatively closed, and many ties linked families, friends and neighbours.

In a group as small and as closely knit as this, reputation mattered a great deal, and people were expected to be straight-forward in business transactions. To be dishonest was viewed with disdain and regarded as stupid. A story was told about a young farmer as an example of how underhand dealing does not pay. This fellow made a habit of watering his grapes when they had been loaded onto the trailer to make them weigh more. After he had been caught twice no winery would accept his produce, and he was forced to sell his farm.

Farming

i] *The land-tenure system* In the early years the land-tenure system was unclear, and much confusion occurred. The Crown Lands Consolidation Act of 1913 was an attempt to set out the responsibilities of the commissioner in matters pertaining to the settlement of irrigation areas.[11] It stated that he had full powers to subdivide land into blocks that could be classified into irrigable, non-irrigable, and townlands; and he could assess the capital value and grant applications.

The house in which a family lived on the farm was defined as the "principal place of abode" of the lessee. If a block was held conjointly only one of the lessees and his nuclear family were permitted to live there. When two or more members of one family, say a father and a son or two brothers, each had a property in his own right, however, and their two farms were within walking distance of each other, they could live under one roof providing they obtained the consent of the Special Land Board. Permission was granted only when one of the parties was unmarried. In effect, therefore, extended households could not develop.

An additional important provision of the act was that a farm was liable to forfeiture if the registered owner did not hold or use it for his exclusive benefit. The object was to avoid dummying monopolies, or the operation by vested interests of a number of farms as one unit.[12] No horticultural farm was sharecropped although this would have been permitted. The income from such a farm was reasonable only as long as the family was the main working unit. It could not support a sharecropper.

Originally the twenty hectare blocks were for dairying, the then major industry. As soon as the commissioner realized that these were too small he suggested making forty hectare blocks available. The settlers opposed him, maintaining that blocks of this size would have led to land jobbing—big farms would have destroyed the "democratic trend of land legislation". They also feared that the larger areas would have encouraged the production of sheep, cattle, and cereals rather than fruit and vegetables, as was originally stipulated.[13] The settlers felt that if some men owned large areas, what was regarded as the "socialist egalitarian dream" would have been destroyed. In later confrontations the settlers clamoured for an increase in the size of farms. Friction was most acute in 1925, when a deputation called on the Minister for Agriculture demanding a minimum of 260 hectares to include both irrigated and dry land. Little was done to re-design large farms, however, until 1926.

Decisions on the sizes of farms had been determined by what was referred to as a Home Maintenance Area (H.M.A.). Mr. Justice Pike's definition of the concept of a H.M.A. was the important result of his judgment in the Batkin *v.* Water Conservation and Irrigation Commission case in 1926. He defined a H.M.A. as the amount of land required to enable a man to support a wife and children in a reasonable manner under average conditions. He concluded that after taking debts, risks, and work into account, "a property showing a net return of somewhat over $1,000 per annum" would constitute such an area.[14] The effect was far-reaching. The first settlers to appeal were granted farms of just under 280 hectares, of which about 160 were irrigable.

In the late 1920s sheep and rice production expanded at the expense of dairying. A number of economic crises occurred, and in 1931 the Minister for Agriculture felt that the government ought to write off $6–8,000,000 in the value of properties. In 1939 a sudden rise in water tables brought further disaster to horticulturalists, and many Australians sold out to Italians.

Over the years two types of farms evolved, horticultural, averaging 8–20 hectares, growing citrus, stone fruit, apples, and grapes; and large area farms (L.A.F.), averaging 160–240 hectares, producing primarily rice, sheep, and wheat.

Originally land was not freehold, and farmers had no option but to lease it from the W.C. & I.C.; only recently have they had the choice of leasing or buying. Leasing tended to be more popular because the money paid was tax deductible, and a man did not receive much more for his property if he owned it. Bank managers agreed that most Italians did not seem to know, care, or understand about the various kinds of titles. Their main concern was to obtain irrigated land. At the head offices in Sydney officials were amazed at the demand for non-freehold land.

Farms continue to be under the strict administration of the W.C. & I.C. of New South Wales, which controls sales and water supply. No person can own more than what is defined as a Home Maintenance Area. Farmers are not allowed to grow fruit or grapes on a large area farm, and the amount of rice is also controlled; regular air surveys keep a check. Subdivision is not permitted. The permission of the commission is not necessary for sharecropping but must be obtained for leasing. In practice, however, farmers who leased to vegetable growers rarely applied for this permit, and it was therefore difficult to know exactly how much was leased.

A direct result of such a land-tenure system has been that if a man already had a farm that was a H.M.A. he could not expand in his own name. He therefore bought in that of his son. Gradually an ideal pattern emerged whereby a father aspired to own one farm and buy another for each of his sons. Thus twenty-year olds frequently owned a farm and established their nuclear household close to the parental home.

ii] *Vegetable growing* Although most Italians started off growing vegetables and then moved into horticulture, it was difficult to know how many vegetable growers there were.[15] One reason was that few people bothered to obtain the permission required from the W.C. & I.C. for leasing land; another was that many who did grow vegetables worked part-time at other jobs.

Some horticulturalists grew vegetables in the rows between trees while waiting for them to come into bearing. One estimate was that in 1969 there were approximately 150 vegetable growers, the majority being Southerners. According to the production manager of Griffith Producers' Co-operative they had about 800–1,000 hectares all told. To do well a grower needed about 15–20 hectares and modern machinery. Leases for vegetable land cost between $75–$100 per hectare per annum.

Prices for produce fluctuated enormously. In 1968 a bag

of onions fetched $5 but in 1969 only $1.50. A bank manager told me that twelve hectares of leased land under vegetable cultivation may be worth $32,000, but price fluctuations and floods could ruin an entire crop. Vegetables were thus a risky venture.

I spent some time with a Trevisan woman in her early thirties who had two children aged two and five. She lived with her husband in a derelict house that she somehow managed to keep clean. "My husband and I lease seven hectares of land nine kilometres away and grow carrots and turnips. We pay $100 per hectare per year and $25–$30 for water. I go out each day with him and we do everything by ourselves, apart from special occasions when we hire labour. If we work all day we can each pick, wash, and pack thirty-five 22 kilo bags of carrots and turnips. The trouble is that one day we may get $3 a bag, another day only $1. That is why we try not to use hired labour. It would eat up all our profits. We pick carrots all the year but turnips only three times a year. We have a tractor and a vegetable-washing machine which we leave on the field. We lease a different block every two or three years. Till recently I took both children with me each day, fed them, and put them to sleep in the truck. Now I only take the little one. The older one goes to school, and my sister picks her up at three in the afternoon. Although this is very hard work, my husband prefers it to working for a boss."

I visited another Trevisan vegetable grower who leased eleven hectares about five kilometres from his house. He worked it all alone but hired labour for harvesting (at $1.10 per hour). His wife could not help him because they had five children under eight. Frequently he left home at three or four in the morning, returned for lunch, and then worked again till eight or nine in the evening.

iii] Horticultural farms Tables 10, 11, 12 and 13 indicate the sizes and distribution of farms. For the sake of simplicity I have classified as Australian all who did not have an Italian or Spanish name.

Table 10. M.I.A.: distribution of farms 8 hectares and over

	Total farms 8 hectares and over	8–27	28–48	48.5–67	68–88	89–108	109–29	129.5–49	149.5–69	170–89	190–209	210–29	230–50	251–70	271–90	291 and over
Australian	316 (40%)	100 (19%)	10 (38%)	3 (50%)	1 (50%)	2 (40%)	5 (71%)	3 (100%)	11 (85%)	38 (88%)	34 (87%)	33 (97%)	18 (82%)	9 (90%)	14 (93%)	35 (90%)
Italian	467 (59.5%)	420 (80.5%)	15 (58%)	3 (50%)	1 (50%)	3 (60%)	2 (29%)	—	2 (15%)	5 (12%)	5 (13%)	1 (3%)	4 (18%)	1 (10%)	1 (7%)	4 (10%)
Spanish	4 (0.5%)	3 (0.5%)	1 (4%)													
Total	786 (100%)	523 (66%)	26 (3%)	6 (0.75%)	2 (0.25%)	5 (0.75%)	7 (0.75%)	3 (0.5%)	13 (1.5%)	43 (6%)	39 (5%)	34 (4%)	22 (3%)	10 (1.5%)	15 (2%)	39 (5%)
	20 acres and over	20–69	70–119	120–69	170–219	220–69	270–319	320–69	370–419	420–69	470–519	520–69	570–619	620–69	670–719	720 and over

Note: The percentages in this and the following tables are approximations to the closest round figure. For the sake of consistency all measurements in these tables have been converted from acres to hectares. The original groupings in acres have been placed at the foot of each column.

SOURCE: Compiled from the books and records of W.C. & I. C.

Table 11. M.I.A.: distribution of horticultural farms 8–27 hectares

	Total farms 8–27 hectares	8–9	10–11	12–13	14–15	16–17	18–19	20–21	22–23	24–25	26–27
Australian	100 (19%)	8 (12%)	7 (10%)	7 (10%)	7 (14%)	8 (17%)	16 (27%)	23 (27%)	8 (18%)	13 (52%)	3 (27%)
Italian	420 (80%)	56 (86%)	64 (89%)	60 (90%)	42 (86%)	39 (83%)	42 (73%)	61 (72%)	36 (82%)	12 (48%)	8 (73%)
Spanish	3 (1%)	1 (2%)	1 (1%)								
Total	523 (100%)	65 (12%)	72 (14%)	67 (13%)	49 (9%)	47 (9%)	58 (11%)	85 (17%)	44 (8%)	25 (5%)	11 (2%)
	20–69 acres	20–24	25–29	30–34	35–39	40–44	45–49	50–54	55–59	60–64	65–69

	Total farms 8–27 hectares	8–9	10–11	12–13	14–15	16–17	18–19	20–21	22–23	24–25	26–27
Veneti	259 (62%)	33 (59%)	42 (66%)	46 (77%)	20 (48%)	20 (51%)	26 (62%)	33 (54%)	24 (66%)	9 (75%)	6 (75%)
Calabresi	82 (20%)	17 (31%)	8 (12%)	7 (12%)	8 (19%)	7 (18%)	10 (24%)	17 (28%)	5 (14%)	1 (8.3%)	2 (25%)
Abruzzesi	32 (8%)	3 (5%)	4 (6%)	3 (5%)	6 (14%)	4 (10%)	2 (5%)	6 (10%)	3 (8%)	1 (8.3%)	
Siciliani	40 (9%)	3 (5%)	8 (12%)	4 (6%)	6 (14%)	7 (18%)	3 (7%)	4 (7%)	4 (12%)	1 (8.3%)	
Others	7 (1%)		2 (4%)		2 (5%)	1 (3%)	1 (2%)	1 (1%)			
Total	420 (100%)	56 (13%)	64 (15%)	60 (14%)	42 (10%)	39 (9%)	42 (10%)	61 (15%)	36 (9%)	12 (3%)	8 (2%)
Total acres		20–24	25–29	30–34	35–39	40–44	45–49	50–54	55–59	60–64	65–69

SOURCE: Compiled from the books and records of W.C. & I.C.

Table 13. M.I.A.: regional distribution of Italian farms 28 hectares and over

	Total farms 28 hectares and over	28–48	48.5–67	68–88	89–108	113–29	129.5–49	149.5–69	170–89	190–209	210–29	230–50	251–70	271–90	291 and over
Veneti	32 (68%)	8 (53%)	2 (67%)		3 (100%)		2 (100%)		4 (80%)	3 (60%)	1 (100%)	4 (100%)	1 (100%)	1 (100%)	3 (75%)
Calabresi	7 (15%)	2 (13%)	1 (33%)	1 (100%)					1 (20%)	1 (20%)					1 (25%)
Abruzzesi	4 (8.5%)	2 (13%)				2 (100%)									
Siciliani	4 (8.5%)	3 (21%)								1 (20%)					
Total	47 (100%)	15 (33%)	3 (6%)	1 (2%)	3 (6%)	2 (4%)	2 (4%)		5 (11%)	5 (11%)	1 (2%)	4 (8.5%)	1 (2%)	1 (2%)	4 (8.5%)
70 acres and over		70–119	120–69	170–219	220–69	270–319	320–69	370–419	420–69	470–519	520–69	570–619	620–69	670–710	720 and over

SOURCE: Compiled from the books and records of W.C. & I.C.

A horticultural farm was essentially a family business that could not under normal conditions support a manager and an absentee landlord. Most people agreed that the peak prices paid for farms in 1969 were highly inflated. But even allowing that this was so, it was significant that a farm equal in quality in Leeton, sixty kilometres away, cost only half as much. Italians were anxious to live as close to the centre of the town as possible, and the prices rose accordingly. An estate agent told the story about the Italian who came to Griffith wanting to buy a farm. The agent offered him a good farm for a reasonable price in Leeton, to which the prospective buyer replied: "I've already migrated once; I don't want to migrate again!"

In 1969 a good 34 hectare vineyard would have fetched $100–120,000. This was a big area; about 20 hectares was the more usual size. The harvest that year on the 34 hectare farm was 460 tonnes at $64 per tonne, a gross of approximately $30,000. After expenses the taxable income would have been about $10,000. Ten years previously this kind of place could have been bought for about $44,000. An average 20–24 hectare citrus orchard cost about $80,000, the gross takings of which would have been about $20,000, leaving a taxable income of $7,000. About eight hectares of citrus yielded an old couple gross takings of $4,000, or a taxable income of $2,500, just enough for them to live on. Prices dropped steeply at the end of 1969 but rose again in 1973.

The greatest problem was fluctuation in prices and demand. The cost of packing and transport was so high that many farmers preferred to sell the fruit direct to the local cannery or wineries by the truck-load rather than run the risk of packing each piece of fruit or cluster of grapes for the city markets. Much depended on the weather and the labour available. During rain periods the mud prevented tractors from moving between the trees to bring out the fruit.

An acute shortage of seasonal pickers occurred for the first time during the 1970 harvest. In previous years the workers came south from the Queensland cane fields, but recent mechanization reduced the number of cane cutters to such an extent that the symbiotic relationsip between them and the farmers in the M.I.A. was thrown out of gear. This explains why many farmers who formerly grew for the city markets delivered instead to the canneries or wineries. Some others picked their fruit, (oranges do not drop off), collected them into mounds, and let them rot. Packing was too expensive and selling locally impossible.

A man and his wife could manage a ten hectare citrus orchard by themselves apart from a few weeks at harvest. An elderly couple who owned twenty hectares brought in contractors to pick the fruit, but the man did the pruning during the winter with the help of his two sons. Otherwise he managed everything alone. A man with a vineyard of thirty-two hectares needed a full-time helper all the year, and during the harvest of eight to twelve weeks he employed six to eight extra workers. In the winter he engaged three men for a month for the pruning. His children were too small to lend a hand. Seasonal workers who came in from the north generally worked as a gang under contract. An experienced man could pick about 25 tonnes a week at just under $10 per tonne, and one without experience could easily pick 12 tonnes.

Deciduous trees such as apricots, peaches, plums, apples, and pears were pruned in June and July. Grapes came later, in July and August. Farmers prepared the soil for irrigation and spraying in August. Apart from oranges and lemons, the harvest time was from mid-November to mid-April, starting with apricots.

In the winter months the men pruned, sprayed, mended fences, machinery, and attended to jobs around the house. They were rarely fully occupied, and many complained of boredom. This was the time for social celebrations, and a great deal of card playing also went on. In the late winter and early spring, before the blossoms, spraying had to be done again and preparations made for further irrigation.

The more specialized the horticultural farm, the more economically could it be run; but many farmers were afraid of the risks.

iv] *Large Area Farm* [L.A.F.] Italians started going into large area farming relatively late. Between 1950 and 1959 four such farms were bought, and between 1960 and 1969 twenty-one. By contrast there were 768 purchases of horticultural farms during the period 1950–69 (see tables 14 and 15).

Table 14. All sales of farms in Wade Shire (1950–69)

	Large Area Farms				Horticultural and Residential			
	Vendors		Buyers		Vendors		Buyers	
Year	Aust.	Ital.	Aust.	Ital.	Aust.	Ital.	Aust.	Ital.
1950	4	–	4	–	29	7	6	30
1951	4	–	3	1	33	5	10	28
1952	2	–	2	–	22	8	4	26
1953	1	–	1	–	32	12	18	26
1954	5	–	5	–	49	13	21	41
1955	2	–	2	–	34	11	12	33
1956	–	–	–	–	37	25	11	51
1957	4$^2/_3$	$^1/_3$ share	3	2	26	25	10	41
1958	5	–	4	1	23	26	7	42
1959	2	–	2	1	26	26	10	42
	29$^2/_3$	$^1/_3$	26	4	311	158	109	360
1960	1	–	–	1	21	20	3	38
1961	7½	½ share	6	2	27	22	12	37
1962	6	–	5	1	18	24	7	35
1963	5	–	5	–	36	42	14	64
1964	4	1	4	1	28	33	7	54
1965	6	1	4	3	14	26	14	26
1966	7	–	2	5	32	27	20	39
1967	8	–	7	1	34	38	23	49
1968	5	–	1	4	27	25	15	37
1969	6	–	3	3	19	24	14	29
	55½	2½	37	21	256	281	129	408
Total 20 years	85$^1/_6$	2$^5/_6$	63	25	567	439	238	768

Note: These cover sales of all properties in Wade Shire marked as "Irrigable Farms". They may include blocks used for residence and not farming. In 1957, one L.A.F. was owned by an Australian and an Italian. The former had a $^2/_3$ share, the latter a $^1/_3$ share. In 1961, an Australian and an Italian owned one L.A.F., each had a ½ share.
SOURCE: Figures collated from the Sales Register of the Rural Bank, Griffith. All sales of farms under the control of W.C. & I.C. must go through the Rural Bank.

Table 15. Percentage of horticultural farms held by Italians (1927–69)

1927	3%
1933	11%
1947	27%
1954	50%
1969	85%

Note: The 1927–54 estimates set out in C. A. Price "Italian Population", included farms of four hectares and over. My tables on horticultural farms started with eight hectares. In 1969 Italians owned 80.5 per cent of farms in the 8–27 hectare bracket. If we added those under eight hectares, the total is likely to be around 85 per cent.

Most farmers believed that a 200 hectare L.A.F., because of the possibility for diversification, had a sounder potential than a 20 hectare horticultural farm. In 1969, at the peak-price period, a L.A.F. of 200 hectares with machinery and stock cost about $120,000. The gross takings would have been about $30,000, leaving a taxable income of about $10,000. Such properties, frequently referred to as rice farms, gave great prestige to the owner.

One Australian rice farmer started with a weed paddock twenty years ago. At the time of my visit he owned a 226 hectare property with tall willows forming an arch along the drive to the house and poplars lining the canals. Thirty-two hectares were under rice, and some paddocks had fat lambs. Other crops were sown with wheat, sorghum, barley, and alfalfa. Eight Italian vegetable growers, one of whom lived on the property, leased 40 hectares.

This rice farmer worked his property with one full-time employee but brought in contractors for harvesting. Crops were rotated, and a rice paddy planted only once in five years. After the rice, wheat followed for one or two years, and the land then served as grazing for three or four years. Unlike horticulture, this type of farming did not demand intensive labour. During the winter the owner planned an overseas trip and left the place in the hands of the employee.

Sharecropping on rice farms was common. The usual arrangement was that the cropper supplied the labour in return for a third of the net income. The owner paid for the machinery, water, electricity, and other expenses. This form of farming was attractive because it did not require a great deal of labour and offered the possibility of diversification. A L.A.F. was a good proposition for many businessmen looking for rural investments to escape taxation.

The younger generation Italians were thinking more and more of rice farms, but some who had tried them out found them too far from the town centre. The wives in particular felt isolated.

The farmers

A number of farmers in their mid-forties and fifties apologized for their houses, which they said were not as modern as they would have liked. "We have altered and added to it so often, it looks really bitsy! But if we were to tear this down and build a new house it would cost $20–30,000, and the value of the farm would not increase, so what's the point?"

The houses of these farmers reflected not only their particular life style but also their aspirations and their degree of adaptation to the host society. Broadly, they can be divided into three categories.

First, there were the shabby old weatherboard or fibrocement dwellings which were usually small, had bare floors and few modern conveniences. Toilets were outside and bathrooms were often inadequate. These were the houses of the early days. When I was in Griffith some poor vegetable growers still lived in them and as a rule felt too ashamed to allow a stranger inside. Those who built another house on the farm kept the old place as a barn or temporary accommodation for seasonal workers.

Then there were the comfortable brick houses that many farmers built in the 1950s. Most of these had three or four bedrooms, a sitting room, and sometimes a separate dining room, indoor bathroom and toilet, a sunroom where women sewed and ironed, and a large kitchen with a fuel and an electric stove and a big table in the middle.

Finally we have the modern farmhouses that look as if

they had been lifted out of the dream-house section of a women's journal. Built in the 1960s, they belong to the married sons with their own farms. They are of brick veneer, have three or four bedrooms, sitting room, dining area, luxurious bathrooms and toilets, sunrooms and well-designed kitchens. The wall oven, hotplates, and refrigerators are all the latest models. Houses of this type have air conditioning, oil heating, and nearly all the machinery and equipment associated with modern living. I did not see a dishwasher; no doubt the first purchase will start a chain reaction.

Most houses were carpeted throughout except for the kitchen, which had a linoleum covering. In the sitting room the chairs were large and comfortable and faced the television set. The bedroom had chenille bedspreads, a dressing table, and frilled curtains. Few of the children had desks in their rooms. The kitchen had a formica-topped table and vinyl chairs. Bowls of fresh fruit stood on the table or the sideboard in the kitchen, and people picked as they walked past. In every house wedding photographs hung on the wall, generally in an oblique line ranging from small to large. In the parents' house were faded photographs of the grandparents' weddings, theirs, and the children's. Sometimes the kitchen had a vase of fresh flowers, but the sitting room was almost always decorated with plastic blooms.

Boxes of fruit, tomatoes, vegetables, bottled fruit, preserves, jams, chillies, and *giardiniera* were arranged in the laundry or shed. Often home-made salamis stood in rows or in an old refrigerator, and stocks of new wine in beer bottles lined the shelves. All this came from the farm or from exchange of gifts.

Lawns, flower beds, trees, bushes, roses, and annuals surrounded the houses. People did the gardening during the quieter periods of the year when work on the farm was less pressing. Most raised chickens for home consumption, a few had a goat or pig and sometimes even pigeons. Dogs and cats were part of the farmyard family.

An observant and realistic Italian, a production manager of a Producers' Co-operative, remarked that when the amount of labour input on a horticultural farm is taken into account the gains are small. "The attraction for Italians is that it offers the intense cultivation to which they have been accustomed," he said. A couple summed up their feelings, and those of most Italians, in the following words: "We work hard, but we don't mind because we're working for ourselves (*lavoriamo per conto nostro*). At harvest we sometimes start at four in the morning and continue till all hours, but at other times if we feel like knocking off we can. In Italy we would have worked like slaves for a hard-boiled egg and a piece of *polenta*; here we set up our children and re-invest. We are attached to the land not because we make so much money but because it is a way of life we love and understand."

I first visited Griffith in May, after the heavy work of summer and autumn was completed, and people were adjusting themselves to more leisure. The harvest had been good, and in spite of the usual grumbles, one father, indicating how content his son was, said, "When Aldo sits himself on the chair he looks comfortable and satisfied."

On my first Sunday with this family the boys, their wives, and young children dropped in to say hello to the mother and father. They had much to talk about: the farm, the harvest, the problems with seasonal workers, the broken-down tractor they shared, the installation of an air-conditioner in the parents' house. The young women listened with one ear, their interest concentrated more on talk about the children, the latest pregnancy, the hospital, next week's wedding, the fashion show, sewing, and knitting. In the talk there was no straining to find a topic of common interest; all knew the people being discussed, and understood the agricultural jargon. The mother divided her attention between the men and the girls and occasionally got up to distribute ice cream and sweets to the grandchildren, to ask for a kiss or to hug them. At no stage did I feel that these visits were a chore, indeed quite the contrary—all seemed to be enjoying themselves.

Before the young people left, the mother took her

grandchildren to see her 87-year-old father who lay in bed flat on his back holding rosary beads. On the wall were holy pictures and a large faded photograph of his parents. On the floor next to him stood a bottle of whisky and one of red wine.

i] *The husband and wife* In Treviso when a mother hit her child "thirty-five faces appeared at the windows and shouted abuse". Life in Griffith by contrast combined the advantages of the nuclear household and the extended household. Husband and wife were at liberty to show each other affection or to quarrel and scold the children in the privacy of the home. At the same time, people had enough kin close by for company and support.

The husband-wife relationship has been, and is, undergoing change, and older couples behaved differently from those who were younger. Yet some things were common to all. The roles were segregated rather than joint, and division in society was along male-female lines.

In earlier days in Griffith all the women worked in the fields with the men, and there were few machines and little specialization. "If it wasn't for the women working the way they did, the men wouldn't have the farms they've got," one woman explained. But the daughters of these women did not work the fields and felt that they had, therefore, progressed economically and socially. The older women, or those who still worked with their husbands either because of poverty or lack of ambition to buy more farms, had a say in the running of the property. Yet it was a basic rule that the husband was the leader, and in any discussion in front of others the wife treated him as the boss.

Wives had little or no say if farmers had specialized in one or two crops or if the cost of machinery had encouraged brothers to work their farms co-operatively. Brothers often made a conscious effort to keep the women out of things because as soon as an argument or conflict between the wives occurred the partnership suffered. Brothers were less ready to find faults with each other than were their womenfolk.

The following descriptions of three farming enterprises will explain why some brothers were more prepared to work together than others.

1. *A man in his mid-forties:* "My wife and I run our twelve hectare citrus farm on our own. We don't need to rely on outside labour, apart from occasional seasonal workers at harvest. We have four daughters and no sons, so there is no point in killing outselves to buy another farm. We start work whenever we feel like it, sometimes at five in the morning, and then knock off at ten, or arrange to work whichever way suits us best. That's the good thing about being your own boss. My two brothers suggested that the three of us form a company for harvesting and marketing. We could then afford to buy bigger and better machinery. Economically it would've been a good thing. I was tempted at first, and if I'd had a son I'd have joined in, but I thought there's sure to be trouble between the women, and you know what that does to the men; well, I didn't. In any case my wife likes working with me so I'm not sorry I didn't go in with them, especially as I know now that there's trouble between their two wives. Still there are some advantages in forming a company. The packing firm didn't accept my fruit this year because they were busy, and I'm only a small grower. The Saletto Brothers have no difficulty because the three of them working as a company are big customers."

2. *A man in his early forties:* "I've got five brothers in Griffith, and all are farmers. Four of us decided to form a company and market together. We work together and divide the income equally. Of course, each farm is in one brother's name. A few years ago one of us said that he was getting too old to work so hard, and anyway he had only two girls, so he got out of the partnership and sold his farm. Now there are three of us working together. A son of one is employed by our company on a fixed wage, but I can see that this'll get difficult because the boy wants a farm of his own. Maybe my brother will also get out and work his farm with his son. I've got a boy and two girls, so I'm hanging on to my farm for

another few years until my son decides whether he wants to become a farmer. He's only twelve and loves the place, but if he decides to do something else I'll sell. What's the point of working so hard? The three of us get on well, but we don't discuss business affairs with our wives because we don't want trouble. My wife doesn't know a thing about the business side of the farm. It's not the usual thing for people to form companies and market together even though economically it's a good idea. In practice it often doesn't work out."

3. *A nineteen-year-old office secretary who had been married for one year:* "My husband has four brothers. Of the five boys, three own one large area farm and the other two one horticultural farm each. The five have formed a company to work everything together. It's permitted to form companies for working, but a company can't own the farms. The father and the brothers work the farms and are happy that way, but the wives don't get on at all. Each one wants something different. The wife of an elder brother, she's twenty-three and now lives on the large area farm, is a real snob. She wants to be Mrs. Large-Area-Farmer or Mrs. Rice-Farmer. She lives about twenty kilometres out of Griffith and doesn't like it because she gets scared and is so far from her mother. Her husband has to wait for her each morning till she fixes the house and baby and drive her to her mother's place. This means that this brother doesn't get to our farm till about ten. They're picking the fruit at our place at the moment. My husband, on the other hand, starts working at four in the morning and it makes me mad to see his brother come so late. This is the only thing I argue about all the time with my husband. I'd rather have two hectares of our own than fifty with the brothers. My husband doesn't like me working here in the office. He'd rather I stayed home and served lunch to him and his brothers when they come in, but I'm not going to do that. I cook dinner for them in the morning before I go to work, and they can get it themselves when they come in at lunchtime. Sooner or later we'll have to split, and, boy, will there be trouble about how to divide things up! My brother-in-law's wife wanted a new car to keep up with her

friends, so we had to cough up $1,000. We've got the utility and the old car, but she has to have the new one. It's not fair."

It may be that the women were trying to tear the brothers apart. The men probably realized that certain things were not fair, but they did not become as agitated as the wives. In the end each husband tended to go the way his wife wanted.

Working the farms together was a sound economic proposition. In a way it could be viewed as a variation of the extended family work unit in Treviso, particularly as almost all the partnerships were made up of close relatives. In the first two examples there was no question that in public and also generally in private the husband was the boss. The division of labour was clear-cut, and each knew his or her role. The third case was an instance of the attitude of the young, in particular of girls who have had an education, held jobs, and felt greater independence. Not all young brothers, however, succumbed to the economic attractions of marketing partnerships. The mother whose family I described on page 76 once told me: "I often think it might be a good idea if Dad and the two boys formed a company and worked the three farms together, but then I think maybe it would start trouble and spoil things."

In cases where members of the family did not market together the finances were kept separate. This did not prevent them from helping one another without payment.

The division of labour between the sexes was most marked in domestic matters. One man remarked, "I'd be ashamed if anybody caught me helping my wife with the dishes or the wash. I've never changed a baby's nappy. After all, it's women's work." The wife added jokingly, "The men let the wives help them on the farm, then when the winter comes they enjoy themselves in the clubs while the women stay and do the housework." Yet it was true that men preferred their wives not to do farm work when this was no longer necessary. As one wife put it, "I like to be on the farm with Emilio, and he likes me to be with him, but he hates me to go out grape-picking at friends' places because he says we're not that hard up. But I like to do it for the company. There isn't much work on our farm now that we've finished picking. Even when I'm not working outside I'm never lonely because he comes in a few times during the day for meals and tea. The worst time for the women is the winter when the men are inside such a lot and get very bored. The clubs are good because they can spend a lot of time there with the boys and play cards and *bocce*. Men get on your nerves if they've nothing much to do and hang around the house the whole time. The women still have to look after the house and children." Another woman added, "I love living on the farm. It's never lonely, but sometimes I get fed up with having the men home all the time. The women cook three times

Table 16. Ownership of farms: male—female distribution (1969)

Italians, 8—27 hectares

	Total		Veneti	Calabresi	Abruzzesi	Siciliani	Others
1 male only	222	(53%)	133	55	18	13	3
2 or more males	44	(10%)	30	7	1	5	1
Male(s) and female(s)	145	(35%)	91	18	12	21	3
1 female only	9	(2%)	5	2	1	1	
	420	(100%)	259 (61%)	82 (20%)	32 (8%)	40 (8.5%)	7 (2.5%

Australians, 8—27 hectares

1 male only	67	(67%)
2 or more males	3	(3%)
Male(s) and female(s)	18	(18%)
1 female only	12	(12%)
	100	100%

Australians and Italians, 28 hectares and over

	Australian		Italian	
1 male only	131	(61%)	8	(17%)
2 or more males	8	(4%)	12	(25%)
Male(s) and female(s)	65	(30%)	27	(58%)
1 female only	12	(5%)	–	–
	216	100%	47	100%

SOURCE: Compiled from information in the books and records of W.C. & I.C.

a day, and the men expect a hot meal for lunch and dinner. They come in on the dot of twelve, and Dino expects a hot *minestrone* every day even if the temperature is thirty-seven degrees!''

If there was no marketing partnership, the husband and wife discussed all aspects of running the farm. One woman confided she felt she had more say than her husband but let him think he was making the decisions and that she just suggested. "We always respect each other. If there's no respect between parents, then how could we expect the children to respect us. I think it's important to show kindness and love to children as often and as much as possible." One husband told me he loved his wife so much that, "Sometimes I feel like swallowing her and then bringing her up again when I want to talk to her. We love being together and talking to each other even after forty years."

In earlier days the farm was usually in the husband's name, but later joint ownership with the wife became more frequent. This may have been the result of the taxation laws that make it more advantageous to distribute property, of a change in ideology, of adaptation to local conditions, or of a combination of such factors. Table 16 sets out the number of farms held jointly.

ii] *Parents and children* Most people said that a family of three children was the minimum and the majority wanted more. One of the priests believed that Griffith had the highest birthrate in Australia, but I am not sure whether this was true. In the twenty years between 1950 and 1969 there were 4,470 baptisms in the four Roman Catholic churches in Wade Shire (see table 17).

Table 17. Roman Catholic baptisms, 1950–69

	Italians	Australians
Yoogali, Hanwood, and Yenda Roman Catholic churches	1,759	–
Griffith Roman Catholic church	997	1,714
	2,756	1,714

SOURCE: Compiled from church registers.

Children were welcome, and families smothered them with love and affection. They were happy in the atmosphere of the farm, and while still young they shared and understood their parents' work. Until recently the boys grew up assuming that at some time they would have farms of their own, and the girls believed they would marry farmers. Parents aimed to set up their sons, and sons helped them to fulfil their ambition.

Both parents were more concerned about the sons. Daughters were loved, but economically they presented a lesser problem. They did not expect to receive a dowry or inherit a farm but rather to marry into one. Parents have only recently started paying boys for their work. "My son didn't want to be paid for his work on our farm, but I insisted," said one parent. "It was like wages, but he didn't draw it. I thought it would be a good idea in case of probate or for when we buy a farm in his name." One girl said to me, "My girl friend is marrying an only son with four sisters. Think how lucky she is, walking straight into a big property; not like me and my husband with his four brothers."

Sons affected the farmer's attitude to his work. Parents valued girls but hoped to have at least one boy in spite of the fact that daughters simplified matters as they did not receive farms. When one girl married an Australian boy her mother informed the young man, "We Italians are only concerned to set up our sons. As far as the girls go we give them a trousseau, and they'll share in what is left in my name when I die. Dad's properties will go to the boys. If you think we'll get a farm for you, you're all wrong. It's up to your parents to look to that."

This woman did not know that there was a limit to the amount of irrigable land a man could hold and had never heard of a Home Maintenance Area. Later I discovered other women who were equally ignorant about the land-tenure system; but all regarded it as natural that parents should aim at buying farms for their sons as soon as possible. What had obviously begun as an adaptation to an institutional rule became an accepted aspiration.

Most women telephoned or saw their married daughters frequently. "Sometimes I talk to Diana three or four times a day, so it's just as though she was next door. I talk to all my kids every day. I have an enormous telephone bill. Jimmy phoned and told me all the things that happened yesterday. To-day his seasonal workers didn't turn up, so Dad and I will go over tomorrow and help him pack the grapes. We'll do this as long as he needs us. The contractors have finished picking on our farm. But I wish his farm was closer. It's a ten-minute drive, but we'll do anything to help the kids."

Berto, her husband, was kind and gentle and loved children. He summed up his attitude, "I'd never adopt children, but I'll give money to help orphanages. I only want children of my own blood living with me."

More recently, with soaring prices, a father with several sons was unlikely to be able to afford to buy for them all. Table 18 indicates the number of families who owned more than one farm and how many each owned. Thirty Veneto families owned two irrigation farms each. These may have belonged to a father and son, or two brothers, or possibly to distant cousins. I did not check on the exact relationships but assumed that people with the same name were somehow related. One group of Veneti with the same name owned thirteen farms. I know that at least five of these were brothers. A group of Calabresi with the same name, six of whom were brothers, owned twelve farms.

Table 18. Number of families owning two or more farms

Region of Origin	Number of families	Number of farms										
		2	3	4	5	6	7	8	9	10	11	12
Veneto	61 (68%)	30	9	7	7	3	2	1	1			
Calabria	18 (20%)	8	6		1	1	1				1	
Abruzzi	6 (7%)	2		1	3							
Sicilia	5 (4%)	4	1									
Other	1 (1%)	1										
Total	91 (100%)	45	16	8	11	4	3	1	1		1	

SOURCE: Compiled from the books and records of the W.C. & I.C.

In some cultures, in Vasilika in Greece for example, people freely acknowledged that the parents' paying for a young son's training in a trade or profession was adequate compensation for his loss of land.[16] In Griffith, however, no two families had, as yet, the same notion of what was proper. One woman's father, who had died in the early 1950s, left two-thirds of his estate to his son and one-third to be shared equally by his two daughters. Although at the time the woman did not find this unfair, she remarked, "I think it's really right to leave the same to all the children. I'd like my children Anna and Tony to inherit the same amount, but it's difficult because most of our assets are in the farm, and if Tony is going to take it over when he gets older I'm not sure how we'd do it." One girl married a younger son who was studying accountancy. She fully accepted that he would continue working in an office and that his brother would take over the father's property. In this family the parents had not succeeded in buying a farm for the eldest son, and he continued working with his father and expected to own it when the latter retired or died. Many parents were reluctant to admit the possibility of conflict even though the eldest boy could have an estate worth perhaps $60,000 while the youngest had to be content with a wage or salary. "The kids are aware of the difficulties, but in our family we just don't talk about it," one housewife confided. "The boys are very close to each other and wouldn't want anything to spoil their relationship. A lot will depend on the wives. That's why I always praise my daughters-in-law. If one of them hurts me I shut my eyes."

On Sundays the sons and daughters and their offspring visited both sets of parents. Usually they lunched with one pair and had tea with the other. Without waiting to be asked, the men mowed the lawns, fixed the tap in the kitchen, or attended to anything else that needed doing.

One day on a farm I was visiting city buyers arrived to pick and take away grapes. A son came over from his farm and negotiated with them. When they had finished he went into the kitchen and handed his mother $400. She wanted him to keep $200, but he refused. "He hates accepting money from us, but I'll give him the $200 when he takes his family for their holidays. The boys are so good to us. If I know that one of them is having trouble with, say, a tractor, I ring up the other boy and suggest that he might go over and help. Of course, he does so if it's at all possible. That's how we stick together."

When father's and son's ambitions and occupations coincided, the relationship was relatively free from the friction and antagonism so characteristic of rural communities where the boys wait until the old man dies before inheriting. What was so noticeable in Griffith was the camaraderie rather than superordination-subordination. In instances where language was a problem, the son interpreted for his father not just out of filial duty but because their interests were the same. Sons were better equipped to deal with the numerous official organizations such as the W.C. & I.C., the C.S.I.R.O., etc. with which the M.I.A. abounded. In many ways then, fathers relied on sons. Mothers took pride in their sons and the relationship of their men. The girls never asked their mother for financial aid but regularly came to her for help with the children, the sewing, the knitting, and for moral support if they were in strife with the mother-in-law or the husband's family.

A twenty-year-old daughter of a local well-to-do family married a boy who had two brothers. The three boys and their parents had four farms bought in quick succession and were thus heavily in debt. When prices dropped catastrophically soon after the last purchase they were in great difficulty. The mother of the girl was worried about her, but there was no mention of cash. When she took a part-time evening job to earn a few dollars the older woman was distressed but said that this would enable the daughter to buy a few things for herself and the baby. Direct financial assistance would have meant giving money to the husband's family.

iii] From birth to marriage Baptisms were an intimate affair and only close relatives and friends attended. As a rule no more than twenty people came, and dinner was held at one of the clubs. Uncles and aunts frequently acted as god-parents to the older children, friends to the younger ones. This was a way of bringing people who were not related closer together. To the older generation the *compare-comare* relationship, and this appellation which they always used when addressing one another, was more meaningful than to younger couples.

The youngsters rarely went to kindergarten but played round the house in the care of older siblings. The mother's prime job was looking after the children, and although many young Italian girls worked in shops and offices, few continued to do so after marriage. Virtually none worked after the arrival of the first baby. If a woman needed a sitter she asked her mother or sister or else took the baby to one of them. She rarely had to ask a neighbour, and only very oc-casionally was she obliged to pay anyone.

The grandmother, baby clinic, and women's magazines influenced young wives in their methods of child rearing. They took great pride in the baby's appearance. Grand-mothers were constantly helping with the sewing and knit-ting. An Australian shopkeeper insisted that Italians sewed, knitted, and mended far more than Australians, and my observations confirmed her view. I was struck by the amount of re-making of old clothes that went on. The grandmother's old skirt became a girl's winter dress, and grandfather's trousers were cut up to make a son's winter pants. The sunroom of many houses looked like a workshop.

Parents with little formal education themselves could not help children with schoolwork. I observed one thirteen-year-old girl trying to do her social studies homework. She was in the sitting room in front of the television set. Her ex-ercise book rested on a schoolcase, which she balanced on her knees. She managed to answer two of the twenty-four questions and then asked her father for help. He took one look and turned to me, "I think it is terrible that children should be made to work so hard at such difficult questions!"

The wealthier Italians, and Northerners in particular, tended to send their children to Catholic schools, and about 600 attended. The same number made up about a quarter of the pupils at the public schools. The headmaster of the primary school informed me that Italian children of the third generation who spoke only English performed just as well as Australians of Anglo-Saxon descent, but he thought that bilingual children lagged a little and newcomers with no English had a lot of trouble. It seemed that parents who were well established were more anxious for their children to continue at school, but as about half of them did not speak English their communication with the teachers was necessarily slight.

According to the headmaster at the public high school language problems as such did not exist, but in first year the Italian students performed badly in I.Q. tests, though later on they improved. In 1969 of the 104 final-year high school students, eleven had Italian names. In the previous year, of the thirteen university scholarships awarded two went to Italians, both girls. One is now studying medicine, the other science. Italian girls stayed at school longer than boys, many completed the School Certificate (fourth year high school), and some went on to the Higher School Certificate. Parents who were better off preferred their daughters not to work on the farm and to continue at school.

Until 1968 the Catholic High School had classes up to fourth year only; pupils wishing to complete fifth and sixth years had to go over to the state public school. The financial plight of the Catholic school was so bad that the priests threatened it would have to close unless parents paid their fees. At that time the sum of $30,000 was needed to keep classes going.

Most of the students enrolled at the Griffith Technical College started there after completing the School Certificate. About half were girls doing either secretarial or dressmaking and millinery courses. Boys attended classes for apprentices in which they trained for branches of the building industry or mechanical and motor engineering. A department of rural studies offered courses in sheep farming and wool classing, but the majority of students were more interested in branches of the building trade. Of the 1,000 enrolments at this college in 1969 nearly half were Italians.

Almost all Italian girls were bilingual and found no difficulty in finding employment in shops or, if they had taken a secretarial course, in offices. Banks, accountants, real-estate offices, lawyers, and shops all tried to have at least one bilingual Italian girl on their staff and preferably more. Doctors also needed them as interpreters. (Apart from the dialect which they learnt at home, many now studied Italian at school.) Australian girls, on the other hand, found difficulty in getting jobs, and they often left Griffith on this account. Some Italian girls attended teachers' colleges, but on the whole parents were reluctant to allow daughters to leave home. They preferred them to work in Griffith and then marry.

Unlike southern Italian girls, those from the north were allowed to go out alone with boys. The different conventions of courtship no doubt contributed to the relative lack of intermarriage between Northerners and Southerners. No southern girl could go out with a boy unchaperoned. One Calabrese girl told me, "We girls don't have much fun till after we're married. Most of us get married in our late teens." Table 19 sets out the rate of intermarriage.[17]

Table 19. Rates of intermarriage 1950–69, Griffith, Hanwood, Yenda, and Yoogali Roman Catholic churches

	1950–54		1955–59		1960–64		1965–69		Total in 20 years	
Calabrese and Calabrese	26	(21%)	33	(22%)	35	(25%)	40	(25%)	134	(23%)
Veneto and Veneto	75	(61%)	90	(59%)	62	(45%)	67	(41%)	294	(51%)
Veneto female and Calabrese male	2	(2%)	–		1	(1%)	4	(2%)	7	(1.5%)
Veneto male and Calabrese female	7	(6%)	9	(6%)	16	(11%)	11	(7%)	43	(7.5%)
Veneto female and Australian male	3	(2%)	4	(3%)	11	(8%)	8	(5%)	26	(4%)
Veneto male and Australian female	5	(4%)	11	(7%)	11	(8%)	23	(14%)	50	(9%)
Calabrese female and Australian male	1	(1%)	–		1	(1%)	3	(2%)	5	(1%)
Calabrese male and Australian female	4	(3%)	5	(3%)	1	(1%)	5	(4%)	15	(3%)
	123	(100%)	152	(100%)	138	(100%)	161	(100%)	574	(100%)

SOURCE: Compiled from church registers.

Weddings were a never-ending topic of conversation. The scarcity of jobs and the parents' unwillingness to allow girls to go to the city ensured that they would marry early. Doubtless the risk of premarital pregnancy was thereby reduced. Veneto boys and girls met at school or at the many balls, dances, and functions held by the churches or other voluntary organizations.

The wedding was the most important *rite-de-passage* in a person's life. No matter how poor, the family spent much money, time, and effort on the preparations. A considerable sum also went on photographs. Veneto weddings closely resembled those of Australians, with bridesmaids, best man, and formal breakfast. An affair with 400 guests was regarded as large, in contrast with a Calabrese marriage, where anything from 800–1800 guests was the rule. Although almost all the relatives were invited, I have heard one Veneto woman say that they had so many of them, she thought about 200, that if they had invited them all as well as friends the affair would have been unmanageable.

Among Veneti it has recently become the custom for the parents of each of the parties to pay for their own guests, but a few years ago the bride's family accepted the responsibility alone. Everyone attends many weddings; one Trevisan woman told me she was invited to between eight and ten weddings every year and found them a great expense.

Only older children attended Veneto weddings, and there was more decorum but less *joie de vivre* than at a Calabrese celebration, where children of all ages rushed and skated up and down the floor, flew paper aeroplanes across the tables, and had a wonderful time without any restrictions. When the Australian bride of a Calabrese boy insisted that no children attend the reception only twenty of the guests arrived.

As is to be expected, the relationship between the parents of the young couple was better if the socio-economic standing of the two families was approximately the same. "One of my daughters-in-law comes from a family that is higher (*più alta*)," remarked one woman. "She is more educated and knows how to do things nicely. My other daughter-in-law comes from a family of poor vegetable growers, and I like her better because she's more like me."

iv] *Siblings* Girls liked to have their mothers and sisters near at hand. Time and again in conversation I observed the importance attached to being in touch with the sister, telephoning her, visiting her, and helping her with the children. Sisters frequently arranged to go shopping together or attend a fashion show or make-up demonstration. Brothers did not speak about their mutual attachment as freely as sisters did, but I often observed their affection in the home and in the clubs. One man in whose house I was living rose from the breakfast table and explained, "My brother's wife has had a baby, so I'll go over and give him a hand with the picking to let him visit her at lunchtime." A young married woman confessed, "My husband won't let anyone say a bad word about his younger brother even when he knows the fellow is taking advantage of him. It makes me mad." And a mother confided, "We bought the farm for the older boy before we bought the second one for the younger. Naturally we buy for the older boy first. It so happens that the second farm is quite a bit bigger, and Gino, the younger fellow, earns more. I don't think it worries his brother. Well, at least he doesn't say anything."

During one winter month when I was living with the parents of these two, the pair of them, with the help of a work manual, put together a big truck that the younger had come by cheaply in a wrecking yard. He intended to use it on his farm and had also bought all the missing engine parts. The older brother came each day and worked for hours. There was no question of payment. Their undemonstrative affection, the harmony, and their obvious enjoyment of one another's company prompted the mother to say, "It makes me so proud to see them together, Gino always asks his older brother Tony for advice. Most younger brothers look up to the older ones."

Brothers felt a sense of responsibility toward their sisters, especially if the latter needed help. But the greatest camaraderie tended to be along sex lines.

v] Relatives Since each nuclear family had its own house, people could choose the relatives with whom they wished to maintain close contact. Some had so many kinsfolk that they could not possibly be in touch with everybody. Even with a small circle it was unusual for all to get on equally well.

One woman had not been on speaking terms with her brother and his wife for over a year "because of what one of them said." Yet their daughters were inseparable, saw each other daily, went out together, and attended the same teachers' college. In Italy the proximity of living would have led to overt fighting and abuse, and the girls would have had to take sides. In Griffith the rift was not aired or discussed in public, and the parents had no objections to the cousins' going out together. Tacit new rules dictated that disagreements should, where possible, be conducted in a "civilized and gentlemanly manner."

The church

The Griffith and Yenda churches were established before the Second World War to cater for all Roman Catholics regardless of their background. In the early years, however, the Italians attended reluctantly and irregularly. Anticlericalism was widespread; many hesitated to mix with other people, particularly at the Griffith Roman Catholic church which was run along Irish lines, unfamiliar to Italians. Common excuses for non-attendance were too much work and lack of transport.

The first priest to minister specifically to Italians was a Veneto, Father Modotti, who before the war came to the district on short visits. Then in 1939 a church was erected in Yoogali for Italians. Father Bongiorno, an Aeolian, organized the members of the congregation into building it themselves, and even the most bitter anti-clericals co-operated. To have their own place of worship made them feel at ease, even if they had no intention of visiting it for anything other than births, marriages and funerals. A second Italian church, at Hanwood, followed after the war.

On Sundays there were six masses at the Griffith church,

two morning masses at Yoogali and Hanwood, and at Yenda one in the morning and one in the evening. People dressed well for church. All the women had their heads covered, and the men wore coats and ties. Apart from an odd crying baby or a child who made a noise, the congregation was quiet and attentive. Announcements and the sermon were given in English and Italian, and the service lasted about forty-five minutes. At the end of the mass people did not stand around or talk for long. They met and greeted each other, and frequently I heard them say, "See you later at the club." At one Sunday mass in Yoogali I counted 357 people. The service finished at about ten and fifteen minutes later everyone had gone home.

The Veneti and the post-war immigrants tended to be better church-goers, according to the priests, than the Calabresi or earlier arrivals. Few of the Calabresi came to church until the importation of a plaster copy of a Madonna from one of their home villages. They carried the statue ceremoniously into the church and placed it on the altar. One of the men then rushed from the congregation, turned to the people, and shouted "*Viva la Madonna!*" The congregation responded with enthusiasm, "*Viva! Viva!*" The priest who told me the story asserted that there has been a definite improvement in attendance since.

Italian priests went to church balls and other secular functions and joined in the singing. They were part of the social scene. Church and social life overlapped to a considerable extent through the activities of the vigorous church clubs and the Catholic school.

I was fortunate to become friends with one Trevisan priest. A hardworking man with a sense of humour and a great deal of insight, he was becoming increasingly influential in the community. He dropped in to visit people, joined them at dinner, or came in afterwards to show slides of his last trip, arrange a school committee meeting, or whatever needed doing. He was at ease with both Northerners and Southerners, and people talked to him as a friend or family confidant. Many called him by his first name.

Italian priests aimed at coaxing rather than exerting moral pressure to get people to come to church. In an Italian sermon one of them said, "In Italy people were ashamed not to go to mass because of what their neighbours would think. Those inside the church would point a finger at a man passing outside and say, 'He is a communist!'. Here, people come of their own free will, no one forces them, and this makes them better Catholics. Here we have left behind the old traditions and are guided by the Holy Spirit, and this to me is a miracle of faith." He did not translate this part into English.

Some Veneti, however, were still anti-clerical. One of my main respondents, who came to Australia in the early 1930s, told me that he never went to church, not even on Christmas Day or Easter. He was sure the rise in attendance started with the post-war immigrants. Those who came in his day were either communists, anti-fascists, or anti-clericals. He did not like priests and assured me that whether a man attended church or not depended on the insistence of his wife. He was also reluctant to allow his children to go to the Catholic school, though on this point he gave in to his wife. She was unhappy about his attitude, "Australian Catholic girls really push their husbands to go, but Italian girls can't force a husband if he really doesn't want to," she told me.

The father and brothers of this man did not attend church either, but when one brother married an Australian girl in the Anglican church the old man was angry. He was annoyed not at the different sect but because, "The man should be the boss, and even if he never goes to church the wife should marry in his religion—they should have been married in the Catholic church." In spite of anti-clericalism, my respondent thought that people should marry in church, "even if the next time you're there is for your funeral; to marry in a registry office is somehow not right." He made no donations to the church but was most generous with gifts to other voluntary organizations because "they help everybody". He was the only one who spoke frankly to me of his feelings.

How much church going was guided by true religious sentiment was hard to judge. In thirty years only three Griffith girls and two boys have entered Holy Orders. In conversation on Sundays people often mentioned that they had already been to or still had to go to mass, just as they might mention whether they had had dinner, "We'll come over after tea, but we still have to go to mass first."

Italians were reluctant to donate money to the church or pay fees at the school. Irish and Australian priests and Australian Roman Catholics disapproved of their attitude.

At the home of a Veneto professional man married to an Australian Catholic a discussion raged over this subject. He was influential within the community, welfare-minded, devout, more assimilated than most, and as much at ease in Australian as Italian company. The argument was with an intelligent and well-educated man who had come to Australia as an adult from another province in northern Italy. The conversation ran like this:

Alfonso [Veneto]: "I went to the Griffith church meeting last night and Father George [Irish] and the other Australians said how terrible it is that Italians just will not contribute to the church or the school. It makes me sick too, the way you can never get Italians to do anything for anybody except their own families. Fifty per cent of the parish at Griffith church is of Italian descent. I'm prepared to form a committee of Italians from the church to go from house to house and put the following questions to each household:

1. Do you think the state assists the church?
2. Do you know the position of the church?
3. Do you know the financial state of the schools?
4. Do you think the state assists Catholic schools?
5. What do you expect from the Catholic church?
6. Do you know how much the priest gets?

After all, in Italy the priest was the most important person in the village. Everybody gave to the church a portion of his harvest, money, and so on. Why don't they give here? I want to prove to Father George that he isn't getting the message across to the people!"

Domenico: "This is exerting pressure on the people, and I don't think it's right, nor is this the right time. This'll take a generation. You're dealing with migrants who've had a very hard time."

Alfonso: "If Father George would go to some of the Italian houses and just say hello to Antonio and Maria and pat the kid on the head or sit down at the kitchen table Maria would feel so honoured. Even if they can't communicate he'd be doing a good job."

Domenico: "Father Niccola [now transferred to Melbourne] had the personality and could do this, but another person is just wasting his time. Father George would be better employed doing something else. The trouble is that you want to force too many things too quickly. Many things have already changed. But you need a certain personality to go to these people. You need a natural flair or instinct to hit it off with certain people, and Father George just hasn't got it."

Alfonso: "What do you want, a miracle?"

The point Alfonso had missed was that people in Italy did not donate to institutions unless they were pressured into doing so. In Griffith they helped one another, but the assistance was direct person-to-person, to members of the family, friends, and *paesani*. It may have been along a horizontal line, from people of equal standing, or along a vertical line, similar to a patron-client relationship. Domenico understood, but Alfonso did not appreciate that it was only the more assimilated of the Italians who would be likely to donate to an impersonal institution such as a church, school, or voluntary association.

The priests in Griffith did not attempt to bring individuals into disrepute, as they did in Treviso by announcing from the pulpit that someone was a communist. But the Italians in Griffith turned to the church only for spiritual guidance; they sought advice on all other matters outside.

Voluntary associations

If an outsider asks an Italian in Griffith what makes the place so much pleasanter to live in than any other, the reply invariably is, "The social life, the clubs; there's always something on." The town's reputation has spread far among Italians in Australia. During Easter 1970 a visiting priest came to see how the clubs operated for the explicit purpose of starting something of the kind in Western Australia.

To understand social life in Griffith today we must take a number of factors into account: the proximity of farms to the centre and to each other; the size and density of the ethnic group; and the background of feuds, animosities, and frictions out of which the type of social intercourse we find today evolved.

It is likely that Italians would have formed associations even in a friendly environment. Australian xenophobia of the early days, however, had the effect of developing a more closely knit Italian community than would otherwise have been the case. Had Italians been able to join existing Australian clubs or been unmolested in the pubs, they would have had less incentive to form clubs catering for their own social needs. These new groups accentuated and made more apparent the Australian/Italian division. Further factors encouraging the proliferation of organizations were the frictions between the religious and the anti-clerical Veneti, and between the Northerners and the Southerners.[18]

Many ethnic groups form associations to maintain institutions from the old culture and cushion the shock of the new environment.[19] In an urban setting, however, where there are numerous types of organizations, they tend to be less all-embracing. They therefore do not as a rule create the same cleavage between immigrants and the indigenous population.

I listened to one man reminiscing, "I remember the early days when we were terrified to go into town, especially anywhere near a pub. The place was full of Australians, mainly returned soldiers, and they'd always pick a fight. They'd call us 'bloody dagoes' or 'spags' and say we smelled of garlic and onions. We only went into town when we had to. On the other hand, we had some wonderful times. We used to get together and sing and enjoy ourselves, and whenever there was a wedding we'd celebrate for two or three days. We stuck together like one big family. Today we aren't so close any more because there are so many of us, and people are mainly interested in their own family and friends."

i] *The development of the clubs* I spoke to numerous people, sometimes singly, sometimes in groups, about the development of the clubs. Some had been instrumental in forming several. Although there is no documentary material available, I found remarkable corroboration in the stories. Gaps in memory of one respondent were filled by another.

In the early years the Italian community was made up largely of Northerners, most of whom knew one another. Although the group was tightly-knit, transport was a problem. Until the mid-1930s the only occasions when all came together were weddings, Christmas, New Year, and Easter. It became traditional at Christmas and New Year for all to go to the river, have a picnic, and play *bocce*. On such occasions four men made up a band.

In 1936 these four bandsmen formed themselves into the Yoogali Amusement Company and built a small meeting place there, which they called the Coronation Hall because it was completed in 1937, the year George VI was crowned.

To comply with the stringent drinking regulations, they built two small rooms on the adjoining block of land, formed a club committee, and started the Italo-Australian Club. Each member was now allowed by law to have his own locker in which to store liquor under lock and key. In this way he could drink on the premises. The Italo-Australian Club had 300 lockers and charged a nominal fee of five shillings (50 cents) per annum. Coronation Hall and the Italo-Australian Club were officially two separate entities, and drinking was permitted only in the latter. The procedure was to buy discs, profits from which went to the Amusement Company at the Coronation Hall, and present them to one of the partners who worked at the Club. The latter then opened a locker, took out the liquor, and served it to the club member.

One of my respondents recalled, "It wasn't a club in the real sense; it was supposed to be a get-together place, like a *trattoria* or *osteria* back home, and also a kind of business enterprise. We were supposed to make some profit on the sandwiches, drinks, and *bocce*. Saturday night and Sundays were the big days. There was a hall, bar, and *bocce*. On Saturday night there was a dance, and we all put on our best clothes. Australians used to come and get drunk, make trouble, and refuse to leave at closing time. Often they were seasonal workers. Also Australian girls came unaccompanied and went for the Italian boys. This also started fights. The Italian girls always came with their parents. Sunday was the day when the women brought the little kids, and all the family was there. We used to make cakes and sandwiches. The kids had games, the men played cards and *bocce*, and everybody loved it."

This small social centre offered a regular meeting place for Italians at weekends. To the partners of the company it afforded a part-time occupation. They all either had farms or other employment. After four years all but one of them, Dino, pulled out.

In 1946 a committee headed by the bishop of Wagga offered to buy Dino out, but he would not agree. The members of this group then formed themselves into the Catholic Club, to which only Catholics were admitted—though Calabresi, permitted in the Italo-Australian Club, were excluded. In effect, the club was made up of the more religious Veneti. They built a clubroom at the back of the church at Yoogali. Within a week of the formation of this organization the committee of the Italo-Australian Club formed themselves into the Yoogali Club, and Dino leased the premises to them.

A number of Yoogali Club members also belonged to the Catholic Club, and the more prominent now began concentrating on this latter organization. The split was primarily between the more and the less religious Veneti.

One of the Yoogali Club initiators recalled how, "The Calabresi used to come and often started fights. One day I called in their head, a fellow called Joe, and said to him, 'Why do your boys always pick fights? It makes it tough for the rest of the members.' Joe slapped the table with the palm of his hand and said, 'O.K. Peter, from now on there'll be no more fights!' Sure enough, there was no trouble after that. Calabresi are like that. There's usually a leader, and they do as he tells them."

In 1949 the Yoogali Club bought land across the road and started planning new premises. The Catholic Club also aimed to have a new clubhouse a few hundred yards away on land belonging to the church. In 1956 the new Yoogali building was completed, and the Catholic Club premises were finished a year later.

Now that the Yoogali Club had moved, a further organization, the Coronation Club, came into being. It leased the now-vacant Coronation Hall and rooms. For a short period Dino managed it with the help of a committee, but in 1957 he sold the property to a Calabrese who still owns it. The club occupies the premises on a lease. It has become progressively more and more identified with Calabresi. As we saw, the Catholic Club was associated from the start with Veneti. The Yoogali Club was, and still is, mixed and includes Australians. At the end of the 1950s the jealousies died down, the clubs started playing *bocce* against each other, and membership became more fluid.

At the time of the opening of the new Yoogali Club premises in 1956 it had the best facilities, much bigger and more luxurious than those at the Catholic Club. Many were keen to serve on the committee, and trouble between committee members soon bubbled to the surface. One cause of friction was the desire of some to expand still further. The opposition accused those who wished to do so of seeking profits from building contracts. Another problem was that Calabresi, unlike Veneti, always voted as a bloc under the direction of an unofficial leader. By the mid-1960s most of the committee members were Calabresi. At length the additions were built, and debts began to mount. Many of the Australians withdrew when the new Leagues Club and Ex-

Servicemen's Club premises opened in the centre of Griffith in the early 1960s, and profits from drinks and poker machines dropped dramatically.

In 1956 a group of Hanwood farmers formed the Hanwood Catholic Club (the Catholic Club at Yoogali then became known as the Yoogali Catholic Club). Many say that jealousy induced the Hanwood committee to start, but others say that the Hanwood people wanted their own club although Yoogali is only a six-minutes' drive away. This new club met in two rooms near the Hanwood church and school. Impressive modern premises were opened in 1965.

The sequence of events suggests that the formation of one club may well lay the foundation for the emergence of more, either through a schism or as a result of blanket exclusions.

The clubs served the purpose of bringing together Italians and helping them to cope with the strange and frequently hostile environment. To soften the shock of change, immigrants try to retain as many of the familiar institutions as are compatible with the new circumstances. It was here that Northerners and Southerners sometimes clashed. The different clubs thus did not have varying functions but rather catered for identical needs in ways that were familiar to the respective regional groups.

Australians, however, regarded all the clubs at Yoogali as simply "Italian".

ii] The Continental Music Club In the early 1950s minimal social contact took place between Australians and Italians. The latter were even reluctant to seek advice on farming methods from agricultural advisory boards.

In 1947 a new Irrigation Research and Extension Committee (I.R.E.C.) was formed with the aim of guiding research, advising farmers of the latest scientific techniques, and raising production through planned extension programmes. It had twelve government representatives, twelve farmer representatives, and one from the University of Sydney. The first fulltime secretary-treasurer, appointed a few years later, was Albert J. Grassby, who had settled in the area in 1950.

He had been a specialist information officer with the Commonwealth Scientific and Industrial Research Organization (C.S.I.R.O.) and then with the New South Wales Department of Agriculture.

Members of the I.R.E.C. were aware that to institute more effective farming they needed the co-operation of the large Italian community, and that to do so they had first to establish better contact and rapport.

In 1951 Grassby and four Italians started the Continental Music Club. His aim was to bring all Italians together, including the women, and through the club win their confidence. From the start they liked his manner and personality. Born in Australia of Irish-Spanish descent, he was able to keep a foot in both camps, the Australian and the immigrant.

Using the club as a point of contact, Grassby's objective was not only to propagate information about agriculture, but also to bring Italians into the community and as he put it, "tear down the wall of prejudice". (This was a time when the Returned Servicemen's League was trying to have a resolution passed prohibiting the use of foreign languages in public.)

The first committee consisted of three Veneti (one of whom became the president), one Abruzzese, and Grassby as secretary. On all occasions he acted as master of ceremonies.

The club met each Sunday evening in the Coronation Hall, though it was not connected with the club. They danced, sang, and played records. Grassby then started inviting Australian community leaders and their wives to attend. On one occasion the shire president and his wife came, on another the head of the R.S.L., and in 1954 Harold Holt, the then Minister for Immigration, danced till the early hours of the morning. Intentionally Australians were in the minority, surrounded by people speaking Italian. On some evenings the committee arranged to meet other groups—Germans, Yugoslavs, Spaniards, Irish, Poles, and others.

Under Grassby's initiative the Music Club started

bilingual radio programmes, one hour on Thursday evenings and half an hour on Sundays. Italian films were also shown. Handicraft demonstrations encouraged Italian and Australian women to exhibit needlework and embroidery. [20] The committee joined with the Good Neighbour Council and Agricultural Extension to arrange special nights for balls and carnivals to foster interaction between the numerous small ethnic groups.

After 1960, when relations between Italians and Australians had greatly improved, and there was no longer overt animosity, the activities of the club waned. Today there are still regular radio features, one Sunday lunch-hour radio programme when Grassby comperes a session of "Songs and Music from Around the Globe". Between records he chats to his listeners, telling them titbits of local news. It is a popular programme, and most families enjoy listening to the songs and to "Our Al". The other is a Thursday evening request programme.

Some refer to the Continental Music Club as "The club before the clubs". It would perhaps be more appropriate to call it the club that bridged the clubs.

iii] The Good Neighbour Council In 1953 a local branch of the Good Neighbour Council was formed.[21] The fact that this body was part of the Immigration Department gave it additional standing and facilitated direct contact with official bodies, institutions, and parliamentarians. It became the formal arm of the Continental Music Club with which it joined in organizing social functions and inviting influential people to the area. It was a co-ordinating body with which most church, welfare and social organizations in Griffith were affiliated. On its committee were representatives from most churches and clubs in Griffith, including the R.S.L. The aim was to harness their assistance in encouraging popular support for migrant integration.

Until a few years ago the branch met once a month to deal with problems such as reuniting families, naturalization, securing nominations for entry permits to Australia, and so forth. It appointed the first bilingual liaison officer for the Extension Services, provided interpreters for the hospital and baby clinics, and attended to numerous requests for help. Today it meets every three months.

iv] The clubs today I shall not go into the hundred-odd voluntary associations or organizations such as the Parents' and Citizens' associations, Boy Scouts, cat clubs, and pony clubs because few Trevisani are involved with these.[22] I will concentrate instead on the seven social and four service clubs (Australian and Italian), around which much of the life of a large section of the population revolves (see table 20).

The social clubs
Each of the social clubs has its own premises. Three are situated in the centre of Griffith and are regarded as Australian. The other four are thought of as Italian, three within a few hundred metres of each other in Yoogali, and the fourth at Hanwood. A striking characteristic of all seven is that they are the province of men only. At three, women can be associates (Yoogali, Ex-Servicemen's and Leagues), but even here they do not look upon the club as an integral part of their social life.

(i) *The Jondaryan* was started in 1928, and originally the membership was restricted to a hundred prominent Australian property owners and professionals within a forty-eight kilometre radius of Griffith. The entrance fee was high, and without doubt this was and still is the most prestigious club in the district. Today, the main club activities are bowls and billiards. Dances are not held, and there is no restaurant, though snacks are provided. By today's standards the facilities are poor. The income from poker machines is small, and in order to provide even modest comfort the policy has had to be changed to admit many new members. Until a few years ago it was not easy for an Italian to join, and of those who have now gained entry few feel at ease in the conservative establishment atmosphere. The first Italian was admitted in 1959, thirty-one years after the club's incep-

Table 20. Membership of clubs

Club	Year Established	First Italian admitted	Total Membership	Australian Members	Italian Members	Veneti	Calabresi	Comment
Social clubs								
Jondaryan	1928	1959	700 (100%)	662 (94.8%)	38 (5.2%)	34 (4.8%)	1 (0.4%)	There were 2 Sicilian and 1 Neapolitan members.
Ex-Servicemen's Club	1938 (new premises opened 1964)	1950	about 4,000 (100%)	about 3,500 (87.5%)	about 500 (12.5%)	?	?	I have lumped members and associate members together.
Leagues Club	1958	1958	about 1,400 (100%)	about 1,220 (87%)	about 180 (13%)	?	?	
Yoogali Club	1946 (new premises opened 1956)	1946	about 1,750 (100%)	about 420 (24%)	about 1,330 (76%)	?	?	There are said to be approximately equal numbers of Veneti and Calabresi.
Catholic Club, Yoogali	1946 (new premises opened 1957) 1956	1946	780 (100%)	85 (10.9%)	695 (89.1%)	670 (85.9%)	25 (3.2%)	
Coronation Club	1956	1956	600 (100%)	100 (16.7%)	500 (83.3%)	20 Veneti and others (3.3%)	480 (80%)	There were no books available; the numbers I quote are estimates given by the "head Calabrese".
Catholic Club, Hanwood	1956 (new premises opened 1965)	1956	800 (100%)	76 (9.5%)	724 (90.5%)	640 Veneti and others (80%)	84 (10.5%)	
Service clubs								
Rotary	1944	1955	73 (100%)	67 (91.8%)	6 (8.2%)	6 (8.2%)	—	
Apex	1954	?	40 (100%)	40 (100%)	—	—	—	There has been one Italian member.
Lions	1963	1963	37 (100%)	24 (64.9%)	13 (35.1%)	11 (29.7%)	—	
Junior Chamber of Commerce	1967	1967	24 (100%)	21 (87.5%)	3 (12.5%)	2 (8.3%)	—	This club was started by an Italian lawyer.

SOURCE: Compiled from the club membership books of various organizations.

tion. Of the 700 members, 38 are Italian (34 Veneti, 2 Siciliani, 1 Calabrese, and 1 Napoletano). The committee is made up of eleven Australians. Although this club is no longer in its heyday, it still has prestige. The entrance fee is $4.20 and the yearly subscription $10.50.

(ii) *The Ex-Servicemen's Club* originated in 1938 as an R.S.L. club and changed its name in 1940. Only persons who have served overseas are eligible for full membership. Of the 963 full members 30 are Italian; of 3,044 male associates 467 are Italian. Of the 850 women associates 25 have Italian names (I have not included them in table 20).

The new building, dating from 1964, has excellent facilities for bowls, darts, snooker, and cards, as well as a restaurant, bar, and poker machines. It is a meeting place for drinking and eating and is closed only on Christmas Day. The main profits are derived from poker machines and the bar. Saturday is the big night, when couples come to dine and dance, and almost as many women as men are present. On Saturday nights approximately 500 meals are served. On other days women when shopping drop in for lunch. The staff of seventy includes four chefs and eight waitresses.

The first Italian was admitted in 1950, but in 1970 there was none on the committee of fifteen. The entrance fee is $5.20 and the yearly subscription $2.10.

(iii) *The Leagues Club* is also conveniently situated, right opposite the Ex-Servicemen's Club. The manager calls it the "working man's club". It was started in 1958, and the buildings were put up in the early 1960s. Friday is the big night here, when members play snooker and the poker machines and drink, dine, and dance. The club organizes and runs football and cricket teams. Light luncheons are available seven days a week but dinners only on Thursdays, Fridays, Saturdays, and Sundays. About 400 light lunches and about 200 dinners are served each week.

Italians were able to join from the inception, and today, of approximately 1,440 members 180 are Italian. There is one Italian on a committee of ten. The entrance fee is $4.20 and yearly subscription $2.10.

(iv) *The Yoogali Club*, as I mentioned, was started in 1946, and when the new premises were opened in 1956 it was the first in Griffith to offer all the amenities of a modern club. There is a large dining room, ballroom, bar, and facilities for a number of sports. As in all Italian clubs, there is great emphasis on *bocce*, a type of outdoor bowls that is a favourite national sport. Tuesday nights are especially devoted to snooker and billiards, Wednesday nights to darts and carpet bowls, and Friday nights to *bocce*.

Australians frequented the Yoogali Club more often until the Ex-Servicemen's and Leagues Clubs built their present premises in the 1960s. Meals are served on Saturdays and Sundays, and on Saturday nights there is always a dance. Australians tend to predominate on Saturday nights and Italians and their families on Sundays. A large percentage of the Italian attendance is Calabrese, indeed it is unusual to see a Northerner and a Southerner drinking or playing *bocce* together at this club.

People frequently choose the ballroom and dining room for such functions as debutante balls or weddings when there may be as many as 400 guests. (The larger Calabrese weddings are accommodated in a shabby building at the showground.) Club profits come primarily from poker machines and the bar, but these have dropped since the opening of clubs in the centre of town, and the Yoogali Club is now in financial difficulties.

Of approximately 1,750 members about 420 are Australian. Officials estimate that the remainder is made up of equal numbers of Veneti and Calabresi, as well as some Abruzzesi, Siciliani, and others. Of the committee of thirteen, ten are Italian. The entrance fee is $6.30 and the yearly subscription $2.10.

(v) *The Yoogali Catholic Club*, like the Yoogali Club, was started in 1946, and new premises were opened in 1957. It is smaller than the Yoogali Club and is also known as the Veneto Club. Full membership is restricted to Catholics, but non-Catholics may become associates. It is well run and does not depend on the five poker machines for income. A large bar has tables set for cards, and people also play carpet bowls, billiards, and darts. Adjoining is a dining room to which part alone, women are admitted. Dinners are available only on Sunday nights, and the predominance of men then is striking. Of about 170 meals served, only about 20 are for women or children. On Saturday evenings the club caters for private functions.

In the summer more women and children accompany their men and sit outside watching *bocce*, but they regard this club as very much for men. Wives and young children accompany the men for dinner on special occasions such as birthdays, baptisms, or anniversaries. On Mother's Day the dining room is packed with couples and their offspring.

Of 780 full members 670 are Veneti, 85 Australian, and only 25 Calabresi. There are 70 non-Catholic associates. Few Australians drop in and when they do it is usually in the company of an Italian friend or for a particular occasion. Business connections are an important reason for their joining but frequently business and friendship overlap. An Australian Protestant who is a close friend of the Veneto president arranged for his daughter's wedding reception to take place in the clubrooms after the ceremony at the Anglican church.

Eight of the nine-man committee are Italian. The ninth is an Australian lawyer married to an Italian. The entrance fee is $6.30 and the yearly subscription $2.10.

(vi) The *Coronation Club* is located in the shabby old Coronation Hall and was started when the Yoogali Club shifted in 1956. It is regarded purely as a Calabrese organization and ranks lowest of all in prestige. The facilities are poor, although *bocce* is, of course, catered for. There are only three poker machines, and profits come mainly from the brisk bar trade. No food is served, and frequently people go across to the grocery a few doors down the street to buy bread and salami. When I visited this club a number of card games were in progress, and numerous Australian workmen came in for drinks and a quick game with the mini pool or poker machine. While other clubs shut at midnight or 1:00A.M., this one stays open till all hours. Saturday and Sunday nights are the busiest.

I was told by the unofficial head of the Calabresi, that there are about 500 Calabrese members, about 100 Australians, and about 20 Veneti and other Italians. The manager said that the Australians "are good members because they are steady and reliable drinkers". This was certainly the only Italian club where I saw a steady stream of Australians coming and going. Apart from *bocce*, the Calabresi play *briscola*, a Calabrese card game and members join *bocce* competitions. The club owns just under one hectare of land on the other side of Griffith on which it hopes eventually to build.

Until five or six years ago the entire committee was Italian, but now there are eight Australians and three Italians (all Veneti). The entrance fee is $4.20 and yearly subscription $2.10.

(vii) The *Catholic Club*, Hanwood, began in 1956, and its new clubhouse was opened in 1965. Non-Catholics can be full members. People are agreed that this is the only true "family club", where all feel at home and where Veneti and Calabresi drink and play cards and *bocce* together. Their *lingua franca* is a mixture of Italian and English.

Men drop in frequently after work during the week for a drink or a short game of *bocce*, cards, or carpet bowls. Sunday is the big day—it is called Ladies' Day, and the restaurant is open to women and children, who together make up nearly half the customers. The club is particularly popular with teenagers because, unlike the other Italian organizations, it runs dances every Sunday night. It also seems to be the club where people from different regions mingle most easily.

The area of Hanwood has the largest concentration of Abruzzesi and Spaniards, and many of them belong to this club. Of a total membership of 800, 387 were Veneti, 233 Abruzzesi and Siciliani, 84 Calabresi, 76 Australians, and 20 Spaniards. As far as actual attendance is concerned, it would appear that at any given time there are approximately just as many Southerners as Northerners present. The large number of Veneto membership is deceptive because of the tendency of Veneti to belong to numerous clubs. The committee is wholly Italian. Entrance fee is $6.00 and yearly subscription $3.00.

The service clubs
The service clubs are Rotary, Lions, Apex, and Junior Chamber of Commerce. Unlike the others which are primarily social, these also have philanthropic aims and collect money for various welfare causes. Once again the service clubs, like the social clubs, are all-male clubs and a man can officially belong to only one. None has its own clubhouse, and rooms are rented for the regular meetings from the social clubs, generally the Leagues or the Ex-Servicemen's.

(i) *Rotary* is affiliated with Rotary clubs throughout Australia and the world. Rotary has a rule whereby each branch has only one member from each profession—there should be only one pharmacist, one real estate agent, one lawyer, and so on. Inevitably this regulation makes entry difficult, but to my certain knowledge four accountants belong.[23] This apparent exclusiveness helps make Rotary the most prestigious of the service clubs.

Rotary meets every Tuesday evening for one and a half hours, and a guest speaker is always engaged. Meetings are preceded by dinner costing $1.10. Unless excused, members may not miss more than four consecutive meetings without being forced to resign. Attendance is therefore about 85 per cent.

The prime function of the club is to accumulate funds for community projects, club service, and international service. At a carnival in 1969, $5,000 was raised. The money is used for such things as community shelters, television sets for the school, and a kindergarten. The biggest night of the year is when the office bearers are elected and wives are invited. A ladies' night also takes place every three months.

Rotary started in Griffith in 1944. Membership today is seventy-three of whom six are Italians (a nurseryman, a real estate agent, an orchardist, a pharmacist, and two accountants, all Veneti). Persons do not apply but are invited to become members. Before this happens, however, the sponsor has to make a series of preparations.

All ten committee members are Australian. The entrance fee is $5.00 and the yearly subscription $10.00. Many Rotarians are also Masons.

(ii) The *Apex Club* was formed in 1954 and in 1969 had a membership of about forty, all Australians, though at times there have been Italian members. The club meets at the Leagues Club every two weeks for dinner from 6:30 to 9:30 in the evening, when there is a guest speaker.

Like Rotary, the aim is the betterment of the community and financial assistance for worthwhile causes. Joining is not difficult, although prospective members are scrutinized at two meetings before the invitation is sent out. Women may come to a special ladies' night every three months, but wives have their own night once a month (according to one member this is "so that they won't mind so much if the men go out"). Twice a year there are international nights at which a more elaborate dinner ,is served and friends invited. On this occasion also there is a guest speaker. Each member must attend at least 70 per cent of meetings.

(iii) The *Lions Club* was started by a Sicilian lawyer in 1963. There are thirty-seven members, thirteen of whom are Italian (eleven Veneti, one Siciliano, and one Piemontese).

Meetings take place at the Irrigana Motel twice a month. Again, there is a guest speaker. A person seeking to become a member must be nominated, and if he passes scrutiny is invited to join. There is a ladies' night every three months.

The quarterly bill for membership and dinners is $15. There is no entrance fee. Of a committee of eighteen, five are Italians.

(iv) The *Junior Chamber of Commerce [J.C.s]* was formed in 1967 and has twenty-four members, of whom about eighteen are active. A condition for entrance is that the person must be under forty. After the fortieth birthday he becomes a senator, an honorary title that does not carry any power. J.C.s meet every second Tuesday at Hanwood Catholic Club, where they have a dinner from 6:30 to 8:30 in the evening. There is a ladies' night every three months.

Like the other service clubs, the aim is to raise funds for worthy projects such as children's sheltered workshops; each year money is donated to a different charity. Every twelve months the members are expected to work for ten hours at an approved task, say picking tomatoes at $1.50 an hour, and this is then their contribution towards the running of the chapter.

It is easy to become a member, and in fact from time to time there is a drive for new ones. A president can serve for only three years, the rest of the committee indefinitely. Changeover of officers takes place at the annual dinner. J.C.s are less demanding on members, office bearers alone must attend at least one meeting in three or send apologies. Up to date there have only been three Italian members, two Veneti and one Abruzzese.

All the Service clubs have a combined ball once a year, and also a dinner to which only men are invited. Both are held at the Yoogali Club.

The clubs: conclusion Overlap of club membership is considerable. Most Veneti belong to at least three and those who aspire socially or seek business connections to many more. Persons with multiple club affiliation tend to frequent one or two regularly and the others less often. Nominal membership is, therefore, not as significant for personal interaction as actual attendance and participation. At the same time, the overlapping ensures that when disagreement or conflict occurs, a definite cleavage does not develop. The priest and manager who helped me were surprised to find that only eighty-four Calabresi were members of the Hanwood Catholic Club. They asserted, and the Calabresi themselves confirmed, that most of the time there are just as many Calabresi in the place as Veneti.

Hanwood alone has the reputation of being the club

where people from all regions drink and play together. Furthermore, the facts that husband and wife regularly dine there and teenagers hold weekly dances, have prompted many to contrast Hanwood with the other organizations and call it a "family club". Why is Hanwood so different from the others?

Obviously there is no single explanation, but it is possible to put forward some suggestions. The club was formed at the time when schisms and alignments at Yoogali had been going on for a number of years. The presence of a large number of Abruzzesi in Hanwood had the effect of diluting the Veneti and Calabresi and fostering greater contact between them. It is also possible that Northerners and Southerners had tired of the Yoogali frictions and were prepared to meet with more goodwill at Hanwood. The Sunday dances attended by young people who had grown up together also encouraged interaction. (It is true that Calabrese girls are unlikely to be regular attenders, but some come chaperoned by their parents.)

The original separateness in Yoogali has been maintained and is hard to break down; Hanwood started on a different footing. If another club is formed there, it will be interesting to see whether a split will take place and if so where. At the moment there is no sign of a separatist movement, perhaps an indication of increasing communication between Veneti and Calabresi.[24]

Clubs were not a feature of rural society in the Veneto. In Treviso people met friends, played cards, and drank at the *osteria*. We could regard Griffith clubs as an adaptation of the *osteria* and simultaneously as media for partial assimilation. The Italians, by learning to organize clubs and serve in various capacities on committees, acquired new cultural symbols that doubtless were instrumental in bridging the gap between them and Australians. The Continental Music Club is a prime example.

The numerous clubs give scope for many leaders. Where the purposes are diverse—educational, philanthropic, social, sport, or regional—a handful of men hold offices in more than one. They are then in a position to exert power and influence and enjoy greater prestige. But in the Italian clubs the purposes are identical. It is unlikely, therefore, that the same men will hold office in more than one. To my knowledge, indeed, nobody does in fact serve on the committee of two Italian clubs.

The clubs are also associated with different Italian regions. Hanwood Catholic Club is the exception in being regarded as neither Veneto nor Calabrese. It may well turn out to be the Italian melting pot.

Other recreations

All the men played *bocce* and some of the younger ones and the boys football.[25] This apart, Italian farmers had no interest in sport. A handful who were not farmers played golf or tennis, rowed, or belonged to the aero club, but these were exceptional.

As mentioned earlier, social life was divided along sex lines. Clubs catered for men, and women remained on the fringe. A man might drop into the club five or six times a week, but his wife probably appeared no more than once every couple of months. Apart from the occasional critical remark, such as "This is a man's town!", women did not feel hard done by. They arranged their own gatherings. When, then, did husband and wife as a couple meet other people outside the family?

The quiet winter season was the time for balls, dinner-dances, and weddings. On these occasions husband and wife appeared together. From May to October there was a ball or major function on every Saturday—the Hospital Ball, the Debutante Ball, the Catholic Ball, and so on. There were also a number of less formal affairs on Fridays and Sundays.

Younger couples attended balls more regularly than their elders, but much depended on what they could afford. It cost little to drop into the club, but balls, which demanded dressing up, were an expense. It is not surprising that the eleven hairdressing salons should have worked non-stop on Saturdays. Weddings also required the wearing of formal dress. Here I noticed what Friedl has called "lagging emulation".[26] The styles resembled those worn in Sydney or Melbourne several years before.

An old Veneto custom that some re-instituted in the past twelve years or so was the party to celebrate *la classe*, when people born in the same year came together. I have a photograph of a group celebrating *la classe di 1924* with thirty-three Veneti, one Australian, one Calabrese, and one Abruzzese. Men and women joined in, brought along their spouse and children, enjoyed a dinner and dance, and had a photograph taken. Those interested met a few months before and decided on the date, place, and menu. People started celebrating *la classe* in their early thirties and then every five years or so.

I lived with one well-to-do farming family where the head was among the dozen or so important Veneti. He belonged to the following clubs: Jondaryan, Rotary, Ex-Servicemen's, Leagues, Diggers' at Yenda, Catholic at Yoogali, Yoogali, Catholic at Hanwood, and Food and Wine. Without doubt the one in which he was most interested was the Catholic Club at Yoogali, of which he was a leading committee member. He attended this five or six times a week and also Rotary once a week, Food and Wine once a month, and the Leagues and Ex-Servicemen's two or three times a week during the day or late afternoon. While I was living with the family his programme for one particular week was:

Sunday: Catholic Club, Yoogali—alone
Monday: Food and Wine Society dinner—alone
Tuesday: Rotary meeting—alone
Wednesday: Catholic Ball—with wife
Thursday: Catholic Club, Yoogali, committee meeting—
           alone
Friday: Catholic Club, Yoogali—alone
Saturday: The Canova Dinner at the Catholic Club,
           Yoogali—with wife.

He had also been to the Leagues and Ex-Servicemen's with other male relatives and friends for a drink and quick game of cards during the day. Although he always had a busy social life, he could keep up this kind of pace only during the winter months when work on the farm was light.

It would be incorrect to assume that everybody went out each night. The point I wish to stress is that anyone could do so if he wished. Couples who were trying to save visited at home and played cards instead of meeting elsewhere. They saw each other two or three times a week during the off season. Calabresi were less club conscious than Veneti and also preferred visiting.

One Veneto put it this way, "Griffith is different from any other Italian place in Australia. Take Ingham, Innisfail, Tully, or Halifax in Queensland, or any other place; on Sunday everything is dead, you can't even get a meal in Queensland towns after six on Sunday. But here on Sunday everything is hopping."

The egalitarian ethos

Social stratification and the egalitarian ethos in Griffith are not my concern here, but I must touch on these to give a better understanding of social interaction.

Wealthy graziers lived in the Riverina but were not part of the social scene in Griffith. They visited one another, had house parties, organized picnic races, yet rarely went into town. The drop in wool prices in the second half of the 1960s meant that their wealth and prestige diminished.

Griffith is about sixty years old. Not many have lived there for more than forty-five years and most for a shorter time. There was no aristocracy or squattocracy as in many old towns in New South Wales.

Italians who came to the area espoused an egalitarian ethos, within their stratum.[27] The land-tenure system which, as we saw, limited the amount of irrigable land a man could own, aided the feeling of social equality and theoretically set a ceiling to aspirations. Thus a man with daughters who owned one farm could rationalize that he had no less prestige than the man with two sons and three farms. The clubs that impinged on the lives of Italians in particular were not exclusive. Members and waiters interacted as equals and all addressed one another with the familiar *tu*.[28]

Bank managers, headmasters, and teachers who had worked in other country towns agreed that the egalitarian ethos was more noticeable in Griffith. A bank manager told me, "There's no place like this for egalitarianism. When I first came here and introduced myself as Smith to the shopkeeper, he said, 'We don't use Mr. here, only first names.' An official who came here a few months ago was disappointed because no red carpet was put out for him. When he went to Leeton it was different. When a new school head said to me how appalled he was by the prices of houses fit for his position, I said to him, 'We don't worry about things like that here.' Compared with Goulburn, Lismore, and Orange, where I've also lived, Griffith is brash and immature, but here everybody can mix if he wants to. Doctors don't mix, they stick to themselves and not one belongs to Rotary, and you never see them in the clubs. Lots of bank managers and headmasters and their wives are not happy here because people don't make the fuss of them that they do in other country towns."

One Veneto described the situation, "Let's face it, we were all peasants and servants before we came here. Some of us have done well and made money. Take Paolo; he came from Italy thirty-five years ago and is one of the really big wine producers and must be a millionaire. Maybe he learnt to sign his name a few years ago. At the club though he is just one of the boys. Giovanni's wife sometimes puts on airs because her husband is rich. But she wouldn't know how to receive the ambassador. Nobody here would."[29] A Calabrese tailor's view was, "The best thing about Griffith is that everybody is equal, nobody cares whether a bloke he talks to is rich or poor." A Siciliano added, "In Italy, with four cents you became 'your excellency'—it's not like that here." A wealthy Veneto farmer, anxious to belong to the group of influentials, was the only person who mentioned the word class. To him, money was the important thing and made a person feel superior. "You can classify Griffith into the average worker with wages," he said, "and the more well-to-do class. Many don't come to the clubs because they feel inferior; they don't have the money to go out a lot." But a Veneta who came out after the war with her husband and two small sons—they now have three farms—spoke about some of the old wealthy settlers as "people who are higher" (*gente più alta*), who "know how to do things nicely". She felt inferior to the wealthy Veneto mentioned above in spite of the fact that financially she did not lag far behind him. A young secretary confided, "Girls whose parents grow vegetables are not as highly regarded as those coming from a family that has moved out of vegetables. Anna gives herself airs because her parents are well off, but we put her in her place." An Italian businessman confessed, "I reckon I'm a cut above the other mob, but I wouldn't want them to know how I feel."

Obviously many are conscious of a form of stratification, yet the majority believe in, or at least pay lip service to, an egalitarianism. Time and again people cite examples. "... take Doug and Glen McWilliams, the wine people, they're probably the wealthiest people in Griffith, but they live in modest houses. Some of us have better houses than they. They work as hard as any bloke, and they'll talk to anybody."

Two recent studies of towns in New South Wales highlight different attitudes to stratification. In Bradstow, a conservative centre, a respondent said, "... snobbery is a necessary thing ... society has to have these differences to exist properly."[30] In Kandos, a fifty-year-old cement manufacturing town, on the other hand, people do not say they are classless; rather, "The different sections mix well here."[31] In Griffith it would be difficult to find anyone who would admit freely that "snobbery is a necessary thing"; he would be more likely to follow the Kandos line.[32]

Earlier I suggested that the land-tenure system went hand in hand with an egalitarian ethos; but I would stress that it alone would not bring this about. Numerous Australians have told me that in Leeton, with the same system of holdings, people are class conscious and do not attempt even to pay lip service to classlessness.

AL GRASSBY AND THE NEW CAMPANILISMO

The emergence of a new *campanilismo* could be largely attributed to, and linked with, the rise of Al Grassby, who was the federal Labor member for the seat of Riverina from 1969 to 1974.[33]

Albert Jaime Grassby, better known as Al Grassby, was born in Brisbane in 1926 of Irish-Spanish descent. He settled in Griffith in 1950 and in 1962 married a local girl. Until his election to the New South Wales State Parliament in 1965, Grassby was employed in a number of capacities concerned with the dissemination of agricultural information and advice to farmers.[34] Shortly before the 1969 elections he switched from state to federal politics and defeated the sitting Country Party member with a swing of 16.8 per cent. Those who knew the area and the people did not regard the swing as a shift in allegiance from the Country Party to the Labor Party, but rather as a personal vote for Grassby.[35]

"Al is the first real spokesman Italians have had here. He pulled them up. He sort of makes them proud to be Italians and to be Australians," said a thoughtful Italian. From the start Grassby's flamboyant unpatronizing manner and undoubted sympathy endeared him to Italians. To them his stubborn perseverance in matters concerning their welfare, and his ability to help them to overcome bureaucratic hurdles, were further proofs of his sincerity.

"Before Al ran for Parliament I always voted for the Country Party. Armstrong used to come round and talk to us quite often.[36] He is a nice fellow and real gentleman, and he said that country people should vote for the Country Party. I don't believe in the Labor Party because I believe in private enterprise, but we've all known Al for years. We all had great times at the Continental Music Club. Even though he's an important man now he's never changed. He's always his old self; it just hasn't gone to his head. If Al walked into the kitchen unexpectedly and we were eating without a tablecloth it wouldn't worry us because Al is like one of the family. Lots of us Veneti vote for him because we like him, not the Labor Party. I dreamt the other night that he became Prime Minister, and by gee it wouldn't surprise me if he did."

Italians are generally not interested in politics or issues outside their immediate ambit. At dinner one evening I remarked, "We mustn't forget to watch Al on T.V. to-night." "Oh sure we must," replied my host and added, "What's he talking about to-night?" "The wheat crisis," I answered. "Oh gee no, I'd rather watch the other channel. I'm not interested in wheat. It's fifty kilometres down the road."

A high Australian official at the W.C. & I.C. described Grassby in this way: "I'm not a Labor supporter—in fact I can't stand them—but as far as Al is concerned, I've known him for twenty years and I'll swear he never has more than a month's salary in his pocket. He's a jolly nuisance to us. Even if he's trying to help some poor little Italian vegetable grower, he never lets up. He's like a flea in our sides. Unfortunately, I can't see the Country Party regaining this seat while Al's around. Nobody could get through to the Italians the way he can."

Grassby was a household name. I once saw a child in the main street of Griffith pull at his mother's skirt and say, "Look Mum, there's Al," then turn, wave, and cry out, "Hello Mr. Grassby!"

To the Calabresi Grassby was a champion. Frisina, their unofficial father, gave him his unqualified support. Shortly before the 1969 elections Grassby had an accident from which he emerged intact, though the car was badly smashed. Frisina told me, "We all worry about Al's driving; he drives too much and too fast, often at night when he's dog tired. After his last accident we boys got together and decided that Angelo had the best car among us, so we told Angelo to hand over the car till Al's was fixed. We took turns at driving him around. I drive for him whenever I can. Before the elections I drove him to Euston, about 240 kilometres away. There are 114 Italian families there, many with tiny farms growing grapes. Most are Calabresi. At the election before that, none of them voted for the Labor Party. But after I told them that Al was our man and introduced him to them, the Labor Party got all their votes. When Al is with us he's like one of us. He comes to our weddings and celebrations and acts as master of ceremonies. When Calabresi support somebody, then you can rely on it that all of us will do the right thing. The Veneti, they're different; they may all say they vote for him, but I know that plenty don't." When I asked him "Why do they do that?" he, a deeply religious man, replied, "Christ, too, was a perfect man." One priest said jokingly, "When a Calabrese loses his head he goes to Frisina to ask Grassby to find it for him."

One evening I was discussing Grassby with three wealthy Veneti who told me that they voted for him, but their sympathies lay with the Liberal/Country Parties. One elaborated, "After all, I don't consider myself a Labor man. Why should I? I'm comfortably well off. I like Al, he's a good bloke, but sometimes I think it isn't such a good idea to have a member who's always in the Opposition. If the government thinks that he is in for good, they'll never spend any money on the area. We hoped that when Al switched from state to federal politics a Liberal or a Country Party guy would get the state seat, but the Labor fellow got it. He only got it because of Al." I was always conscious of a difference in the attitudes of Veneti and Calabresi towards Grassby. Veneti respected, admired, and felt they owed him allegiance. Frequently, however, they expressed regret that he did not belong to the Country Party. The Calabresi, on the other hand, revered him and did not care what party he represented.

In spite of cultural differences, Calabresi and Veneti did not live in airtight compartments; they used the same schools, shops, churches, and general facilities. An example of the concern for the wellbeing of Italians as a whole was the formation of what has been called *il comitato di aggior-*

namento. Literally translated this means "the committee for keeping up to date". It was made up of a number of prominent people who undertook to give talks one evening a fortnight during the winter months.

They spoke on matters of general interest to whoever cared to attend. Recent speakers have included, a Sicilian and an Australian lawyer married to an Italian, discussing the problems of drawing up wills, a Veneto pharmacist explaining Medical Benefits and Hospital Funds, Frisina, the Calabrese, setting out the procedure and eligibility for applying for Italian pensions, a Calabrese real estate agent outlining the pension system in Australia, and a Veneto accountant giving an account of eligibility requirements for government assistance to farmers. The speakers mainly used Italian, but sometimes simultaneous translation in either Italian or English was provided. Attendances were good. Grassby went to the first meeting.

People talked affectionately of Griffith as *paese*. When a woman said she was going to town she said, "*Vado in paese.*" Alda, a young woman in her twenties, came to Griffith in 1965 with her husband, a waiter. She told me, "I've never been lonely or cried since I came here. I miss my parents and hope one day to go just for a visit to show them my children, but I never want to leave Griffith. We have lots of friends and play cards two or three times a week. My sister-in-law goes with me to the hospital to interpret, but otherwise it doesn't worry me that I can't speak English."

Not everyone in Griffith was blissfully happy, however. One woman, married to a carpenter, with eight children, wanted to leave because she couldn't see a future for her family there. Another told me that her husband drank so much she was ashamed to go outside and wished she lived in a city where people would not know her on the street. An important Veneto, however, knew of only one family that had returned to Treviso in the past three years—when the man inherited a big block of land. Others who inherited land sold it, or arranged for it to be sold, when they returned for a visit. It was exceptional for Italians to leave Griffith willingly. Some went after they had had bad luck with crops for two or three consecutive years, some for medical reasons, and some for the sake of the children's tertiary education.

An article appeared in a Sydney paper recently about a reunion dinner for former Griffith residents. The organizer had asked Al Grassby to bring a flagon of "magic potion", or channel water, for the occasion. "The water is said to make former residents of Griffith 'nostalgic' and is also claimed to have magic properties ... The function would not be the same without 'channel water' ... it was traditional for former Griffith residents to drink the water. They feel that if they drink the water they have to return to Griffith. They can never really get away from the place and neither do they want to."[37]

Over the years a conscious effort to accommodate, co-operate, and restrain ill-feeling has emerged. Italians frequently said, "Things are good now, let's keep it that way." That ethnic relations are in fact good now is in no small measure the result of Grassby's efforts, of his years of drawing together the diverse groups and imbuing them with a new sense of *campanilismo*.

CONCLUSION

The economic life of Trevisani in Griffith was again based on agriculture, but instead of following a peasant economy they established themselves as commercial farmers. The rules of land-tenure did not permit extended households, but telephones and cars allowed easy communication with relatives while each one retained a nuclear family's privacy. In the early days lack of formal education did not significantly handicap the immigrants—they were familiar with agricultural work. Later all the young received formal education. The church influenced but no longer dictated people's actions. Farms were also dispersed in Griffith, but to visit a relative or friend rarely entailed more than a ten to fifteen minutes' drive. The clubs became the social centres, a substitute for the inns, though here as in Italy there was sex segregation.

Conditions in Griffith enabled Trevisani to retain, adapt, and, as they said, improve upon a number of old pre-World War II core institutions. The land-tenure system and the possibility of buying farms from Australians created a favourable environment for their adaptation. Most important was the fact that since a farmer who already had a Home Maintenance Area could not expand his property, he was obliged to buy in the name of his son in order to keep the additional purchase in the family. Each additional farm belonging to a son in his own right increased the parents' sense of achievement: "We look after our sons and set them up." Sons depended on fathers to help them acquire a farm, but fathers in turn relied on sons to look after all their interests in dealing with the numerous institutions in the M.I.A. Thus many owned farms at an early age, and father-son relationship developed into one of camaraderie rather than superordination-subordination. This, then, created a different kind of family interaction from what is usual in most rural communities.

The land-tenure system, the clubs and the fact that Griffith was a relatively new town, originally settled by poor people, all helped to reinforce the egalitarian ethos in which most of the townspeople believed, and to which the rest at least paid lip service. Certainly there was a reluctance to admit that a class hierarchy existed. The presence of a political leader like Al Grassby, who did not belong to one minority group but straddled several, and acted as a spokesman for them all, achieved two important results—it united the groups vis-à-vis outsiders, and it gave them a new sense of identity and common allegiance. Integration was achieved not by denying origins or past heritage but by encouraging respect for them.[38]

To ensure viability of farms it has become increasingly necessary to specialize and mechanize. Farming is thus more expensive, profit margins narrower, and the formation of companies for marketing a logical economic proposition. Where this has occurred friction between the wives was common.

Mechanization in the Queensland canefields has brought about a diminution in seasonal workers, and fewer come to the M.I.A. these days. Further uncertainties have thus been added to the rural economy. Perhaps the Griffith farming community has reached a watershed.

In the next few years it is likely that fewer sons will follow in their fathers' footsteps and more will leave the land and enter the trades and professions. The community will not be as closed as before, and a gradual shift away from the egalitarian ethos may occur.[39]

Improved socio-economic conditions, lagging emulation, and assimilation to many aspects of Australian life have changed the Italian stereotype of earlier years. "My daughters don't work in the fields like I used to; I wouldn't want them to. They read magazines and worry about how the house looks, clothes, and new recipes. In the early days here we were glad to just have *pasta* and *minestrone*, but our girls now go in for *pavlova* competitions."[40]

Unlike the situation in Griffith, in other Italian rural settlements in Australia there was no limit on the amount of land a man could own.[41] The head of the household bought as much as was practicable in his own name. The relationship between him and his sons thus tended to be hierarchical. In many cases there was open hostility. Generally the sons had to wait until the father died before taking over. Even if for some good reason he handed over nominally during his lifetime he never relinquished his right to give directions.

In recent years it has become more usual for offspring in most ethnic groups to own properties sooner than they would have done twenty or more years ago. The main reasons are that commercial farmers are becoming increasingly keen to avoid high taxation and probate. They therefore distribute the ownership of property among members of the family. It seems unlikely that in Griffith before the mid-1950s fathers would have bought farms for their sons if they could have added to their own. The stringent land-tenure laws of the M.I.A. and the advisory branches of the C.S.I.R.O. made things difficult for the father who rarely spoke English and thus prevented him from exerting the kind of pressure that he could have done elsewhere.

In Griffith, apart from a few marketing partnerships, the finances of farms were kept separate. The relative satisfaction and independence of many sons thus created a type of family interaction that was different from that found in other communities. As more and more young people seek occupations outside farming in the M.I.A., however, decisions concerning the form that inheritance should take will increasingly occupy people's thought, and the atmosphere may well change. As present conventions of inheritance are in a state of flux, it is too early to forecast what form they will take and what tensions will arise.

All Italian farming in Australia demanded labour-intensive methods but relatively little financial outlay. Most immigrants had been accustomed to garden agriculture with pick and spade. This training facilitated their adaptation to the economic opportunities they found in rural areas in Australia. Cultural differences that allowed Italian women and children to perform tasks Australians could or would not undertake enabled the newcomers to take advantage of the depression years of the 1930s. They soon realized their ambition to become self-employed landholders. Australians sold out because the Italians were such willing buyers.

The depression years demonstrated that people with an un-Australian cultural background could easily carve out a niche for themselves while the members of the host society hung back. The immigrants' attitudes, especially to women's labour, rendered them more adaptable to the exigencies of fluctuating prices for agricultural products.

But the second and third generations are unlikely to submit to conditions previously accepted. Second-generation Italian girls are no longer willing to work in the fields. They have come to accept Australian values and also feel that with the state of comparative rural affluence their labour is unnecessary. Perhaps already, and certainly soon, the

Australian farmer of Italian descent and the old Australian will be competing on equal terms.

In Griffith more boys who would like to remain farmers are thinking of moving out of horticulture into large area farms. To date few have done so, but when, or if, they do it is likely that their views on kinship rights and obligations will need to approximate more closely to what Australians regard as usual. Modern farming methods are not compatible with traditional Italian values that accept intensive family labour.

Social life was different in Griffith from that in other Italian rural settlements. The M.I.A. system of distributing small horticultural farms around the town enabled people to drive from one end to the other in less than fifteen minutes and encouraged social interaction and club attendance. In contrast, the Ovens Valley and Queensland settlements were long thin strips extending for many kilometres. The Ovens Valley, Phillips wrote, was more a territorial segment of a metropolitan community based on Melbourne; it was not isolated and therefore unlikely to encourage a community spirit.[42]

In Griffith the egalitarian ethos and the emergence of a political leader who straddled all the ethnic groups fostered a kind of interaction that approximated more closely to a *Gemeinschaft*-type community. Doubtless this will alter as the economy changes, overlaps of interest decrease, and groups re-form. One woman commented, "We wouldn't dream of leaving Griffith. This is our home, and we have a good life, but in the old days when things were harder people stuck together a lot more than now."[43]

NOTES

1. For a definition of *campanilismo* see page 49, n.14.
2. For more details on the M.I.A., see T. Langford-Smith, "Landforms, Land Settlement and Irrigation on the Murrumbidgee" and *Water and Land*.

3. For greater detail on the Italian population of Griffith see C.A. Price, "Italian Population of Griffith". For an analysis of chain migration and its influence on settlement in Australia see C.A. Price, *Southern Europeans in Australia.*

4. C.A. Price, "Italian Population", p. 12.

5. T. Langford-Smith, "Landforms", pp. 98–99.

6. There were about 150 Spanish, half a dozen or so Greeks, a handful of Dutch and Scandinavians, and a number of other nationalities. These together formed but a tiny minority.

7. According to the 1971 census, the total Christian population of Wade Shire was 17,470 of which the largest groups were: Roman Catholic 9,168, Church of England 4,445, Presbyterian 2,187, and Methodist 1,001. The 53 per cent Roman Catholic population here is almost twice the average in the Australian population where Catholics and Roman Catholic total 27 per cent (1971 census).

8. Commenting on the separation of Northerners and Southerners, N. Glazer and D. Moynihan (*Beyond the Melting Pot*, p. 184) quoted L. Covello who wrote that, "wherever Italians might go, they were already divided into two groups". For a discussion of the differences between Northerners and Southerners in Carlton (Melbourne), see F.L. Jones, "The Italian Population of Carlton".

9. As L. Coser pointed out in *The Function of Social Conflict*, p. 38, "A distinction has to be made between conflict and hostile and antagonistic attitudes. Social conflict always denotes social interaction, whereas attitudes or sentiments are predispositions to engage in action. Such predispositions do not necessarily eventuate in conflict."

10. C.A. Price, *Southern Europeans*, pp. 193–94.

11. Irrigation Areas must not be confused with Irrigation Districts. In the former the Water Conservation and Irrigation Commission controls sales and water supply; in the latter the water supply alone.

12. T. Langford-Smith, *Water and Land*, p. 42.

13. Ibid., p. 38.

14. Ibid., p. 65.

15. The strict anthropological definition of horticulture is "cultivation without ploughs". In this book I use it in the same sense as the farmers and agencies use the word. By rights what they call horticultural farms are either orchards or vineyards or a combination of the two. In Mirrool Irrigation Area (Wade Shire) there were about 1250 farms, 400 of which, called residential farms, were under two hectares. People who owned these generally worked elsewhere, but some grew vegetables as a side occupation.

16. E. Friedl, *Vasilika: A Village in Modern Greece*, pp. 48–49.

17. The resistance to marriage between people who came from different parts of Italy crops up in the literature time and again. J.S. Macdonald, for instance, writing about Rivertown in Australia, said that there was no marriage across regional or provincial boundaries.

Italians married fellow provincials or Anglo-Saxons (see "Migration from Italy to Australia", p. 261). R. Firth, also, found that in London Italians displayed a marked preference for intra-regional marriage. He thought that this was an extension of the traditional Italian *campanilismo*, which also made for antagonism between Northerners and Southerners and prevented marriage between them (see *Two Studies of Kinship in London*, p. 90).

18. Simmel (in L. Coser, *The Function of Social Conflict*, p. 31) argued that, "... no group can be entirely harmonious, for it would then be devoid of process and structure. Groups require disharmony as well as harmony, dissociation as well as association; and conflicts within them are by no means altogether disruptive factors ... on the contrary, both 'positive' and 'negative' factors build group relations. Conflict as well as co-operation has social functions."

19. For a discussion of ethnic associations in Australia see J. Martin, "Migration and Social Pluralism" especially pp. 106–8.

20. J. Tully, "Experiences in Integrating Italian Farmers into an Extension Programme and into the Farming Community of the M.I.A.", pp. 124–34.

21. Unfortunately no documents were available about the early years of this organization in Griffith.

22. For a list of these organizations see appendix 6.

23. R. Wild, in his study *Bradstow*, p. 87, noted that many loopholes can be used to admit more than one person of a given occupation to Rotary.

24. It may well be that, in Simmel's words (see L. Coser, *The Function of Social Conflict*, p.72), "Contradiction and conflict not only precede unity but are operative in it at every moment of its existence ... there probably exists no social unit in which convergent and divergent currents among its members are not inseparably interwoven ..."

25. When men attended the clubs to play *bocce* or cards on weekends they generally wore suits, white shirts, ties, and often hats.

26. E. Friedl, "Lagging Emulation in Post-Peasant Society".

27. J.S. Macdonald described the socio-economic power system of the Alps as "egalitarian—associative" ("Migration Versus Nonmigration: Regional Migration Differentials in Rural Italy", p. 5). Elsewhere he maintained that "There was no class struggle in the Alps because there was no distinctive class stratification." (See "Italy's Rural Social Structure and Emigration", p. 444.) C. Jayawardena ("Ideology and Conflict in Lower Class Communities", p.414) wrote: "Typically, notions of human equality are dominant in the subgroup to the extent that it is denied social equality by the wider society or its dominant class."

28. Only six Italians, all Veneti, belonged simultaneously to Rotary and Jondaryan, the two clubs considered exclusive.

29. Most of the very wealthy Italians made their fortune through business or real estate, but these were in the minority.
30. R.A. Wild, *Bradstow*, p. 84.
31. H.G. Oxley, *Mateship in Local Organization*, p. 96.
32. C. Jayawardena, "Ideology and Conflict in Lower Class Communities", p. 440, said of peasant solidarity and conflict, "... it is not individual success in itself that is disapproved but the use or suspected use of such gains to repudiate the relationship of equality."
33. For Grassby see also appendix 4. For a definition of *campanilismo* see p. 49, n. 14.
34. See the Continental Music Club, pp. 101–3.
35. M. Mackerras, *Australian General Elections*, p. 78.
36. Armstrong was the Country Party member up to the 1969 elections.
37. *Sun-Herald*, 4 June 1972.
38. "There is nothing so shallow or sterile as the man who denies his own ancestry. The one-hundred-per-cent American or Canadian is commonly one who deliberately suppressed an alien origin in order to reap the material benefits of a well advertised loyalty. There can be little hope of noble spiritual issues from such a prostituted patriotism." (Watson Kirkconnell in P. Bosi, *Farewell Australia*, p. 30.)
39. E. Banfield (*The Moral Basis of a Backward Society*, p. 10) attributed "amoral familism" to the high death rate, the land-tenure system, and the absence of the institution of an extended family. Silverman also attributed this ethos primarily to the land-tenure system and family organization. In her paper "Land Reform and the Creation of Cultural Traditions" she discussed the initial phase of a field study in a southern Italian agricultural reform region. She felt that if she selected an area where the agricultural organization had been drastically altered it might be possible to determine whether changes in social structure would bring about changes in ethos. She found the kind of settlement she was looking for but could not prove her hypothesis because there was no room for expansion into farming for the sons. The children had to leave home and seek employment in towns. The rural organization had no perseverance over time. Griffith might well have been her ideal experimental station.
40. The dancer Pavlova inspired the naming of this cake. It consists of a meringue base filled with whipped cream topped with passionfruit and strawberries. In Griffith, as in other rural areas, it is a top favourite, and numerous variations are served on important occasions.
41. See the section on Australian studies of Italian rural communities in appendix 3, pp. 219–21.
42. D. Phillips, "Italians and Australians in the Ovens Valley Area".
43. As Simmel maintained (see K. Wolff, *The Sociology of Georg Simmel*, p.87), "... a group upon reaching a certain size must develop forms and organs which serve its maintenance and promotion, but which a

smaller group does not need. On the other hand, it will also be admitted that smaller groups have qualities, including types of interaction among their members, which inevitably disappear when the groups grow larger."

PART 3
SYDNEY

INTRODUCTION

In the previous section I discussed how economic opportunities affected Trevisani who settled in Griffith. We saw
that the new environment was conducive to their setting up
as commercial farmers, and to the introduction and adaptation of a number of older institutions which helped cushion
the difficulties of adjustment.

In this section we will look closely at a network of eight
Trevisan families living in Sydney. As before, the study aims
to demonstrate the influence of economic factors, to indicate
whether these people abandoned, retained, or altered old
core institutions, and to look at their pattern of settlement.
The eight families came from the same socio-economic
background as the group in the M.I.A. but migrated to
Australia after the war, between the mid-1950s and the mid-
1960s. As we shall see, the shift from rural to urban life and
the consequences that followed were not conducive to the
retention or adaptation of any specific traditional institutions. Economy based on agriculture, the extended
household, and seasonal migration all disappeared.
Qualitative changes in attitudes to the church and personal
interaction also took place. Lack of suitable training and
education to cope with the new city conditions were persis-
tent handicaps. I must emphasize, however, that difficulties
encountered by these immigrants were not the result solely
of their being foreign, as is often implied; they were bound
up with such factors as their earlier background and the unfamiliarity with the urban setting and culture.

As mentioned earlier, in 1947 48.3 per cent of Italian born
immigrants in Australia lived in cities, 51.6 per cent in rural
areas. At that time only 1,000 Italians lived in central Sydney
and almost all were Southerners.[1] By 1966, however, 87.5
per cent were living in urban and only 12 per cent in rural
regions.[2]

The reasons for certain groups settling in particular places
depended not only on the process of chain migration but
also on the economic conditions in Australia at the time of
arrival, and on fortuitous meetings and experiences during

the first weeks and months in this country. Before 1947 most Trevisani became farmers and agricultural labourers in South Australia, New South Wales, and Queensland.[3] The earliest Trevisan immigrant to Sydney I met, arrived in 1949. He knew of no one from Treviso who had settled here before that date.

MIGRATION AND URBANIZATION

People taking part in internal and international migrations have to cope, not only with the physical environment and the mechanics of life in the city but also with mental adjustments. Oscar Handlin summed up the situation:

> ... broken homes, interruptions of familiar life, separation from known surroundings, the becoming of a foreigner and ceasing to belong. These are the aspects of alienation; and seen from the perspective of the individual received rather than of the receiving society, the history of immigration is a history of alienation and its consequences.[4]

There was something both real and symbolic in the example Simmel used in "The Metropolis and Mental Life", "If all clocks and watches in Berlin would suddenly go wrong in different ways, even if only by one hour, all economic life and communication of the city would be disrupted for a long time."[5] From my respondents I gathered that agricultural workers in Treviso regulated their lives by the sun and the seasons. A clock mattered only as a prestige item. In Sydney this was no longer so.

My concern in the following paragraphs is to select those aspects of urbanization mentioned most frequently by writers on that subject, which either contrast or compare with village life, and which affect or relate to the people who moved into an industrial urban area.[6]

People with similar backgrounds and needs tend to select or drift into the same section of the city: living in an industrial setting is more conducive to the setting up of nuclear than extended households, particularly where there is social and physical mobility; there is a highly developed division of labour in the society; although physical contact is greater in the city, residents are less likely to know one another; bonds tend not to be as strong, personal, or long lasting among co-residents in an area with a high turnover of population; the husband-wife relationship is likely to be more joint than segregated under such conditions; the city offers a greater number of alternatives and a greater range of attitudes; and finally, in the city there is greater geographic and social mobility.

Problems of assimilation in these conditions have inspired numerous recent studies on internal migrations. In Italy a rough calculation indicated that 10,000,000, or about 20 per cent of the population, moved from one town to another in the ten years 1953–63.[7]

Papers dealing with migrations within Italy described the difficulties encountered by migrants to the industrial regions. Most of the studies concentrated on the reactions of the host population and the industrial combines rather than on the migrants. Yet it is possible to piece together a picture of their problems from the descriptions of exploitation and gruelling physical conditions they experienced.

I refer to Italian studies on internal migration in order to support my contention that the problems of Trevisani in Sydney are only partly caused by the Australian situation.

The following quotation from an article on immigrants to the upper Milanese area is informative not only for what it reveals about them but also for its insights into the indigenous population (not to mention the writer) as well.

> The resentment felt by part of the population towards the new arrivals is more clearly noticeable in the matter of customs. Too often the immigrants do not try to adapt themselves, in those respects where it is right to adapt oneself, to the habits and attitudes of the district which has received them. To maintain some traditions of special value is logical and human, but almost to flaunt one's different background is counterproductive. In one town in the Upper Milanese, at the time of the Limbiate meeting, the walls of all the houses were covered with posters directed at the "Venetian Colony", asking for mass

participation in a religious festival, organised by priests come specially from the Veneto, which was to culminate in a procession in honour of a statue of St. Anthony of Padua, also brought from the Veneto. This resembles the case of certain Italian-Americans who celebrate the feast of San Gennaro each year with rites and displays so alien to most other citizens, even Catholics, that they invariably call down on themselves some very unfavourable comments, and what is worse, the accusation of obstinate refusal to assimilate to a reasonable extent.

These are unimportant episodes in themselves, but it is precisely little things like this, repeated and multiplied by thousands, which give rise to the intolerance and coolness which are often felt towards the immigrant groups. Sometimes, folklore apart, the irritation is based on facts having a very different impact on the life of the native population. In a town in the Comasco, for instance, quite similar in economic and social structure to those of the Upper Milanese area, Venetian immigrants, when they had established residence qualifications, succeeded in voting out the traditionally socialist administration and replacing it by Christian Democrats. Similar episodes could happen in the Upper Milanese area too in a few years.[8]

Here in Italy, illegal co-operatives that set themselves up as labour agencies subjected the migrants to constant exploitation. At times they worked for half the wages of local labourers doing identical jobs. "They are exploited and isolated, they have bitter experiences behind them, there is no one to give them the perspectives, the social, cultural, and political education that they need."[9]

The results of Romano's study of Sicilian migrants from the village of Belmonte Mezzagno to Palermo nearby are interesting. Here were people who migrated to an urban centre fifteen kilometers from their original home. They spoke the dialect and were familiar with the cultural, educational and political systems of the town. Cronin, commenting on this research, stressed that although adaptation to the new environment should have been quick and easy, this was not so.[10]

These studies shed light on the disorientation of rural migrants and are illustrative of some of the urbanization problems which are exacerbated when these people moved from one cultural milieu to another. It is true that they often found themselves in hostile territory and that the host society did not welcome them, especially when they were a threat to the current economic, political, and religious systems or had a different cultural background. In industrial regions of Italy, the host community was easily able to exploit these rural workers if they could not fend for themselves.

The findings in Italy support the point I made earlier when speaking of rural migrants to urban industrial regions—that these are people whose main handicaps are lack of formal education and the insecurity that results from their inability to understand or deal with the various bureaucratic institutions of an industrial metropolis. In Sydney they must additionally cope with a new language.

SYDNEY

Stages in settlement

When I began my research in Sydney the ages of the children of the eight families on whom I concentrated ranged from four weeks to nine years. One child was born during the period of the study. All eight households were thus in the same phase of familial development (see table 21). Although I met many Trevisani outside the limited group I observed in depth, it would be absurd to speak of statistical significance or to make general statements about all Trevisan families based on my findings. Yet in observing this network of families a pattern of behaviour and attitudes emerged that suggests specific stages leading ultimately to permanent settlement in Australia. This appeared to be accompanied by changes in the orientation to life and shifts in reference groups which I will discuss later.

The following is the set of sequences frequently found in the process of settlement:

Stage 1: The man came to Australia alone, either by paying or borrowing his fare or accepting assistance as an im-

Table 21. Summary of eight Trevisan families in Sydney

Family	Date of birth of wife	Husband's arrival, year and passage	Wife's arrival year and passage	Marriage	Relatives in Sydney at time of arrival	Accommodation after marriage	Deposit on house	Children and their ages	Suburb where living in 1968	Return to Italy
1. Rosa and Claudio Varese	1931 (Crespano)	1950 paid	1953 paid	on day of arrival 4 guests	none	on farm in a country town	one year after marriage	2: 4 and 9 years	Leichhardt	1963 for 5 years
2. Ida and Nico Gori	1933 (Fonte Alto)	1955 assisted	1957 assisted	on day of arrival 3 guests	husband's brother	rented room in Leichhardt	one year after marriage	2: 6 and 9 years	Forest Lodge	1967 for 8 months
3. Alda and Tonio Lorenzin	1933 (Paese)	1956 assisted	1958 paid	8 days after arrival 3 guests	husband's cousin	rented room in Annandale	end of first year	4: 2, 6, 8, and 9 years	Campsie	no plans
4. Lucia and Guiseppe Bresci	1935 (Casone)	1958 paid	1960 paid	on day of arrival 40 guests	none	rented rooms in Leichhardt	three years after marriage	2: 4 and 7 years	Haberfield	plan for 1969
5. Maria and Sandro Pieranti	1937 (Sta. Cristina)	1957 paid	1960 paid	married in Treviso when husband returned	none	rented rooms in Leichhardt	one year after marriage	3: 4 weeks, 5, and 7 years	Leichhardt	1967 for 10 months
6. Gina and Paolo Tomasielli	1942 (Castelcucco)	1955 assisted	1964 paid	8 days after arrival 60 guests	none	put deposit on a house in Leichhardt immediately		2: 1 newborn, 3 years.	Lakemba	End of 1968 for 3 months
7. Anna and Giovanni Santrin	1943 (San Zanone)	1961 paid	1963 assisted	3 days after arrival 35 guests	none	rented rooms in Glebe	five months after marriage	1: 3 years	Leichhardt	plan for 1969
8. Melia and Luigi Crespani	1945 (San Zanone)	1960 paid	1965 paid	married in Treviso when husband returned	none	rented rooms in Leichhardt	ten months after marriage	1: 2 years	Ashbury	plan for 1972

migrant. He first worked in the cane fields of Queensland, lived frugally, saved a big sum in a short time, and then went south to Sydney where excellent opportunities existed for unskilled labourers in the building trade.[11] (The majority of the men were not married, but the few who were, also migrated alone. Their wives and family followed them one to three years later. Many of the children are now of marriageable age, but none of my respondents belonged to that particular category.)

Stage 2: Two or three years after his departure from Italy either the fiancée followed him to Sydney or he returned briefly to Treviso, married, and came back.

Stage 3: The money saved before marriage and immediately after, enabled the couple to put a cash deposit on a house during the first twelve or eighteen months of marriage. With obsessive determination they then aimed to pay off the whole sum within about five years. About three additional years of saving financed their trip home to Treviso. At first they hoped to re-settle in Italy but were aware that as unskilled labourers their standard of living in Australia was higher. They knew that they would probably return to Sydney as many had done before them. Regardless of cost, however, the trip was essential to give them, as they put it, "peace of mind". Before leaving Australia they sold everything they could not take, thus severing all material ties.

Stage 4: The trip itself generally lasted from six to twelve months. It was a time of conspicuous consumption to impress the family and fellow *paesani*. After a time, disillusionment with former friends and family set in and convinced them that they no longer fitted into village society.

Stage 5: They returned to Australia, started afresh, and now oriented their life and ambitions to permanent settlement. They had ceased to straddle two worlds.

Table 21 is a summary of facts about the eight families illustrating the stages set out above. I have numbered the families according to the ages of the women, the oldest first, the youngest last. I wish to stress again, however, that most of the information gathered in Sydney came from observing and being with the women and children. Accordingly the report is slanted from this angle. Although the bulk of the study was carried out in 1968, I kept in touch with those who remained in Sydney during the following couple of years.

Family 1, (the Vareses), is atypical in many ways. First, there was much tension between the husband and wife, and secondly, they had lived in both Sydney and in a country town. They married in 1953 and for the first three months were in the country where the husband had already been growing vegetables for a year. Rosa, the wife, hated the place and left for Sydney. The husband then worked in Queensland for three years. She put a deposit on a house in Sydney, worked in a factory as a machinist, and took in boarders. At the end of three years the husband joined her, and they had their first child in 1959. After ten years in Australia they sold everything and returned to Treviso. There they built and furnished a house but found after five years that as an unskilled worker he could not earn enough to make ends meet. The wife wanted him to go to Switzerland as a seasonal worker, but he refused, and they returned to Australia early in 1968. "This time we didn't make the mistake of selling up, we rented out the house in Treviso and hope to return there when the children have finished school here. That's why we have to start all over again now. We haven't a penny," Rosa said. When I first met her she was living in a room and garage. Of all my respondents she was the only one who had the *terza media* (intermediate certificate indicating eight years of schooling). She was the only girl in the village to have attained it. She was also my sole respondent who did not grow up in an extended household. Her father and mother lived apart, and she was an only child. The father remained with his family, and the mother returned home after a few months with her mother-in-law, with whom she did not get on. Rosa stayed with her mother and aunt in the village, but her father was good to her, and she saw him almost daily. She trained to be a machinist although she would have preferred to be an office worker. Her husband had only three years of schooling and was, and felt himself to be, intellectually inferior. She often talked about divorce and told me that she thought the church ought to permit it as long as there were no children. Before her marriage she had been engaged to a man who was found to have a congenital ailment, and the engagement was broken off. When a short time later her husband proposed by letter, she agreed to follow him to Australia. They married on her arrival in Sydney and proceeded the same day to the country where the husband had a sister.

i] *The man's migration* Unlike migrations before World War II, those after the war were conducive to social changes. Men who came out sent home some of their earnings, but their prime concern was for their own future welfare. They no longer aimed to subsidize the extended household economy but to save so that they could form their own nuclear family. Furthermore, going overseas did not now connote years of separation and hardship. Some who left for Australia utilized the assisted passage scheme, others saved or borrowed the fare in the knowledge that they could easily repay it. Unlike political émigrés, however, most of them had no intention of remaining in the new country. The idea of seasonal migration was familiar, and now they came to look, work, save, and decide later.

There were several reasons for leaving home—to escape parental domination, to earn a lot in a short time and enjoy the resulting prestige, and to avoid conscription. The men retained material and psychological ties through letters that cost little, and they knew that if necessary they could be back in two days by air or four weeks by ship. A single man did not find it difficult to save the fare. Of course, they still took their inheritance of land for granted.

Those who came to Australia were almost always unskilled, single, and aged from 18 to 28. Their assets were physical strength and willingness to work hard for long hours. They preferred outdoor employment because it was familiar and the pay was better.

One respondent recounted, "My husband comes from a family that's well off. He has only one brother and a sister. My father-in-law was very poor. When he married he lived in his extended household but then left and set up on his own. He saved like a maniac and bought land—he didn't inherit any. He and his wife worked like horses and lived like pigs. Giovanni, my husband, left for Australia because his parents were so hard and mean. His father had more land than most of the peasants in the village so the two boys didn't learn a trade; in fact Giovanni's reading and writing isn't so hot. They expected to go on working with their father. Giovanni worked for his father all the week using the tractor. The father never paid him wages, just doled out about 30 cents each week as pocket money. Whenever the two of us went to the pictures I paid even though my family was really poor. But the last straw was when his father wouldn't let him buy a motor bike. The family had just one between them.

Giovanni then decided that he'd had enough of his father, and when he heard of the assisted passages he decided to apply and go to Australia. A travel agent who heard about his plans and knew that the family had money went to the father and told him that all assisted-passage migrants were starved for the four weeks and persuaded the father to pay the fare. One reason why the father didn't hit the roof as he normally did was because he thought Giovanni was going to be called up, and this was a way out. When my husband got on the ship he was furious because he saw that, assisted or not assisted, everybody had the same food. But it was too late, and he paid off his father as quickly as possible once he started working.

When he arrived in Australia he met a couple of *paesani*, and they all went up to Queensland together. A few of them lived together and took turns at cooking. In a good week he'd make $200, but if it rained they couldn't work. In the first six months he cleared $1,200. He stayed there for over a year and then came to Sydney.

We'll go back to Treviso when we've paid off the house here. His father is getting old, and when we inherit half his property—the other half will go to his brother—we'll go back on the land. But meanwhile I won't go and live with my in-laws. I'd rather work in a factory and have my own place. They didn't want me to follow my husband to Sydney because they thought that once we got married and settled here we'd never come back."

A second respondent told me, "My husband came to Australia when he was seventeen. His uncle brought him out to his farm in Queensland, but he didn't get on with the uncle's wife and came down to Sydney after six months and got a job concreting."

Another said, "Luigi was nineteen when he came here. He went straight to his uncle's fruit farm in Queensland. All they gave him to eat was fruit, and they only paid him eight dollars a week. He didn't realize at first that this was a slave wage. He slept on straw in a stall with the cows. But what really terrified him was when one night a large goanna stripped its skin over him. So the next day he left and took the train to Sydney. After a week he started working for Melocco, the concreting firm."

In Sydney most single men shared a room. Sometimes they took turns at cooking, but often their landlady cooked, washed, and ironed for them. They each paid between $12 and $14 a week. Thus it was not difficult to save between $50 and $60 if they worked overtime. They earned a great deal but were lonely.

Few spoke enough English to make contact with Australian girls; there were no single women from Treviso; and southern Italians were closely chaperoned and kept at home. After two or three years they either returned to marry or arranged for someone from home to come out. They then set up a nuclear household. Uprooted rural workers thus became urban labourers.

ii] Courtship and marriage All my respondents knew their future husbands before coming to Australia, but few were engaged at the time of the man's departure. Some had merely agreed to correspond providing they received money for stamps. Five of the eight had been engaged two or more times before marrying. Multiple broken engagements were not unusual and did not affect a girl's chances of making a good match.

"I knew my husband at school. He went regularly to Switzerland as a seasonal worker until he left for Australia. His intentions towards me were always honourable, but I was engaged twice before I decided to marry him. When Tonio left for Australia I said I'd write if he sent me money for stamps. After he'd been here for seven months he wrote to me, I replied, and three months later we were engaged."

Another told me her story, "When I met my husband I was thirteen and he was seventeen. After a few months he left for Australia, and we said we'd write to each other. We did so for three years. Then he became engaged to the daughter of his boss in Sydney. When he broke off this engagement we started writing again. I was engaged three times before marrying. My sisters were always angry with me because I could never say no. I used to dream that I'd marry a doctor or a lawyer, but that was very stupid of me because those sorts of people couldn't marry an ignorant peasant girl like me. When Paolo asked me to come to Australia he paid my air fare. I didn't bring a trousseau because he said he had plenty of money and I shouldn't bother. Each of my sisters had a trousseau worth $300. We decided not to ask my parents for the money, but when we go back next year and stay with them we won't pay for our keep and that'll make up for it."

Here is an account of a third. "I was engaged to a fellow when I was sixteen. One day this young man brought a friend along to a get-together we were having in the stable. The friend, to annoy my fiancé, sat on a box next to me. We fell in love, I broke off my engagement, and the two of us became engaged when I was eighteen and he was twenty. Shortly after that he left for Australia, and I followed two years later."

All the couples married on the day of the woman's arrival or a few days later. Some had only three or four guests at the wedding. A few had thirty or forty, but the brides were then uncomfortable because they only knew a handful. Regardless of the number of guests, all the women wore a full bridal outfit either brought out from Italy or hired. Invariably a large sum was spent on the photographs that were later displayed in the sitting room and bedroom. A woman who had only three guests told me, "I don't even have a happy memory of a wonderful wedding. My sister-in-law had 100 guests and so many presents that for years she didn't buy anything. I got nothing and had to buy every single plate."

Another told of her marriage at home. "We were married when my husband came back to Treviso. It wasn't a big wedding because the arrangements had to be made in a hurry. After staying with my husband's family for a week we boarded the ship in Genova. In Sydney we rented a room and kitchen from Siciliani. We stayed there for two months and then moved to another Sicilian house."

None of these women had relatives in Sydney, and all dwelt with anguish on those first few weeks.

iii] *The new environment* The sudden change from village to a densely populated inner suburb in Sydney was especially traumatic for the women. Most couples rented a room and kitchen in or near Leichhardt for the first few months. Occasionally they lived with *paesani* but more often with southern Italians. In every case, "We kept ourselves to ourselves and didn't see or talk much to anyone."

One woman recalled how, "We rented a room in Annandale. Our landlady asked me not to look at my husband at the table in case her young daughter was shocked by the way newlyweds gazed at each other. I spent most of my time crying. We then moved into a Calabrese home and stayed there for four months."

Another told a similar tale. "I cried all the time; I was so lost and lonely. After two weeks a girl from Trieste married to a Sicilian friend of the landlady told me to come with her to the factory where she worked. So I started there. I was terrified to stay home by myself in case somebody knocked on the door and I wouldn't know what to say."

During the first few weeks or months the women were afraid to venture out. They found the streets, the crossings, and the traffic bewildering. Fortunately in Leichhardt language was not a problem as shop assistants, pharmacists, estate agents, doctors, and others spoke Italian. Soon after marriage a number started to work in neighbouring factories to which they were introduced by other girls. Most stayed for a few months until they put a deposit on a house or had their first baby.

iv] *The house* At the time of my study a number of respondents were no longer living in the house they had bought. Those who had sold profited by inflation. Most houses were bought and sold quickly, sometimes through agents, sometimes directly. Rumours spread rapidly. "The day after we decided to sell and move to Campsie I took down the blinds to wash them. A little while later a woman from across the road to whom I'd never spoken knocked on the door. She asked whether we were selling. I said yes. That evening we accepted a deposit from a Calabrese *paesano* of hers. She must have seen me take down the blinds."

Most Trevisani put a deposit on a house during the first twelve months or so.[12] They bought in both husband and wife's names, a different custom from that in Treviso. The prices for the first house ranged from $5—9,000.

"We rented a room for five months and then put a deposit of $800 on a house that was to cost $9,000. We spent $1,000 doing it up. We have been trying to pay off as quickly as possible. In the past two years we've paid off $2,000 and now have only $150 to go. The first three years we paid 8 per cent to the lawyer for the mortgage. After that the bank lent us money at $5\frac{3}{4}$ per cent."

Some of the families I visited lived in narrow terrace houses, others in places with a concrete path down both sides. One in an outer suburb had a large garden. The terrace houses tended to be old and musty, but the couples put

Fig. 12. Residential area in Leichhardt, Sydney.

Fig. 13. Downtown Leichhardt.

much effort into renovating and painting them. Usually there were two or three bedrooms, a sitting room, kitchen, and bathroom. The laundry and often the toilet were outside.

Floors were covered with linoleum and the walls painted in pastel shades. The main bedroom had the most expensive furniture, a satin bedspread, and generally an ornate doll sat in the middle near the head of the bed. On the dressing table stood many nick-nacks and snapshots of parents, children, relatives, and wedding groups. If there was a young baby the bassinette stood in the main bedroom.

In the sitting room a large television set had pride of place. The settee and chairs were covered in floral material or vinyl. Sometimes a small sideboard stood against the wall containing glasses, liqueurs, biscuits, and sweets for visitors. On the top were photographs, souvenirs from resorts in Italy, and plastic flowers. In the children's room were the beds, a cupboard, a dressing table with a large mirror, toys, and holy pictures, but as in Griffith, no desk or table for homework.

The only table was in the kitchen, and here the woman did her sewing and ironing and prepared the meals. The family ate at the table and sat chatting over coffee, and occasionally the children used it for their homework. Also in the kitchen was the refrigerator, usually new and large.

The status symbol to which all aspired but none had attained was a wall-to-wall carpet. A woman remarked of a Trevisan acquaintance who had been here many years, "She really thinks she's somebody because they've put in wall-to-wall carpet and a bar. When we went back for our trip home she asked me to tell everybody how rich she was, but I didn't."

The women took immense pride in the house and were constantly cleaning and polishing. The curtains and blinds were generally drawn to prevent fading, and hence the light was poor. In the backyard people grew vegetables wherever possible, and sometimes they kept a few chickens, rabbits, and pigeons. Ground not used for vegetable growing was covered with cement, and pocket-sized front lawns were also dug up and turned into slabs of green concrete. Only one family had flowers and shrubs.

The nuclear family

As I mentioned earlier, the families with whom I was concerned were at a particular stage in their development and settlement. Most of them were either preparing for their trip or had recently returned. They were unsettled and so had formed few close ties. This fact explained in part their loneliness.

During the first year or two most women were sustained in their solitude by the knowledge that in the foreseeable future they would return to Treviso. Earning and saving became the all-important goals and entailed many hardships, though the husband and wife, with common aims, drew closer together. The initial ambition was to pay off the house. Most people were apprehensive about other debts and paid cash for everything except the house. Each woman knew exactly how much was still owed and how long before the payments would be completed.

As soon as the outstanding sum was paid off the trip home became the object for which couples planned. For this at least three more years of saving were necessary.

i] *The husband and wife* In Sydney during the first months of marriage the wife found herself in a different environment, living in rented rooms among strangers. Without kin and with only a minimum of *paesani* to offer advice, she and her husband were forced to turn to each other for companionship, help, and approval. Redefinition of their roles was therefore inevitable.

All couples agreed that ideally the wife's main concern should be the home and family and that the husband should be the sole bread-winner. For practical reasons these ideals were very difficult to achieve. From the start both agreed that they must save money. An income of $100 or more a week was, therefore, desirable (I am speaking of 1968–69).

Only the husbands in households 6 and 8, the Tomasielli and Crespanis, earned as much as this, and their wives alone did not need to work.

I noticed two tendencies which, at the risk of oversimplification, I shall call traditional or conservative and modern or progressive. (The biographies of Antonietta and Grazia given earlier, pp. 40–46, could be taken as an example of each.) In the conservative households of Gori, Lorenzin and Bresci, (2,3 and 4), the husband and wife tended to keep their roles as segregated as possible.[13] Obviously they could not be as distinct as in Treviso, for of necessity on many occasions they had to interchange tasks. For this reason I would still call their relationship "joint" though less so than in the modern group. Working in a factory was not acceptable to these households, but such tasks as taking in unmarried male boarders, minding other people's children during the day, and sewing at home for a factory were. All was well as long as the wife could by some means contribute to the household income without going out to work.

In the modern or progressive households, Pieranti, Tomasielli, Santrin, and Crespani, (5,6,7, and 8) the husband-wife relationship was joint out of conviction as well as need. ("We think it's right that way.") The husband did not object to the wife's working in a factory, though preferably not after the birth of the first child. Gina and Melia in households 6 and 8 said that they would have gone to a factory had this been called for. All had worked outside in Treviso. Maria and Melia, in households 5 and 8, had been trained as machinists and thus could sew at home. Anna in household 7 could not sew and therefore returned to a factory eighteen months after the birth of her baby. She intended to stop as soon as she and her husband had met all their financial commitments and were ready to go off to Treviso.

We can say that the Sydney families had joint conjugal role-relationships. Apart from the husband's workmates with whom he interacted during the day, his wife's and his own networks of friends and acquaintances were identical. The men also knew how to cook, wash, iron, clean, change nappies, feed the children, and attend to the general household chores. The differences lay in the attitude to the performance or exchange of household tasks. In the more traditional group both sexes had definite ideas about men's and women's tasks.

A conservative wife explained, "Whenever I have a baby my husband stays home for a week and looks after the others. He can do everything except sew, but he only does things when I'm in hospital. But he kills and cleans the chickens, something he wouldn't have done in Italy. My young brother Alfonso who came here only three years ago helps his wife with the dishes or anything else in the house. In Treviso people would have laughed at him and said that he wears the skirt. My husband only helps when he really has to, not otherwise; but he never laughs at Alfonso or anyone else who does things for his wife."

Ida (household 2) remarked, "I never worked in a factory—my husband wouldn't have liked it—but I always had boarders and did their washing and ironing and the cooking. But now that we've had our trip and paid off all the debts my husband doesn't want me to work any more. In a way it's no good if a wife becomes too independent and doesn't listen to anything her husband says or wants. When I worked in the fish and chips shop and had boarders my husband helped with everything. He's a better cook than I am, but now that I'm home all the time he doesn't even help to dry a plate; he says he'll do his work and I must do mine, and I think he's right."

This attitude was different from that of the more progressive couples. The wife who worked in a factory told me, "Men in Italy are terrible egoists. They go out and leave the wife at home with the kids and the work. They're not like that here. Here the husband and the wife co-operate, and they're much closer to each other. At night sometimes I wash up and Giovanni does the sandwiches for the next day, at other times he washes up and I do the sandwiches. I suppose that's because there's no interference from relatives. When we go back to Italy we'll just carry on like we do here and won't listen to anyone. But there's no doubt that if the wife works the husband is not completely the boss."

Another expressed similar views, "I'd like to go out to work because I get so lonely at home, but my husband won't let me. He says he earns more than enough, and he's right in that respect. But sometimes he doesn't have a day off the whole year round, and I like company. When I'm sick he knows how to do everything and does it. Even if I'm not sick and we're rushing to go somewhere at night he helps with the dishes. He often gets up at night for the baby and sometimes feeds her without waking me up. Couples are much more united here. If we weren't, that'd be the end."

The wives tended to have greater sway when the problem related to something inside the home, the husbands more influence in matters outside, such as what house to buy and where. All agreed that they discussed everything together before making a final decision and neither went against the other's firm wish. (Here I do not include household 1 where the husband and wife barely spoke to one another.)

The conservative wives told me, however, that although all decisions were joint, they went to great lengths to let the husband feel he was the boss. "I always ask Tonio before buying anything. One of the kids needed new sandals so I asked him whether it was O.K. for me to buy them, and he said 'no'. Then when the doctor said I needed a corset to support my stomach muscles he also said 'we can't afford it this week'. If a wife goes to work though, she can just go and buy things without asking. But I think the man ought to be the boss. When the kids ask me for ice cream and Tonio isn't home I always give it to them, but when he's here I tell them to go and ask their father. He always says, 'yes, go and ask your mother for the money'. He wouldn't like it if I didn't tell them to ask him first. When Tonio decided on a television set, he wanted to buy one for $140, but I said that if we're going to pay that much we should get the best. So we got one that has a radio and gramophone all combined, and it cost

$580. I told Tonio that one day he might buy some records. We used the $60 I'd saved up for my false teeth for the deposit."

One of the more modern wives, however, had said, "My husband thinks that in Australia nobody is the boss. We're both head of house (*capo di casa*). Yet when it comes to deciding about things like furniture and T.V. I think I have more say, but I wouldn't buy anything my husband didn't like. He had more say when we decided to buy this house." Another added, "We decide on everything together, even when I go to buy a dress, but I still think the husband should be the boss."

It would have been unthinkable for one of the conservative wives to contradict her husband in public even though later she might explain to me that she did not agree with him at all and would tell him so in private. The more progressive wives were not so reticent. Without doubt the most assertive was the one who worked in a factory. She admitted at times doing things without her husband's knowledge. She sent her mother a few dollars in an envelope occasionally, and the mother made acknowledgment by putting a cross at the bottom of her letter. Although this woman had her way on many issues, she tried to compromise, and the man also at times, as she put it, "closed his eyes". She told me, "Giovanni hates my using tinned food, but I find it's handy especially as I'm working. He minds it less if the tin has 'Continental' or 'Italian' written on it, so I only buy those." He also disliked her smoking, especially in public, "so I don't smoke if he's around. He wasn't very happy when I got my driver's licence. I think he hoped I'd fail. But I want to be able to get around when I'm on holidays from work. I wouldn't drive when we're both in the car together. He wouldn't like it."

All the couples had joint savings accounts. The Lorenzins (household 3) required both signatures for a withdrawal, but in the other households, that of either party sufficed.

Men always handed the wife their pay envelope unopened. She first gave him an allowance and then looked after the expenses and allocation of funds. Wives who worked did not always tell the husband their exact earnings. They sometimes allowed themselves one or two dollars to buy personal things or send to their mother. It made them happy and avoided arguments.

Obviously a wife who worked in a factory and spoke better English than her husband could become more independent than one who stayed at home and did not speak English. (Working in a factory did not automatically mean that the woman learned English. Her accomplishment or lack of it depended on what language the majority of the employees spoke.) Although smoking and driving a car were relatively unimportant compared with, say, working or speaking better English, such habits were indicative of an attitude more readily found among the younger progressive wives.

Table 22 is a rough impressionistic summary of wives' attitudes. Thus, a woman who scored four pluses was likely to be the most assertive, the one who scored four minuses was likely to be the most submissive. On the whole the table tallies with my findings: Anna in household 7 was the most assertive, and Alda and Lucia in households 3 and 4 the most submissive. Gina and Melia (6 and 8) would have been more like Anna had they worked. As was mentioned, relationships in household 1 were poor. Rosa was aggressive and, unlike all the other women, had no respect for her husband. Ida (2) had an extrovert personality and was always prepared, as she insisted, "to have a go". She learnt some English from two Australian neighbours who used her telephone. Maria (5) was somewhere between the two extremes.

Frequently the women used such phrases as the following to describe Trevisan couples in Australia: *vanno piu d'accordo* (get on better), *sono piu uniti* (are more united), *sono piu vicini* (are closer), and *c'è piu serenita in casa* (there is greater serenity in the home). Although conjugal role-relationships were joint, I have pointed out that present circumstances were mainly responsible. Conservative couples, however, had to readjust themselves more than the progressive. The former stressed division of labour in the household more than the

Table 22. Sydney: the women's attitudes

Family	1	2	3	4	5	6[a]	7	8[a]
Does the wife work or has she ever worked in a factory?	+	–	–	–	+	–	+	–
Does she speak English as well as or better than her husband?	+	+	–	–	–	–	+	–
Does she smoke?	+	–	–	–	–	+	+	+
Does she drive a car or would she drive if they had one?	-c (+)	-c (+)	-c (–)	-c (–)	+c -	+ truck (+)	+c +	+c (+) learning

+   positive response
—   negative response
+c   have a car
-c   have no car
(+)   would drive if they had a car
(–)   would not drive if they had a car

a   Wives in families 6 and 8 did not need to work. Had they needed to do so, it is likely that they wou
    have chosen factory work in preference to anything else.

latter, but much depended on whether the wife was in employment.[14]

ii] *Parents and young children* Most couples did not want more than two children—"If we have only two we can give them everything"—though one respondent with four wanted another. One with three admitted that the last had been a mistake, and a third with two, finding herself pregnant, even sought an abortion.

The most common form of contraception was *coitus interruptus*—"the man must be careful". Two confided that they were on the pill but did not tell anyone "because people associate pills with prostitutes".

Men wanted to have at least one son. A woman recalled how disappointed her husband had been when their first child was a girl, but she added, "You should have seen how he carried on when Steven was born; he didn't mind that the last baby was a girl." The baptism of the firstborn was generally a big affair, especially if it was a boy. Between ten

156

and thirty *paesani* attended the party at home, though only the godparents and one or two friends went to the church ceremony. The godparents (*compare* and *comare*) were almost always relatives or *paesani*.

Babies were all born in intermediate or public hospital wards. All the mothers breast fed the infants for several months and started pot training them after three to six months. I was able to observe only three very young children, all had dummies and were fed on demand. Some of the mothers went to Baby Health Centres but rarely understood what they were told or, if they did, failed to carry out the instructions. The main reason for going was to have the baby weighed. One mother showed me instructions, written illegibly in English by the nurse.

The mothers bought baby biscuits and foods at the chemist, choosing familiar Italian brands if possible. The younger women sought advice from the older or more experienced, who suggested the proportions of milk and water or powder. Mothers nursed and fed the babies when they cried but sometimes put them into the bassinette sucking a bottle of water, milk, or orange juice. One woman wanted to feed the baby "in our way", but another said the chemist had suggested Heinz tinned foods, which the baby liked. "Some people said that apples fried in olive oil are much better for the baby than apples out of a tin, but I just kept on with the tins. My sister-in-law was jealous and spread rumours that I fed the children on tins to save money and that was how we had enough to go on our trip."

The amount of entertainment was limited. Unless the couple had a car or were prepared to take a taxi they stayed at home. It was unthinkable to pay a baby-sitter, and they did not like to make arrangements with neighbours. "These are the sacrifices one must make for one's children," one woman said "I wouldn't be happy to leave them with strangers." (Yet she regularly minded two Greek children whose mother worked.) "It's all wrong. All the parents think about is money, money. The mother works even on Saturday. They bring the two children here at half past six in the morning when mine are still in bed. There they stand and watch with their mouths open when mine are having breakfast. The parents pick them up at about seven or eight in the evening, and they don't have dinner till they get home."

None of the children attended kindergarten but started ordinary school at the age of five or six. The choice depended on proximity. If a convent school was located nearby they went there, but if the public school was nearer the parents were satisfied with that. The mother took the children along in the morning and picked them up in the afternoon.

The children did their homework either on a suitcase on their knees in front of the television set or on the kitchen table. They learnt English soon after starting school and as their English improved, their Trevisan dialect deteriorated. After a year or two many had problems in talking to their parents. One child aged nine, who spoke both languages well, interpreted for his six-year old brother when the latter spoke with their mother. The boys, however, always communicated with each other in English. When the younger boy announced one day that he had been elected class captain, the mother did not understand. Only two of the mothers in the group had ever spoken to a teacher about her children's progress.

Family outings were rare, mainly because the father always worked on Saturdays and frequently on Sundays. People with a car visited Luna Park two or three times a year and the beach occasionally in summer. Husband, wife, and children were always alone on these expeditions. One woman explained this exclusiveness "because more couldn't fit into the car", and another justified herself, "We don't want other people to know how much we spend."[15] Three of the children had been to the cinema once to see *Mary Poppins* on a school outing. The children seldom played outside and mostly sat in front of the television set.

Parents took tremendous pride in the fact that the children lacked nothing and that the mother was home to look after them. The women often repeated that the most important person was the mother. The father worked hard but she was the one who "makes sacrifices and denies herself everything for the children". He left their upbringing to her. When he came home in the evening he washed, had dinner, and watched television. The older children generally joined him.

All parents hoped that their sons would be professionals—lawyers, doctors, accountants, or architects. If they could not achieve their goal, then it was hoped they would be skilled tradesmen such as mechanics or carpenters. Nobody wanted his son to be a manual labourer. To avoid this fate no sacrifice was too much. Girls were expected to become secretaries, teachers, or hairdressers. Nursing was never mentioned.

iii] Organizing the household In Sydney each day and week had the same routine. The couple rose between five and six every morning, had breakfast, and the man went to work shortly after six. As soon as he had left the woman started feeding the babies, dressing the children, and getting the bigger ones ready for school. Generally they had prepared the men's lunches the evening before (a thermos with meat, vegetables and potatoes, and bread, cheese, salami, and fruit). They cut the children's lunches in the morning. From about 5:30 to 9:00 in the morning they had the radio on to know the time. After breakfast they started the housework—washing dishes, making beds, cleaning, and sweeping. They tended to allocate particular tasks to given days: washing on Monday, ironing on Tuesday, and so on. Friday was the weekly shopping day. One who lived on a direct bus route to the markets went there each week. Others shopped at the closest shopping centre, Leichhardt if possible. They liked going there because of the wide assortment of Italian foods and brands.

Whenever the women sat down to talk or watch a midday movie they mended, knitted, sewed, or unpicked old garments for remaking. Many associated the days with television programmes and could recite these without hesitation:

Monday—Showcase, The Saint, and a detective story; Tuesday—Robert Taylor in a detective serial; Wednesday —Peyton Place; and so on. Like the daily television feature, they had a certain menu on a particular day—one kind of meat on Monday, another on Tuesday, etc. On Sunday there was always chicken.

The husbands of all women worked on Saturdays, and if possible Sundays. Two women complained that they could not remember when their husbands last had a day off. Visiting during the week was kept to a minimum. Most watched television for from two to four hours each night and then went to bed. Saturday evening and Sunday were the most popular times for visits, which were rarely pre-arranged.

The one respondent who was in a factory started at six in the morning and finished at two. Her husband drove her to work at 5:30 in the morning then returned home, dressed and fed their small daughter and took her to a friend with whom she stayed until the mother picked her up at 2:15 in the afternoon. He left for work at 6:30 in the morning.

Some of the younger mothers celebrated the children's birthdays and went to Luna Park or the beach occasionally. All remarked on the monotony of the daily routine. There were no *feste* nor seasonal changes which they said had enriched their lives in Treviso; here all they could look forward to were Easter and Christmas.

iv] Relationships with relatives Six of the eight couples had no kinsfolk in Sydney at the time of their marriage. Of the remainder one husband had a brother and another a cousin. In 1968 three of the households had relations:

The Goris [*household* 2] The husband had two married brothers and their wives and children in Sydney. The wife had a young sister who married in Treviso before coming here in 1967. This sister lived with her husband around the corner in a rented room and kitchen.

The Lorenzins [household 3] The husband had a married cousin and his wife and children. The wife had a young brother who had come out in 1965, married a Maltese girl, and now had a baby. They did not live within easy reach of his sister but had a car.

The Pierantis [household 5] The wife's older sister, her husband, and three children had migrated to Sydney and lived in a house on the opposite side of the road.

The attitudes of the women in these households towards the relatives were expressed as follows:

Ida [household 2] "I love having my young sister here. She often drops in after work on her way home, and we talk for half an hour or so. The children really like her and her husband, and we often have our Sunday dinner together. They married a few months ago in Italy while we were there on our trip. They then came to Australia with us. Giovanni started work in a shoe factory after a week. Within a few weeks they bought a fridge and a T.V. Now that they have their own T.V. they don't visit so often in the evening. They don't want to have a baby until they can afford a house. I hope they find one near us. I don't get on with my husband's people. We see the brothers and their wives every couple of weeks or so at the weekend. One sister-in-law is worried about anyone dirtying her floor, so she puts strips of paper down for us to walk on. I told my husband I never want to go there again. The other one is jealous because we've been on our trip and she hasn't. But for all that they've got a much bigger house. She's always jealous about something."

Alda [household 3] "We don't speak to my husband's cousin and his wife any more. They had a grocery shop in Leichhardt and were offended because I didn't buy everything there. But I said to him, 'This isn't Treviso. I have money every week and don't need credit and then pay at the end of the season. If I see something cheaper in another shop I buy it. Why should I buy from you?' So we haven't spoken for a long time even though they're godparents to one of the children. But now I have my young brother here. He came three years ago; his wife speaks good English. She went to school here. We're hoping to buy a big house together in Liverpool, and she could go to work and I'd look after her baby. She'd help the children with their homework. They live in Five Dock now, and that's too far for us to visit them, but they have a car and come to see us several times a week. We get on really well."

Maria [*household* 5] "My older sister and her three children followed her husband to Australia a year after I came. She works in a factory full-time because it is so expensive to bring up three children [the youngest is ten]. My sister is like a mother to me. She's ten years older, and I see her nearly every day, but she's so tired most of the time. When I had the babies she couldn't help me, and my husband had to stay home. We only eat together at Christmas and Easter, and we never go out together. When we move to Adelaide in a few weeks I'm going to miss her very much, but I must do what I think is best for my children.[16] I know the children will miss each other. My sister and brother-in-law don't want to move because they don't want their children to change schools. One is doing her Certificate."

In these households the wife was attached to her own siblings but had little or nothing to do with her husband's brothers or cousin. People often remarked, "In Sydney we can choose whom we want to see and whom we don't." Thus even those who did have relatives saw some and avoided others. It seems likely that sisters not in employment who lived near each other would meet frequently during the day. Brothers who did not work together could see one another only on Sundays. Of necessity the women, many of whom did not want to meet, were brought together. The problem of a married brother seeing his married sister is probably similar and conducive to the kind of friction I found among the Goris (2).

Children were without grandparents in Australia and only occasionally had an indulgent aunt or uncle close at hand. Thus parents were often the sole source of affection and security.

v] *Godparenthood* Although the parents, siblings and other relatives of the couple sometimes acted as the children's godparents, several people told me they preferred to choose friends. "If we like people very much we try to become *compare* and *comare*. This binds us closer together."

When two people married they chose for the wedding a *compare* and a *comare* who were frequently but not necessarily another married couple. Their function resembled that of a best man and matron of honour. Subsequently the two became godparents to the first child. The married couple and the *compare* and *comare* all addressed each other as *compare* and *comare*. When a second child was born the tendency was not to reaffirm the ties but to seek others. One woman remarked, "People ask their relatives to be godparents if they want only a small affair and not much spent on the baptism, but here especially people want to spread their close ties and be in *compare* and *comare* relationship with as many different folk as possible." The child calls his godparents *santolo* and *santola*, Trevisan dialect for the Italian terms *padrino* and *madrina*.

These relationships stayed meaningful only as long as the people saw each other regularly. Of the seventeen children in my sample households, nine were attending primary school (first to fourth class), and most of them did not know who their godparents were. When I asked the mother about it she generally gave such reasons as, "Oh, they moved away and we don't know where they live now", "They've gone back to Italy", or "They were jealous about something, and we no longer see each other". Thus the attempts to create surrogate relatives and extend ties did not always succeed. Four respondents were in *comare* relationship to each other. They felt that they were, therefore, more than just good friends but agreed that they were able to continue in this way only because they lived close together. One day they might quarrel, and that would end the current harmony. In the Lorenzin household (3) the godparents were as follows:

1st child: A couple who had lived in Annandale (*paesani*)

but moved eighteen months ago and no longer
kept in touch.

2nd child: The husband's cousin and wife with whom he
was then on speaking terms.

3rd child: A couple in Annandale (*paesani*) who had no car
or telephone and were consequently estranged.

4th child: The wife's brother and her mother (the child's
grandmother) who was here on a six months'
visit at the time of the christening.

The first three sets of godparents neither sent presents nor
maintained contact. In the Pieranti household (5), the sister
and brother-in-law were godparents to the first two
children, and the Lorenzins (3) were godparents to the third
of the Pieranti children.[17]

Work and savings

i] *The husband's work and earnings* All the men were employed
in the building trade, mostly as concreters. Apart from overtime on Saturdays and perhaps Sundays, they hoped to work
at least an extra hour each day. One woman said that on a
good week her husband did up to 30 hours overtime but
15–20 was more usual. I recall one particular Saturday when
the husband had left at four in the morning and was not expected back until nine in the evening. One man was in
partnership with ten others and regarded himself as self-
employed. The company concentrated on contracts, and
profits were equally divided.

The basic wage in 1968 was about $50, but most brought
home $80–95 a week. Luigi Crespani (household 8) was a
foreman, and, apart from his weekly income of about $80,
the company paid for a car and petrol. Each night he had to
fill in work sheets that required writing and reading English.
He made an effort to learn all new words with the aid of a
dictionary (this was the only house I knew that had one). The
main boost to his income, however, was private concreting
at weekends, when each job earned him from $200 to $400.
To find this kind of work he either looked up advertisements
or put one in the paper himself.

ii] The wife's work and earnings As mentioned earlier, only three respondents were subsidizing the family income. One worked in a factory and earned $34 per week, the second was minding two Greek children during the day for $10 per week, and the third did sewing and knitting jobs at home. Apart from Gina (household 6), all had worked at sometime or another. Those who had had boarders charged $12–14 each per week. They cooked, washed, and ironed for the men. Often two or three men shared a room. One woman had looked after five men simultaneously and earned about $60 a week. Those who sewed tried to do piecework for factories. One woman machined trousers at home at the rate of 95 cents each and often earned $40 per week. Another who made frocks was paid $5 for each and earned between $30–40 without much difficulty. This kind of work was not easy to find, and many factory owners took advantage of the women. Two wives had had evening jobs for a time. One had worked in a knitting factory from five until ten; the other worked in a fish and chips shop from six until ten—a period when her husband could mind the children. Those without spare rooms or sewing skills minded children of mothers, mostly southern Italians or Greeks, who went to factories.[18]

Table 23. Type of work done by the women before this study (1968)

Family	1	2	3	4	5	6	7	8
factory	√				√		√	
sewing at home for the factory	√				√			√
looking after boarders	√	√	√	√			√	
minding other people's children during the day				√				
other jobs		√*						

Note: * The wife in family 2 had worked for some time in a fish and chips shop – from six in the evening until ten. The husband minded the children and the owner of the shop drove her home.

Table 24. Type of work done by the women at the time of this study (1968)[a]

Family	1	2	3	4	5	6	7	8
factory							√	
sewing at home for the factory	√							
looking after boarders								
minding other people's children during the day			√					
other jobs								

Note: a. After the completion of this study, the wife in family 2 started work-ing as a cleaner at Wesley College for four hours every day. She was always home before the children returned from school. The wife in family 8 persuaded her husband to allow her to work in a factory because she was too lonely at home. The husband did not want her to have a second child at this stage and so agreed.

iii] Savings and expenses All the women maintained that a family of four or five could live comfortably on $70–80 per week, especially after the house had been paid off (I am speaking of course of 1968–9). Most lived on $45–60, depending on the number of children, while saving every cent for house payments and the trip. The young sister and brother-in-law of Ida Gori (household 2) both worked, had no children, and rented a room and kitchen. They saved $70–80 a week. The Tomasiellis and Crespanis (6 and 8) had saved between $2,000 and $3,000 in the previous twelve months. The Santrins (7) saved $1,200, and the others had put away $800–1,000. All relied on overtime.

Table 25 shows the approximate weekly income of the men (including overtime) and the average weekly earnings of the wives. In brackets is the maximum the wives had earned in previous years. The amounts are net (after tax).

Table 26 indicates approximate weekly food expenses of three households.

All houses had an abundance of food—a variety of meats, salami, and cheese (generally parmesan). The people ate relatively little fruit and less *pasta* than formerly (meat and

Table 25. Husband's and wife's earnings

		1968 Husband	1968 Wife	
Family	1	$85	$15	($40)
	2	$75	–	($30)
	3	$95	$10	($10)
	4	$95	–	($60)
	5	$90	–	($40)
	6	$120	–	–
	7	$75	$34	($34)
	8	$78 (plus weekend concreting jobs)	–	($35)

Note: The figures in brackets represent the maximum the wives had earned in previous years. The amounts are net (after tax).

Table 26. Approximate weekly food expenses (1968)

Lorenzin family (4 children)	$ c	
groceries	5.00	
fruit and vegetables	4.00	
bread	1.19	
milk	3.08	This family grew some
cheese	0.80	vegetables in their backyard.
meat	7.00	They also had chickens,
coffee	0.25	rabbits, and pigeons, and did
beer and wine	2.41	not need to buy eggs.
lemonade	1.75	
children's lunches	1.20	
Total	**26.68**	

Pieranti family (3 children)	$ c	
groceries	10.00	
fruit and vegetables	5.00	
bread	2.20	
milk	1.20	This family had vegetables
cheese	1.80	in their backyard but no
meat	6.50	animals.
coffee	1.50	
beer and wine	3.00	
lemonade	2.00	
eggs	1.00	
Total	**34.20**	

Table 26. Continued

Gori family (2 children)	$ c	
groceries	6.00	
fruit and vegetables	5.00	
bread	1.20	
milk	2.00	This family did not grow
cheese	3.20	vegetables, nor did they have
meat	5.30	animals in the backyard, but
coffee	1.30	the wife frequently bought
beer and wine	1.30	pigeons (20 cents each) and
lemonade	2.50	sparrows (7 for 10 cents)
eggs	1.10	from a man who came round
Total	28.90	regularly.

vegetables replaced the daily plate of *spaghetti*). None of the families ate lamb. One woman bought horse meat from the pet shop once a week because she thought variety was good for the children. Her husband did not eat *mortadella* because he thought it was donkey meat, but he ate salami because it was made from pork. All the men drank beer in preference to wine; those who continued with wine did so only because it was cheaper. Women often mixed wine with lemonade but also drank beer, and the children consumed vast quantities of orangeade and lemonade.

Many items, such as tinned foods, ice cream, beer, and instant coffee, were adaptations to their new economic situation rather than simple assimilation. Those who had come back from Italy said that relatives who were earning good wages there were also drinking beer and eating ice cream.

In the eight households refrigerators, radios, television sets, and sewing machines were the most common consumer items. Some had been bought secondhand (see table 27).

Gina (household 6) said that she intended to buy as little as possible until they returned to Italy and decided whether they would settle in Sydney. Probably many others were similarly placed. The couples spent little on entertainment and a minimum on clothing. At any festivity the men were better dressed than the women because dresses go out of fashion quickly.

Table 27. Consumer items in the house

Family	1	2	3	4	5	6	7	8	Total
car	–	–	–	–	√	truck	√	√	4
telephone	–	√	–	√	–	√	–	√	4
refrigerator	√	√	√	√	√	√	√	√	8
television	–	√	√	√	√	√	√	√	7
washing machine	–	√	√	√	√	–	–	–	4
radio	√	√	√	√	√	√	√	√	8
tape recorder	–	√	–	–	–	–	√	–	2
gramophone	–	√	√	–	–	√	√	√	5
fan	–	–	√	–	√	–	√	–	3
mixmaster	–	–	–	–	–	–	√	–	1
coffee grinder	√	√	–	√	√	–	–	–	4
floor polisher	√	√	√	√	√	–	–	√	5
vacuum cleaner	–	√	√	√	–	√	–	–	4
sewing machine	√	√	√	√	√	–	√	√	7

iv] Dilemmas and alternatives As I pointed out, men preferred their wives not to work, and those who earned over $100 tried to be adamant about it. The others were ambivalent; on the one hand they wanted to save as quickly as possible, on the other they would have liked to have been the sole breadwinners.

The young brother of Alda Lorenzin (3) was determined that he would never allow his wife to work. "Once a woman has children her place is in the home; it's better to have less and bring up the children properly." Yet three weeks later he was saying, "If we shared a house with my sister and she looked after our baby, my wife could go to work at least till we had enough for a house."

Anna (7), who worked in a factory, admitted, "My husband doesn't like the idea of my working outside the house, but we want to have the house paid off and $4,000 in cash before we go back, so it's either the factory or we don't go for a long time, and my husband is anxious to see his mother. We haven't got space for boarders. But we agreed that if we came back to Australia I'll stop working."

Others, like Melia Crespani (8), who did not need to work and had only one child were bored and lonely. She wanted to do anything that would get her out of the house, especially as her husband worked the whole weekend. He was emphatic, however that she must stay home and did not want her even to visit anyone. "You shouldn't be enjoying yourself while I'm working," he reiterated. Some months after the completion of this study she told me her husband had given in, and she was now in a factory. Again the understanding was that she would not resume when they came back to Sydney.

The women who did not work stressed, "It's better that we should manage on less as long as the children are properly looked after." Those who did work were delighted with their contribution and the rate at which the money was accumulating. Yet those in each category were a little envious of those in the other. They often said, "we're all afflicted with the money illness (*malatia di soldi*). In Italy we didn't have this opportunity. It's something new for us and hard to resist." One day a woman I was accompanying as she went shopping met a *paesano* coming out of a bank, where he had just been depositing money, who said jokingly to her, "I've just put the saints into church" (*ho gia messo i santi in chiesa*).

The trip home was a turning point and climaxed years of planning, working and saving. Afterwards couples expected a reorganization and reappraisal of their lifestyle and, hopefully, fewer dilemmas. Anticipation of the pilgrimage postponed the time for decisions.

The social network

The primary group in Sydney consisted of the nuclear family, perhaps a few relatives, and *paesani*, who often became godparents to the children. The scattering of *paesani* in the metropolitan area, transport difficulties, and long working hours militated against the formation of clearly demarcated circles of friends meeting regularly. The result was the establishment of networks where only some of a person's acquaintances knew one another. Outings and gatherings were not planned, and people just dropped in and met whoever happened to be there. I was present on a number of occasions when people had to be introduced although each knew the host well. Trevisani found it more relaxing to be together because they could speak their dialect.

There was no focal point of contact such as a church or club. The friendship network was made up of: i. *paesani*, ii. workmates who were *paesani* or other Italians, and iii. neighbours, who might be *paesani*, Italians, Greeks, Australians, or of other nationalities. They were most at home with those whose role-sets overlapped most completely, that is, people who were simultaneously *paesani*, workmates, and neighbours. It is with this group that they shared what has been called a "consciousness of kind",[19] the group with whom they relaxed and participated with ease.

i] *Men and women* I have already mentioned that if the members of the nuclear family went out on an outing they were invariably alone. Only the two respondents with sisters spent Christmas and Easter with someone other than just the immediate nuclear family; the rest were on such occasions alone. "For Christmas and Easter we don't like to go to anyone's place in case we disturb," they said. They saw relatives they liked more frequently than friends, especially if these lived nearby or had a car. But few had either relatives or cars.

None of the respondents belonged to a club. Two had been to the Apia once, one to the Marconi once, and one to the Marconi four times in three years. "People think the Apia is a typical Italian club, but it is just for snobs and businessmen. We wouldn't feel comfortable there. Lots of single men go there, but married couples like us don't. The Marconi Club is more of a family place, but it's a long way out, especially if you haven't got a car. On top of it, it costs a lot to go to these places, and I wouldn't go if I didn't have a nice dress. In any case, you don't go out when you're trying to save."

People visited more in summer than winter, but much depended on how close they lived to other *paesani* and whether they had transport. A car and few or no debts were turning points in a family's social life. The following were excerpts from conversations with the women of the eight households.

Rosa [*household* 1]

"Apart from visiting *paesani* once a week or once a fortnight for a chat and a game of cards, we haven't been anywhere since we came back. A lot of people we know are better off than we are. They didn't go back to Italy for as long as we did, and they made quite a bit of money. Now they're putting on airs. I really don't enjoy going out."

Ida [*household* 2]

"We can't afford to spend anything on entertainment. I haven't been to the pictures for three years. In the summer we sometimes go to the beach. We've been to the zoo and to Luna Park. We see friends every few weeks, but not regularly. We see my sister and her husband a lot and my husband's brothers and their family more often than we see friends."

Alda [*household* 3]

"The last time we went to the city was nine years ago. I'd like to go to a club or to the pictures, but I haven't got decent clothes, and I'd feel ashamed. In the past two years we've been to visit friends three times and to my brother and sister-in-law about four times. It gets expensive because we have to get a taxi. It's too complicated with buses. A couple of our friends have cars so they visit us every two or three weeks."

Lucia [*household* 4]

"The only holiday we've ever had was two weeks in Griffith. My husband loved it because of the clubs, but I'm shy. I'd be frightened to live on a farm. It's so far from the next neighbour. We've been to the pictures about four times in eight years and to the city about five times since we were married in 1960. We have people dropping in once or twice a month, and sometimes we go in a taxi. It would be easier if we had a car."

Maria [*household* 5]

"We know five couples here in Leichhardt, but we don't all meet at the same time. They drop in whenever they feel like it because they're close to us. We can't go out much because of the baby, but we drive out to see the Lorenzins every three weeks or so. At the baby's baptism we only had my sister and her family and the Lorenzins, who are the godparents."

Gina [household 6]
"We go out once every six months or so. In the past three years we've been once to the pictures and twice to the beach. Lots of people drop in on us at the weekend. I never know who's coming or how many, but my husband always has a stock of beer. He prefers people to come here rather than go out. He worries in case our kid dirties something or brings in mud on his shoes when we are out visiting."

Anna [household 7]
"We never went out till we got the car. In the past two years we've been to Griffith four times, once to Canberra, and once to Melbourne. We always stay with friends or relatives. Whenever anyone I know goes on holidays it is usually to Griffith or Adelaide, and they stay with people they know. But you've got to have a car first. We sometimes have a drink with our neighbours. We have Greeks on one side and French people on the other. Now that the house is paid off we think we'll join the Leagues Club after our trip if we come back to Australia."

Melia [household 8]
"My husband and I adore wrestling, and we've been to the stadium seven or eight times. Whenever we go to Luna Park or the beach just the three of us go. In Italy visitors were always family, here they're mainly friends. Usually six or eight turn up on Saturday or Sunday night, and we sing or play cards. Some people hesitate to sing the way we used to in case the neighbours think we'd gone mad. When we go out we leave the baby with a Sicilian girl friend in Ashfield."

Compared with Southerners, the Veneti had little time for conspicuous consumption. Marriages, confirmations and births in particular were modest.

The Tomasiellis and Crespanis (6 and 8) who were financially best off, had more people dropping in at the weekend.

I am not sure whether people regarded the men in these two households as advice givers or useful connections, or whether the two couples were the nucleus of a reference group whom the others strove to emulate. Probably there was an element of all three.

It was difficult for friends to help one another—many worked, others lived too far away. Thus friendships were generally not as intense or as permanent as some would have liked. People drifted apart, particularly if they found it hard to meet regularly. When a break-up occurred accusations of jealousy often followed.

Couples hesitated to tell others their financial state or plans. They tended to be secretive and say as little as possible on the principle that one can never speak too little but often too much. The married pair recognized few obligations outside the nuclear family.

Trevisani rarely initiated contact with Australian neighbours and were unsure of how to behave or what to expect. They were concerned with "impression management" and were aware that it was "important to put one's right foot forward at the beginning of a relationship".[20] In the majority of cases any interaction was superficial and took place at the front door between the women. Television programmes and artists performed the invaluable function of providing topics of conversation.

ii] *The women* Of the eight the following saw one another in their homes once or more in 1968.

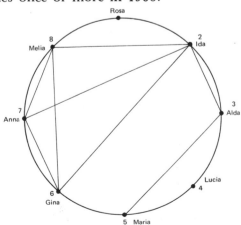

Rosa and Lucia had neither visited nor been visited by any of the others although each knew at least two of the remaining six. When Anna had three weeks' vacation she spent much of the time picking up friends in her car and dropping in on others she had not seen for several weeks or months. One day Gina, Anna, and Melia arrived while I was at Ida's. All were delighted with the novelty of having a car at their disposal and being "girls together". This was the first occasion when a few of them had met without the husbands. Anna, who had no telephone, called up Gina, Melia, and Ida every two or three weeks from a booth.

Each came into more frequent contact with women who lived close to them or whom they met while shopping. Alda once told me about her fears when she ventured further than a few streets. "When we first moved to this suburb it took me two weeks not to get lost every time I walked to and from school with the children. No matter how hard I tried to remember which street to turn into I got lost. Tonio, my husband, goes to work all over Sydney, but usually he arranges to be picked up somewhere. But when I ask him to go to the shops to buy something, he also gets lost even though it's only a five or six minutes' walk. Once I decided to visit my sister-in-law in Five Dock. My son wrote the address on a piece of paper, and I hailed a taxi and showed the driver the piece of paper. When we were just one street away he looked up his road book and couldn't find it. I was too scared and shy to try and tell him that the place was just around the corner. In the end he just turned around and drove me all the way home. That was my first and last attempt at trying to go out somewhere on my own."[21]

Ida Gori was the most gregarious of the women. She chatted in her broken English across the fence to her Australian neighbours who also came in to use her telephone. On these occasions they sometimes stayed for a cup of coffee. "I've got to talk to people, and I can't stand it if there isn't some sort of noise in the place," she said. "My sister is amazed how I talk English, but I told her, 'Giovanna, if there isn't a human I can talk to, I'll talk to the dog on the street.' When

I was shopping in Leichhardt with her I said, 'Let's go into the espresso bar and have a cup of coffee.' So we did. When we came out, sure enough three *paesane* gaped at us and said, 'You've just had a cup of coffee in there!' I was furious and said to them, '*Sacramento*, nobody is stopping you from going in is there?' You can't do a thing without somebody criticizing you. They think we're still in the village, where it's a crime for a woman to have a cup of coffee in an espresso bar.

On Saturday morning I clean the house, so I open all the doors and windows to let in fresh air. But at lunchtime I stop to watch the wrestling on T.V. When I do this I scream and yell at the top of my voice because I get so excited. A few weeks ago my Australian neighbour didn't hear me scream and thought I must be sick. She came in to ask what was wrong, and then I realized that the clock had stopped and I hadn't turned on the wrestling. They all expect to hear me scream every Saturday lunchtime."

Lucia spoke to other women when she went shopping, but her *comare* lived in the same street, and saw her three or four times a week when she picked up the children from school. She also had a Sicilian neighbour whom she saw often, though she did not intend to invite her to her child's communion party.

Gina was often in touch with three *paesane* and a Slav girl married to a Trevisano all of whom lived in the same street. She saw all four between one and four times a week depending on how busy they were. Three of the four worked and visited her when they had time; she hesitated to go to them.

Melia had a Sicilian friend who visited her regularly with the children, but neither husband knew about it. According to this woman her husband was a "dreadful nasty brute", and she came to Melia to pour her heart out. They were the same age and both were lonely. Melia had never used public transport, and when she visited she took a taxi. Although she communicated somehow with her Australian and Greek neighbours, her English was poor. When she went to a hospital or to a doctor who did not speak Italian she always asked Ida to go along with her.

These women did not live within walking distance and therefore met only occasionally. Those who had telephones communicated more frequently. Anna increased her mobility by learning to drive a car. She could now choose whom she would visit and form more permanent friendships. The way in which each of the women responded to the other depended to a large extent on the total situation. The fact that she was working in a factory, spoke better English and learnt to drive a car madĕ Anna more aggressive and self-assured than say Gina or Melia whom I included among the "modern or progressive" wives. Neither of these two worked—their husbands earned well, much more than Anna's. This meant that not only was their attitude toward their husbands different from that of Anna, but that they were also less assertive in their interaction with the other women. Gina and Melia enjoyed the prestige of having successful husbands; Anna took delight in a greater degree of independence.

iii] *The men* The greatest contact the men had was with *paesani* at work, where they introduced one another to the employer. Paolo Tomasielli was one of a number of partners and regarded himself as self-employed. Each afternoon all the partners met at a bar in Ashfield to discuss business and have a few beers. The other seven husbands went straight home from work, and more of their time was spent with their wives and children.

Tonio Lorenzin, his brother-in-law, and another *paesano* went out together to a club once in the past three years. Recently, when a new bridge was completed enabling him to walk to the Apia Club, Giuseppe Bresci started going there on his own every few weeks. He asked his wife to come with him, but she said she'd be too shy and did not want to leave the children. After he had finished paying off his debts, Giovanni Santrin had gone out on two occasions with his Greek neighbour to watch the wrestling at the Leagues Club.

His wife Anna was not happy about it and hoped this would stop. Indeed she threatened that she would start going out alone if he made a habit of it. Paolo Tomasielli brought his wife a large box of chocolates when he went out once.

It was unusual in fact, for these men to go out alone; each wife said the husband felt guilty when he did so. This was indicative of an enormous change from the social life of husbands in Treviso; it was also different from the social life of men in Griffith.

Tensions

The difficulties most Trevisan immigrants encountered were largely the result of their rural background and their unfamiliarity with the new urban setting and its institutions. In Sydney the problems were further aggravated by their being foreigners and their inability to communicate in English which has, of course, the most direct influence. As W.I. Thomas put it " ... language becomes the most concrete sign of unlikeness and the foremost object of animosity. It is certainly true that a man cannot participate fully in our life without our language."[22]

i] *Language and education* Of the sixteen adults in my households, one had had more than five years of schooling and the rest between one and five years. None spoke, read, or wrote English adequately; indeed some could not read or write Italian fluently. To many learning English presented an insurmountable obstacle, and they rationalized their inaction by saying to themselves that there was no point in trying as they did not intend to stay here. One woman explained that she had heard a professor say that although English only had 366 words and Italian over 600, English was more difficult because of the spelling. Two had tried attending classes but stopped after a short time, with such excuses as that it was too inconvenient and they were too tired. Some of the men could not advance in their jobs because of their inability to communicate with non-Italians. The husband who was a foreman was the only one making an effort.

The rest were resigned, particularly if they lived in or near Leichhardt. The lack of formal education discussed earlier was such that few knew how to go about learning English. Although illustrations from my own findings cannot be taken as general because the number of my respondents is not statistically significant, I include nevertheless the following examples because I suspect they are not isolated.

A woman who wanted to give me her friend's telephone number could not find her little notebook. When I handed her the directory it was obvious from the way she set about looking up the name that she had no idea of the alphabet. I took the book from her and said something about the English alphabet being very difficult. She seemed relieved that I had rescued her from embarrassment.

Another told me her husband never wrote anything apart from a few words to his family for Christmas and Easter. She said whenever he had to write a few lines he became very agitated and his temperature rose. Two weeks previously the lawyer had given him four typewritten lines to copy in his own handwriting, sign, and return (it was a document about the purchase of the house). After she had tried day after day to persuade him to do this, his brother-in-law told him not to be a fool and sit down and get on with it. The husband then asked her to do it. She said no and added, "Take the little table out to the front verandah, sit down in the fresh air in peace and quiet and when your temperature goes down, copy out the four lines." Finally he did so and took the paper to the solicitor early next morning.

A man in his late twenties liked his wife to read to him the football section in the Italian newspaper *La Fiamma*. She said he pretended he was too tired, but she knew he had difficulty in reading.

The women occasionally read *Fotoromanze* stories told in pictures with balloons. One woman took *Peyton Place* (in Italian) to hospital when she was to have a baby. She said she tried to read it because she loved watching it on television, but she only read up to page 8 because she found it too difficult.

I asked a woman to point out to me on a map of Europe where her village was situated in relation to Venice. With her finger she started looking for it in northern Holland. When I indicated Venice, her glance turned to southern Italy, and she exclaimed with relief, "We're still a long way north compared with the southern bastards." She was also surprised that Australia was bigger than Italy.

It was inevitable that children of these immigrants would be at a disadvantage compared with the children of educated parents. Two recent issues of the *Quarterly Review of Australian Education* were entitled "European Migrants and Their Children". Findings showed that only one out of 113 Italian-born children had a father in the professional or managerial category. "In fact our own research shows that relatively few of the Italian parents have had more than a few years of elementary education. There were only 14 per cent of students with fathers and 8 per cent with mothers who had had more than primary education. The majority had not even completed the primary school while there were 3 per cent of students with fathers and 9 per cent with mothers who had no formal education whatsoever." Furthermore, research workers found that "it would be incorrect to single out the use of migrant language at home as a direct and principal cause of poor progress at school, for the latter must also be related to the socio-economic, cultural, and ethnic origins of the child".[23]

This made nonsense of the 1960 report of the Commonwealth Immigration Advisory Council which proclaimed that " ... most young migrants settle down well to life in Australia and that, as a group, they are above average in scholarship".[24] A report such as this, lumping together children of rural Greeks, Italians, central European intellectuals, skilled Dutch craftsmen, and others, to evaluate the academic success of migrants, is meaningless.

Although I have heard it said that low scholastic attainment is the result of parental apathy, this was not so with the Trevisani. Parents were ambitious for their children and would do anything to help them move out of the unskilled labouring class. Unfortunately the kind of assistance they needed was beyond most of the elders' capacity.

I asked one woman which school system she preferred, the Australian or Italian. She said the Italian, and when I wanted to know why she replied, "I went to school for only two years, and whatever I learned I knew off by heart. When I ask my niece, who's at high school anything, she says to me 'I'll look it up'. Now if the school was any good she'd know it all off by heart."

One child told her mother that the teacher had said she must buy an English dictionary for school. The mother could not understand because, "After all, the child already speaks English". When I asked had she ever had an Italian dictionary she looked at me in amazement. "What would I do with an Italian dictionary if I already speak Italian?"

Another little girl aged seven did well at school and at the end of the year was awarded a Merit Certificate. The mother was delighted and a few days later bought her a new Olivetti typewriter, telling me she hoped the girl would become a secretary. This demonstrated further that if parents thought a typewriter would help the girl to become a secretary, they would go to great expense to obtain one. Yet the same woman was angry when the girl had said she needed another exercise book. "I bought you one last week," she answered. "Yes, but that was for writing, and I need one for social studies," the girl insisted. "Then use the back of the writing book. Do you think that I can waste money on new exercise books each day?" the mother snapped. The child burst into tears. The six-year old son then came into the kitchen, and the mother turned to him saying, "Show how you can recite the ACB." He remained silent, so she clouted him over the head. He burst into tears and blubbered, "You're stupid, it's not ACB it's ABC!"

A research worker who suggests that these adult immigrants should attend classes is unrealistic. Most see themselves as humble and frequently refer to themselves as "just peasants". They certainly do not want their judgment reinforced by having to reveal ignorance in a classroom.[25] I am sure that well constructed classes on television could be far more useful, not only in teaching English but also in disseminating useful information. The attraction of such a programme is that it can be viewed in the privacy of the home.

ii] Unaccustomed institutions To cope with the complexities of industrial society today requires more education, sophistication, and know-how than ever before. Filling in forms for medical benefit refunds, car insurance claims, taxation returns, or census forms daunts many a middle-class educated Australian. Trevisan immigrants would have found difficulty handling such things in Italy; in Australia the problem is aggravated not only by language but also by the unfamiliar institutions.

None of the respondents had had a bank account in Italy, none had applied for a loan, and none had held an insurance policy. The constant contact they had with bureaucratic institutions resulted largely from their new occupations, new earnings, and new ambitions. Their work brought them into contact with trade unions and worker's compensation; their earnings with the Taxation Department; their ambitions with banks, loan institutions, insurances, municipal councils, and so on; day-to-day living entailed contact with hospitals and medical funds; to drive they had to pass a test; the list could go on and on.

Since arrival in Australia not one respondent had received aid or been in touch with any governmental or private welfare agency such as the Good Neighbour Council, social workers, or any Italian welfare organization. There were several reasons for this. To begin with they did not know that such institutions existed, and even if they had they would not have been aware of how to go about finding them (and the agencies themselves had never made contact).[26]

Whenever they needed assistance in filling in forms or applications they turned to Italian real estate and travel agents, accountants, lawyers, chemists, and doctors. Relationships with such persons had few of the qualities of the traditional

Italian patron-client ties. Whereas the latter tended to continue over long periods with the one patron advising his client on all matters, in Sydney the migrants turned for help to different people, depending on the advice they needed. Frequently they sought assistance simultaneously from several doctors, lawyers, real estate agents, etc., for the one problem. Part of the explanation for this behaviour is frequent changes of address and a basic mistrust of people, especially those outside the immediate family. A proliferation of estate and travel agents, chemists, lawyers, and other professionals, however, encouraged clients to shop around. The dependence for help or advice was thus distributed over a number of people. The chemist filled in the medical benefits form, the doctor wrote out the medical certificate, the accountant attended to the taxation return, and so on. Informal information and advice moved around networks in a garbled fashion from *paesano* to *paesano*.

Two factors partly explained the respondents' hesitation or failure to use certain institutions: they were afraid to appear foolish or ignorant—to lose face—and frequently failed to realize their limited understanding of how such things worked. They were also reluctant to admit their difficulties to each other lest they appear stupid.

The following incidents will illustrate what I mean. I once went with a respondent to the bank to collect her child endowment cheque. The teller made her sign a deposit slip, then a withdrawal slip. The whole transaction took a long time as he had to fill out various parts for her. There was also a language problem and hence misunderstanding. When we came out she was furious. "Every time I want to take out this money he doesn't want to give it to me. I always have to sign and write out bits of paper. After all, it's my money, and I can do with it what I like." In Italy she had never transacted business in a bank, and in Australia she avoided using it wherever possible. She half believed, I think, that there was some conspiracy to stop her from taking money out, and much of what she saved each week was hidden at home. She related this so-called conspiracy not to anything Australian but to the fact that one cannot be too careful about bureaucracy.

Another woman showed me a receipt she had received from a so-called insurance man who had knocked on her door and spoken Italian. He told her that her furniture and other items were worth $2,500 and advised her to insure them. The receipt was the kind sold at a newsagent. She did not realize that it should have had the name of the firm printed on it. My estimate of the value of the contents of the house, including the television set, would not have exceeded $1,000. This confidence man had relied on her ignorance and played on her vanity by saying that the furniture was worth far more.

The husband was at home one afternoon when I visited. He had injured his leg, and it looked as though he would be incapacitated for a few days. I asked him whether he had applied for workers' compensation. He said no, it wasn't worth the effort. Sometime later I spoke to the wife about it and she said: "He's ashamed because be can't fill in the forms and do all the things he's supposed to do to get it, and he doesn't like to ask one of the *paesani* or the foreman because they'll think he's stupid. He'd rather lose the money."

One woman had a boarder for a short time, a young baker from Sardinia. He worked from about 3:00A.M. and came home in the morning. On a number of occasions he told me that he would have liked an additional job. When, after a few days I asked him whether he had found one, he said, "No, I've asked everybody and nobody knows of one." In conversation it was obvious that he did not know how to look up advertisements, and it had not occurred to him to go to an employment agency. He was deeply unhappy and unsure of himself, and one morning when he received a letter from his mother he decided to return home to Italy.

iii] Australia versus Italy Trevisani constantly compared Australia with Italy, stressing on the one hand the material advantages of living here while at the same time pointing out that "life has so much more meaning in Italy". Before the trip their sentiments for and against Australia fluctuated constantly. What they told me one day was often contradicted on the next; attitudes and opinions reflected the feelings of the moment. Much depended on whether there was a letter from home, a week of illness, a large sum banked, or incivility at a government office. People weighed up the pros and cons and each time came up with a different conclusion.

In Australia there was more freedom, less gossip, greater independence, closer relationship with the spouse, but there was also less involvement, fewer friends and relatives, less help, greater loneliness, and less enjoyment.

Trevisan men with whom I spoke had experienced little or no overt hostility from Australians. Doubtless this was related to the full employment the building industry enjoyed. On the whole respondents had had little contact with unskilled Australians. Those they met at work were the people in charge whom they found fair and good to work for. They stressed that Australian bosses were not as class and as status-conscious as Italian bosses.

The aspects of Australia that impressed most were the opportunities to work and save and what seemed to them an egalitarian ethos. "You don't feel like a piece of dirt having to crawl to the back of the queue." But many non-material things were lacking. "In Italy there is more to it, people don't work so hard, and they expect less, but somehow you can enjoy yourself." The new work opportunities had made these people prisoners of their own ambitions. Again and again they said, "We've gone mad, life consists of working for as many hours as you can, putting away $6 out of every $10, watching T.V., and going to bed."

A woman who had been ill and depressed put it this way, "We live like strangers and work like slaves, we don't speak the language and have no friends. We don't seem to be able to do anything except save."

Those who came here in the mid-1950s had a less rosy picture of Italy than those who came in the 1960s. The latter in particular dreamt of living in Italy on an Australian income, though in their rational moments they realized that this was unlikely.

Of the eight couples one was naturalized. Another couple said that they would became naturalized if they returned, and still another that they had decided to become Australian citizens in the near future. A week later these last reversed the decision. The husband thought naturalization would prejudice any Italian pension he might be entitled to. One man said he did not want to become Australian although he wished to live and die here. His reason was, "If we went on another trip home and got sick and had to go to hospital, they'd charge us double if they knew we had Australian passports. They all think we've made a million." Another thought he would be liable for call-up if he became Australian.

One woman told me she felt ashamed when she heard that her brother in Adelaide had become naturalized. "I will never give up my *patria*", she proclaimed. She was resigned to the fact that her children would be Australian. Most women suffered from "headaches and nerves" as they called it, caused no doubt by the tension of conflicting worlds. The extent of their insecurity was brought home to me when one of the babies, born with a congenital ailment, died. The body was sent to Italy for burial. The mother explained, "We'll probably live in Australia for the rest of our lives, but if we decided to go back I couldn't bear the thought of my child buried here and nobody to look after the grave. This way I know that my relatives will always look after it."

iv] *Hearsay* On one occasion a group of us were chatting over a cup of coffee, and one said she had liked Mr. Holt because he was *simpatico*, but didn't like Mr. Gorton. "How can anyone vote for a man with a nose like that?" she asked. She had never heard of Mr. Whitlam. Two of the women present were eligible to vote. One said, "I vote so as not to get into trouble, but I don't care who gets in; all politicians are crooks, so I just put a cross on the piece of paper. My husband does that too." A Yugoslav girl then remarked that if she were naturalized she would vote for the D.L.P. because "it's democratic and it's labour, so what else would you want?" Like a large proportion of the Australian population, the immigrants do not understand the workings of the electoral system and certainly not of preferential voting.

In the section on unaccustomed institutions I described the relationships between the immigrants and welfare institutions, lawyers, doctors, chemists, and so on. I mentioned in passing that informal information and advice moved around networks in garbled fashion from person to person. The following are some examples of the kind of things I heard.[27]

Alda said to Maria: "In Adelaide you have to be naturalized to buy a house. That's why houses are much cheaper there." The day before Alda left Sydney in the train for Adelaide, she told me, "We're going to be very hungry on the train because we're not allowed to take food if you cross from one province to another." (Doubtless this referred to the fruit-fly regulations.) One man insisted, "It's better to take your money out of Australia when you get old because the government takes half of it when you die." Ida confided, "I wouldn't want my mother to come here to stay because in Australia a pensioner gets only $12 a month; in Italy they get much more." (At the time the pension was about $50 per month.) Lucia was worried because she had heard "that the Vietnamese are trying to invade Australia, and the men will be called up". Two women were discussing a third and explaining why she could not have children. "She had an operation for haemorrhoids and the doctor made a mistake and sewed up her womb instead." Another confessed that she had suffered badly from worms for many months, and had spent $200 on a herbalist who could not cure her. A pharmacist (whom she called a doctor), then gave her injections every second evening "to replace the blood the worms were eating up". The pharmacist, she added, attributed her problem to the fact that the previous owner of her house had not kept the floors clean. Eventually an Australian neighbour recommended a red worming medicine which cured her in a few days. When a woman who lived a few doors down came in with her baby who was suffering constantly from gastroenteritis my respondent suggested they move because "the foundations of your house are too low on the ground and this always causes stomach sickness".

v] The church Unlike Greeks, Jews, and Muslims, Trevisani in Sydney did not have their own churches but linked up with parishes already established. The church was therefore not necessarily a rallying point.[28]

Italians found Irish Catholic services strange, and those who lived in outer suburbs came to the Leichhardt Italian church (St. Fiacre's), where the atmosphere was familiar, for the Easter and Christmas services. The rest of the year they attended irregularly. One woman told me that she had tried to confess in Leichhardt on a couple of occasions. There was a queue, and the priest rushed her. She decided not to go again. She also had no intention of confessing at her local church in English. There were only a handful of Italian priests in Sydney, too few to minister satisfactorily to the large number of Italian immigrants. One cheerful American-born Italian-speaking priest told me, "In spite of the fact that I am of Italian descent and speak fluent Italian, I cannot establish the kind of intimate rapport I'd like to have with parishioners. Most of them are Southerners and would prefer not just an Italian-speaking priest but one who comes from their region."

When one of my respondent's babies was baptized the parents arranged for a priest from their village, now working in Melbourne, to come to Sydney and officiate at the ceremony.[29]

The constraints that the church exercised in Italy were loosened in Sydney. I once found one of the women sitting at the table looking pale but struggling to teach her little son the catechism. She explained that she had had an abortion the previous day. On my attempting to sound her out on the subject of legalizing abortion she insisted that she would be horrified if the state or church were to allow it. "After all," she said, "it is killing something." "Then how come you had one?" I asked. "What could I do? I already have two children, and I don't want more. I can't afford it," she replied.[30] Another woman admitted that she was on the pill but added: "If the Pope allows women to take the pill or priests to marry I'll stop being a Catholic."

To these people flexibility on the part of such an institution as the church was a demonstration of weakness, and their reaction was a loss of respect. The women agreed that the individual was not perfect, sinned, was uncertain, faltered, and put expediencey before morality. But the church ought to be different, they said. A person respected and had faith only in institutions with immutable moral rules.[31]

When a woman took the pill or had an abortion she contravened the rules, but it would be wrong to assume that she therefore wanted the ideology or rule altered: quite the contrary. The church was the only pillar left on which she could lean or come back to after she had deviated. Its strength and appeal lay in its steadfast resistance to innovation. One woman explained, "I don't want to wake up once a week and find that the Pope has made a new law or changed an old one. One day St. Christopher is in, next day he's out. For years we weren't allowed to eat meat on Friday, now it's O.K., I never cared what I ate, but I still don't think they should have changed it. It makes one lose respect if they change their minds all the time." She admitted that although rules were contravened at home in Italy, it was easier in Sydney to take pills, have abortions, not go to church and so on. "The Metropolis," wrote Simmel, allows the individual "a kind and an amount of personal freedom which has no analogy whatsoever under other conditions."[32] The new alternatives relating to the church frequently precipitated spiritual dilemmas and were therefore a mixed blessing.

Although the people wanted to benefit from the changing material world and their values altered to accommodate what was new, they were more conservative in their attitudes to things spiritual. Migrants from rural to urban regions in Italy no doubt had greater opportunities to take pills or have abortions than in the village; but in Sydney, where there were even fewer constraints, other problems arose. Unfamiliar services and language difficulties in confession were more likely to loosen ties with the church.

The media

Television, radio and newspapers Television was the most popular. People knew the times of the programmes by heart and preferred the commercial channels to government stations (A.B.C.). They tended to listen to the news only when a dramatic event occurred. So when Robert Kennedy was assassinated in June 1968 they watched all the programmes and repeats of the event. Some cried. When they did listen to the plain news, however, they frequently misunderstood. One day Lucia, who was obviously upset, explained that she had just heard that all men under the age of forty-five were to be called up. I had difficulty convincing her that this could not be right. An hour later we listened together. President Thieu had ordered all men under forty-five in South Vietnam to register for national service.

Peyton Place is a favourite programme with the women. Once when the story was more complicated than usual Maria did not understand what was happening and so could not sleep. One of the men loved watching old war films, especially those set in Italy, and his wife said he often cried while watching. People loved talking about television stars and their private lives. A neighbour called Melia to the fence to ask her whether she had heard that an actor they knew well from the screen had cancer. Melia had not heard and was most upset. She immediately phoned Ida to tell her. To some extent this fascination with screen personalities replaced gossip.

Few listened to the radio when television channels were transmitting. In the morning people switched on the radio to find out the correct time, and in the evening many enjoyed an Italian programme on a commercial station compered by a well-known Italian radio personality.

None of these households had a newspaper delivered apart from the local weekly, which came free of charge. Some looked through this for bargains or second-hand furniture. Most bought Italian newspapers from time to time.

Rosa [*household* 1]
"I buy the *Fiamma* occasionally, I like to read Lena's column, but my husband rarely looks at any paper. I also like *Fotoromanze*."

Ida [*household* 2]
"We get the *Sun-Herald* on Sundays and *La Fiamma* once or twice a week and sometimes also *Sette Giorni*. I like Lena's column, and my husband reads the football results."

Alda [*household* 3]
"We never get any papers apart from the one they leave in our letter-box at the gate. My husband looks to see if there's any second-hand furniture. My eldest son reads it out to him."

Lucia [*household* 4]
"My husband occasionally buys the *Fiamma* for the football, and then I read Lena's column."

Maria [*household* 5]
"We get the *T.V. Times* and every two or three weeks the *Fiamma*. Sometimes we also get *Oggi*. I like reading *Fotoromanze*, and quite a few of us swap these round."

Gina [*household* 6]
"We don't get any newspapers delivered but every two or three weeks we get the *Fiamma*. My husband likes to look at the football page, and occasionally we get *Sette Giorni*. I buy *Fotoromanze* sometimes."

Anna [*household* 7]
"We get *La Fiamma* sometimes. My husband likes me to read the sports page to him. He sometimes looks at the N.R.M.A. paper which comes in the mail. I love *Fotoromanze* but don't

have time to read them except sometimes at the weekend."

Melia [household 8]
"My husband gets the *Herald* on Saturday to look up advertisements for concreting jobs. He also looks at the local paper for this. We get the *Fiamma* sometimes because my husband likes to read the sports page."

Recently an editor of one of the Italian newspapers stated that he felt sure it was politically influential, and he may well be right. In support of the statement he quoted the extensive circulation, and I have no reason to doubt his figures. Only a small minority of the people I spoke to, however, bought papers regularly or read or were interested in world events or political articles. The most common reasons given for buying the paper were the sporting pages and Lena's column (a type of personal advice section). Although, as I have pointed out, the number of people I met is statistically insignificant, I am certain that it would be misleading to attribute political influence unquestioningly to the Italian press on grounds of the size of its circulation. Most Italians I have met prided themselves on their lack of interest in politics.

The trip: a new rite-de-passage

Early in this section I outlined stages in the pattern of settlement of Trevisani immigrants and referred to actual manifestations of group behaviour. I suggest that there were shifts in the dominant reference groups that consciously or unconsciously reshaped attitudes and affected conduct. "That men act in a social frame of reference yielded by the groups of which they are a part is a notion undoubtedly ancient ... There is, however, the further fact that men frequently orient themselves to groups other than their own in shaping their behaviour and evaluations ... "[33] The sense of insecurity from which most suffered up to the time of their return to Australia may have resulted largely from influences exerted by two or more reference groups.

Sociologists are aware that people may be affected by the

life-style, norms, and values of reference groups to which they can or sometimes can never belong. Here, however, I have tried to discover which reference groups were dominant at particular stages of settlement, concentrating on those to which the immigrant could belong.[34] For heuristic purposes I risk oversimplification and suggest four as dominant.

1. The peer group in Treviso of which the immigrants felt a part and to which they hoped to return.
2. The group new immigrants emulated and then became part of (the group in the process of leaving Sydney and returning home).
3. The group recently returned to Sydney.
4. The group of well-established and permanently-settled Trevisani in Sydney who no longer straddled two worlds.

At the time of this study all the respondents were affected by one or more of the first three.[35] At no stage were the reference groups simple and clear-cut; overlaps accompanied the shifts. If the behaviour of these people was typical, then it would seem that a move through the first three was necessary before aspirations to the fourth could occur. At the completion of my field work none belonged to this last group, although those who had returned were beginning to move towards it.

i] *The trip home to Treviso* The aspiration and transition to the second reference group, and later to the third assumed the importance of a *rite-de-passage*. The preparation and departure to Treviso had an important ceremonial quality. When word passed round that someone was leaving, flocks of *paesani* visited the household each evening to say good-bye, cry, sing, feel homesick, express envy, and send messages and parcels home. These were unarranged but not unexpected visits.

Most *paesani* sold the house and most of their furniture and appliances, thus severing material connections here, and returned by ship to Italy with many new goods such as tape recorders, transistors, hairdryers, etc. This kind of departure was different in quality from the quick farewell at an airport.

Trevisani never regarded the journey as a waste of money nor failed to understand why yet another family had gone back. The trip cost anything from $4,000 to $8,000 depending on how long the couple and their children stayed away. Apart from fares they needed money to purchase gifts and to support themselves in Italy for from six to twelve months. Although they stayed with relatives they were expected to contribute to the household expenses, and also, as they put it, "We need money to live it up." Thus, having left Treviso as penniless unskilled labourers they arrived with tangible assets and thereby gained self-esteem, status, and prestige.

One woman recalled how, "Before we drove into the village I put on slacks and a long flowing scarf. As we drove in some children called out '*Ecco Americani*'. My father didn't believe that I, too, could drive, so we put a chair out for him and sat him down while I drove round and round the courtyard. He just gazed in amazement that his daughter knew how to drive."

Another reminisced, "It was wonderful to be back and to see my relatives, especially my mother. We brought them all presents. All the sisters got the same nightdresses, and all the men got shirts. I brought my mother and my mother-in-law quilted dressing gowns. I know they'd never use them at home, only if they went to hospital or something like that, but they thought they were beautiful."

After a time the joys of conspicuous consumption faded. The relatives began exploiting the visitors and made unreasonable demands. In addition, the years of working together and confiding made the husband and wife different from married couples who had never left Treviso. One of my respondents told me how, "When Sandro, my husband, and his friends were together at the inn they'd suggest that they go here or there or do something on Sunday, and so on. My husband always answered, 'I'll ask Maria'. After this had happened several times they said, 'Tell us, who wears the pants in your house?'. So from then on, instead of saying

'I'll ask Maria,' he said 'I'll think about it'; but he still always asked me in the evening. His mother was angry because he took me to the pictures. She said a son should take his mother not his wife. We couldn't stand this sort of life after Australia."

The women found life in Treviso so different from what they had grown accustomed to in Sydney that they no longer felt comfortable. Generally they did not get on with the mother-in-law, with whom they often had to live. She tended to view her newly returned daughter-in-law with suspicion and could not understand the feelings of her son. Others found it hard to renew the intimate rapport they once had with their siblings. One recalled, "Before I left for Australia my sister and I were very close, and we always told each other everything. Now she works in a factory, her husband is a mechanic, and they live in a house away from my parents' home. I found that we just couldn't talk to each other the way we did."

A crucial point to keep in mind is that during the years that Trevisani spent in Sydney the social structure of Treviso itself had been continually changing. As I indicated, many people moved away from agriculture, from extended to nuclear household, and young people received better education and training, thereby gaining social and economic mobility. Although the respondents in Sydney came from Treviso after the war, the changes had been gradual, and when they returned they found that not only were they themselves different, but that Trevisan society as a whole had continued to change. The degree and direction of these changes, however, affected individuals in different ways.

A man who eventually came back to Sydney said in agitation, "The thing that really rubbed me up was the way people crawl when they go to a government office. When I had to go to fix up some documents my mother said to me, 'If you see the priest or the mayor (*sindaco*) be nice to them.' So I said to her that the best thing I learnt in Australia was not to crawl and I'd be damned if I'd be nice to those bastards.' My mother didn't like them, but she was scared of them. I wouldn't mind going back to Italy for trips, but I couldn't live there again."[36]

ii] *Back in Australia* Many would still have stayed if they could have lived as comfortably as in Sydney. In Treviso, to build and furnish a house as they wanted it on a small block of land would have cost about $12,000 in 1968. They could have brought this sum from Australia, but the earnings of a labourer in Treviso would not have allowed them to live in the manner to which they had grown accustomed. The ambition of most was to have an independent business such as a restaurant, grocer's shop, or some other sort of shop. One woman asserted that to live comfortably on a small business would have required taking $60,000 to Italy. Some achieved this, but the majority did not.

After spending between four and twelve months at home the visitors found they no longer felt at ease. They realized that they had more in common with their settled compatriots in Sydney, the third reference group. Australia also no longer connoted a migration into the unknown. They were therefore closer to severing the umbilical cord that had bound them to their village. If they inherited or expected to inherit land, they sold it or perhaps made arrangements to give it to a brother on the understanding that the gift was a contribution towards the mother's maintenance.

Many times I heard Trevisani in Sydney say they must go back at least once for their peace of mind. The functional aspect of this return was that it fostered greater satisfaction and identification with Australia. Certainly their orientation to permanent settlement became more positive. They returned to Australia, a place they now knew, to start again, resigned to the fact that they would always be foreigners but suffer less homesickness. When at length there was no further inheritance and the parents were dead the bonds were completely severed. "I'm glad I went back, especially because I wanted to see my mother, but I couldn't get used to the family interference and the gossip any more. We all have to go back to see this and get it out of our system."[37]

CONCLUSION

I have now outlined the sequences that most respondents followed in the process of settlement in Sydney. The initial decision to move to an industrial metropolis rather than to a rural area was a function of the economic opportunities available. After World War II, particularly after the 1950s, Trevisani could, within a few days of arrival in Australia, find work and a steady income without need for investment. We have already seen how different these conditions were from those prevailing before World War II when people were forced to look for a livelihood in the country.

My findings in Sydney also clearly show that most core institutions ceased to exist when former rural workers became urban labourers. Unlike Trevisani back in Italy, the immigrants lived exclusively in nuclear households with at most one or two relatives nearby. Those who had kin were rarely able to call on them for help—they either lived too far away or were busy with their own work. The husband and wife were thus forced to redefine their roles and work out a fresh relationship. Close primary associations also gave way to loose networks of acquaintances, and although people attempted to set up ties by means of godparenthood, these seldom endured. A dearth of suitable Italian-speaking priests made it difficult for the church to exert much influence, and as a result there were fewer constraints.

The problems agricultural workers faced, particularly those who had had little schooling, when migrating to an industrial region within their own country were accentuated in Australia by inability to communicate in English. The pattern of behaviour was thus a function not only of foreignness but also of background and unfamiliarity with industrial institutions.

In discussing Italian migrations I stated that almost all had been voluntary. But I did not imply that all Italian voluntary migrations followed the same lines. Respondents told me that, unlike the Trevisani, few Friulani even contemplated returning home for good.[38] The reasons were that these latter came from a poorer area and rarely had expectations of inheritance in land. Heiss found that in Western Australia also, immigrants from southern Italy showed greater satisfaction with life than immigrants from the north, where conditions were better.[39]

Thus we can say that the stages of settlement that evolve among voluntary migrants from the same country will differ not only according to the environmental and other conditions prevailing in the receiving country but also according to the varying social, political, and economic structures of the different regions of the homeland.

With the improved economic conditions in Treviso today fewer immigrants like my respondents will settle in Australia. Young men would be discouraged by the loneliness, especially now that Trevisan girls prefer to marry local men who have a trade and can find work either close to home or at least in northern Italy. Although some of the single men who recently came to Australia married Southerners, the majority returned for good.[40]

Postscript: 1972

Of the eight households I studied, four are still in Sydney. The Lorenzins and the Pierantis have moved to Adelaide. Last Christmas I had a card from the former telling me that they have had a fifth child, so I doubt whether they are contemplating the trip. The Brescis and the Santrins are in Italy. The Santrins expect to inherit a large block of land and will probably stay. The Goris have bought a new house in Annandale and are now letting their old place.

Late in 1971 I attended the baptism of the Tomasielli's new baby boy—the reception celebrating it was held in a restaurant and fifty guests attended. Early in 1972 I was present at the confirmation of their daughter. The confirmation dinner was an intimate affair—just the Tomasiellis, two sets of godparents, and five friends including me. During the evening the baby was brought in and introducd as Dr Pietro Tomasielli.

As on most such occasions, there was more singing and improvising than talking, and by midnight most suffered acute sore throats. The evening was memorable as much for the bonhomie and banter as for the menu. We started at seven in the evening and carried on till the early hours of the morning. The first course consisted of a full plate of *antipasto* (salamis, anchovies, olives, etc.), followed by a large helping of *lasagne*, then *minestrina* (thin soup). After an interval the hostess first served thick slices of veal and spinach and then cheese (parmesan and romano). An hour later we had thick slices of beef and peas, again followed by cheese. At midnight Gina appeared with a full platter of turkey and *radicchio* (a Veneto speciality somewhat like green salad). We then carried on with the confirmation cake, pastries, and coffee. On the table were numerous bottles of beer and lemonade but no wine, confirming what I have heard said on many occasions—that most people prefer beer and drank wine in Italy because they could not afford beer. When Gina cut the cake, however, Paolo cracked a bottle of champagne and the rejoicing grew louder.

Postscript: 1974

In September 1974 I visited Anna and Giovanni Santrin in Treviso. Before I left Sydney a number of people told me that Anna was gravely ill with a "terrible disease", and that she had already been in hospital for several months.

On arrival in Treviso I made straight for the hospital at Crespano del Grappa expecting the worst. I was delighted to hear that she was better and had been discharged on the previous day. She was home when I knocked on her door.

I knew that Anna had been apprehensive about returning to Italy and the possibility of having to live with her in-laws. So it did not surprise me that she was suffering from a gastric ulcer requiring long hospitalization. She is still not well and may need surgical treatment in the future.

The Santrins have been back in Treviso four years. Until the completion of their house nine months ago, they lived with Giovanni's parents who had a large property which Giovanni and his only brother will eventually inherit. With this in mind, Giovanni and Anna wanted to build their own house on the property (just as his brother had already done for himself and his family), but the father demanded that they pay for the land. Anna refused, so they bought a block in a new housing subdivision in the town a few minutes' drive from the family property.

They completed their house with a minimum of outside help, utilizing every spare hour they had after work in the factory and on the farm. It took them three years. The house is set in a small garden surrounded by other new houses. It is a two storey building consisting of two self-contained appartments. The lower flat is let and the Santrins live upstairs. They have three bedrooms, a lounge, a large kitchen containing a fuel and an electric stove, and a large bathroom which includes a bidet and a separate shower room. The garden is cultivated with vegetables, flowers and shrubs. The carport accommodates Anna's small car, Giovanni's larger Fiat and the motorcycle he uses much of the time to save petrol.

At the time of my visit Giovanni was working in a tile factory earning about half of what he earned in Australia. Anna, until her illness, worked in a clothing factory earning as much as her husband but she would now find it difficult to get a job. Many factories have closed down while others have cut production and there is increasing unemployment. Anna thinks they will be able to manage on Giovanni's income, fortunately they have few debts, but will probably need to sell her car. She stressed that their financial situation would have been really bad had they returned say a year ago. The house for instance, would now cost twice its original price.

Anna told me that people were worried about the political and economic situation in Italy. Unemployment and the rate of inflation were accelerating at an alarming rate. People who had previously been anxious to sell blocks of land were now reluctant to do so. Indeed more and more cultivate their plots after working in the factory, growing fruit and as many of their vegetables as possible. The great desire to turn away from the land to industrial work has slowed and many seek security by labouring on the land and in the factory at the same time. Giovanni, Anna insists, works harder now than he did in Sydney or on the farm before he emigrated to Australia. He is in the factory from seven in the morning until two in the afternoon and spends the rest of the day, often till ten at night, on his parents' property.

We visited Anna's in-laws who live in an old stone house built around a courtyard. Many rooms are now locked, some still containing the old furniture. On marriage, almost all the couples move into more modern flats or houses.

Giovanni's mother looked much older than her fifty-eight years. She obviously knew about all that was going on on the farm and had her say. They grew several kinds of fruit and vegetables, grapes from which they produced wine, and even potatoes and peanuts. Chickens and turkeys ran round the courtyard and in the stalls under the house were pigs and cows that had been brought in for the winter. This ensured a steady supply of milk from which they manufactured butter and the ricotta cheese they used. From time to time they slaughtered cattle and stored the meat in a large deep-freeze in Anna's house. The freezer and its contents (300 kilos of meat the day I saw it), belongs to the old couple and Anna explained she never touches it. It stands in one of her bedrooms because the electricity supply on the farm is inadequate. The only gift Anna and Giovanni received from the parents was some wine that had recently been pressed. The old people's prime aim is to produce as much of their food requirements as possible and sell the surplus they cannot easily store. A few years ago, Anna said, there was more crop specialization. Now people are worried and so are diversifying to ensure a greater measure of self-sufficiency.

In the town and the surrounding fields stand many houses belonging to people who have returned from Australia. These were built and furnished with money earned abroad. Recently, however, the number returning permanently had decreased.

In some respects Anna prefers living in Italy, in others she prefers Australia. In Italy, she says, they go dancing once a week and feel at home. Many of their friends are like themselves, people who have returned after a number of years abroad. The aspect of life that she dislikes most in Treviso is the fact that they work harder than ever, and feel constrained by numerous family commitments. Her parents-in-law are demanding and never satisfied with the amount of help the young couple give them. Although Giovanni neither receives payment nor a share in the harvest (apart from some wine), the parents expect him to be at hand and work with them each day after he finishes in the factory. Anna summed up the relationship with, "They are never, never, satisfied, it drives us mad." Obviously the degree of pressure that can be exerted by the old on the young in this way varies with circumstances. The larger the expected inheritance, the greater is the pressure that parents are likely to exert on the younger generation.

Anna speaks with nostalgia about her years in Australia. She vaguely hopes to return for a visit someday, "or perhaps for good, who knows? It's a beautiful country," she added.

NOTES

1. C. A. Price, *Southern Europeans in Australia*, p. 154.
2. Department of National Development, *Atlas of Australian Resources: Immigration*, p. 11.
3. C. A. Price, *Southern Europeans*, p. 162.
4. O. Handlin, *The Uprooted*, p. 4.
5. K. Wolff, *The Sociology of Georg Simmel*, p. 413.
6. I refer here in particular to the classic urban writers of the German school such as Georg Simmel and Max Weber as well as Robert Park, Louis Wirth and Ernest Burgess of the Chicago school.
7. G. Fofi, "Immigrants to Turin", p. 269.
8. C. Manucci, "Emigrants in the Upper Milanese Area", pp. 260–61.
9. G. Fofi, "Immigrants", p. 284.
10. C. Cronin, *The Sting of Change, Sicilians in Sicily and Australia*, pp. 262–63.
11. In 1957 83.3 per cent of cane cutters were migrants who had arrived since 1947. Of these 71.3 per cent were Italian (see J. A. Hempel, *Italians in Queensland*, p. 169).

12. Whether or not the husband saved a substantial part of the deposit for a house before the wife came out, was of utmost importance. It certainly helped Trevisani over a crucial hurdle. I heard that the main problem that faced Siciliani who came here as assisted immigrants with their families after the floods in 1967 was lack of money for a deposit on a house (and of relatives who could help them). The husband's weekly earnings in Sydney barely sufficed to pay the high rents and buy food, let alone allow for savings. With several children to look after, the wife was unable to work. A considerable number of these clamoured to return, and, I understand, many were repatriated. Henderson, in *People in Poverty*, pp. 140–41, stated that, " ... the typical Southern European ... arrives with little or no money or even in debt, his wages make it hard for him to save and he does not know what services are open to him or how to avail himself of them." He did not mention, or may not have been aware of, the custom whereby some immigrant men come out first and thus help to solve this problem.

13. See n.21, p.50.

14. This contrasts with Griffith, where conjugal roles were segregated; if one of the older women worked, it was invariably on the farm under the direction of the husband. If one of the younger wives worked, she generally did so in a shop or office and stopped as soon as she had a child. Thus although the roles were more strictly segregated among the middle aged than the young, the attitudes of the newly married to division of labour and individual interests resembled in many aspects the conservative households in Sydney. But whereas all Griffith couples could turn to parents, siblings, and relatives for comfort and approval, in Sydney they could not. Here, conservative and progressive husbands and wives of necessity turned to each other for support.

15. Jean Martin in *Refugee Settlers*, p. 25, pointed out that refugee immigrants who took part in community life incurred many more obligations than those who did not. "In one way the migrant certainly travels fastest who travels alone: not alone in that he lacks a helpmate, but alone in the sense of being isolated from the distractions and obligations of sociable living."

16. The young brother of Alda Lorenzin (household 3) visited a brother in Adelaide, returned to Sydney, and announced that he was moving there because housing was cheaper. Although they had already put a deposit on a house in Liverpool, the Lorenzins decided to go also. The decision was reached overnight, without the husband visiting Adelaide. Three months after they had all moved, the Pierantis (household 5) visited them for five days. While they were there they put a deposit on a house, returned to Sydney, put their old place on the market, and started making arrangements for the move. They went towards the end of 1968.

17. One respondent said southern Italians were so anxious to spread their ties that if A and B were in *compare/comare* relationship, the siblings of A and B also addressed each other as *compare* and *comare*. This would appear to be a case of classificatory godparenthood. Cronin (see *The Sting of Change*, p. 194) did not mention this kind of extended godparenthood when she wrote about *compare/comare* relationships among Siciliani in Sydney. Mintz and Wolf ("An Analysis of Ritual Co-Parenthood", p. 187) made the point that in Latin American communities, " ... ritual ties between contemporaries seem to have become more important than those between godparents and godchildren." This would appear to be true among Trevisani in Sydney. Zubrzycki noted the increasing importance of the godparenthood (*kum*) relationship among Ukrainians in Australia, who substituted this for kinship ties particularly where there were no other relatives (see *Settlers of the Latrobe Valley*, pp. 112–13).

18. Most respondents had lived with southern families immediately after marriage. (It was unthinkable for southern women to take single men as boarders.) For one or two rooms they charged about $15. A Trevisan woman letting two rooms to four men, and doing their washing, ironing, and cooking, could expect about $60 per week. Many more married southern women worked in factories than northerners. C. Cronin mentioned that Sicilian women worked in factories from six in the morning until five in the evening and were away from home from ten to eleven hours a day. They left the children with neighbours. "This is such a common practice, that it is not even mentioned as something special." (See *The Sting of Change*, pp. 170–72.) F.L. Jones ("The Italian Population of Carlton", p. 204) found that in Carlton a significantly higher proportion of southern wives were in the work force than those from the north.

19. M. Gordon, *Assimilation in American Life*, pp. 53–54.

20. E. Goffman, *The Presentation of Self in Everyday Life*, see especially the introduction and chapter 6.

21. A few months after the completion of my fieldwork this family decided overnight to move to Adelaide. The idea of moving from Sydney and the long train journey did not terrify this woman because the nine-year-old boy was going with her (the husband and other two children went in a friend's car), but her main consolation was that she was getting onto a train here and did not need to move out until she reached her destination. She foresaw no problems entailing enquiries or decisions.

22. M. Jonowitz, ed., *W. I. Thomas On Social Organization and Social Personality*, p. 205.

23. J. J. Smolicz and R. Wiseman, "European Migrants and Their Children", pp. 10–11, 17.

24. Ibid., p. 17.

25. J.A. Nagata et al. found that this factor had to be taken very much into account when English classes for immigrant women were set up in Toronto. (See J. A. Nagata, J. R. Rayfield and M. Ferraris, "English Language Classes for Immigrant Women with Pre-School Children".)

26. In this respect they were not unlike West Indians in London where voluntary welfare associations " ... are usually available to all migrants who apply, but in practice only a small minority take advantage of them either because the majority are ignorant of their existence or because not all migrants are willing to apply for assistance of any kind." See S. Patterson, *Dark Strangers*, p. 263.

27. My reason for inclusion of examples is not to draw attention to the ignorance or lack of sophistication of many immigrants on matters relating to institutions of industrial society (many Australians are badly informed on relatively simple facts also), but for the benefit of social workers, school teachers, or anyone directly connected with immigrants and their welfare. It is only through close contact with the people that many of their misconceptions come to light.

28. For a contrast of the influence of the Greek Orthodox and the Roman Catholic churches on ethnic groups, see J. A. Petrolias, "Post-War Greek and Italian Migrants in Melbourne", especially chapter 6.

29. C. Manucci described how Veneti arranged for priests from their own region to come to Limbiate in Northern Italy for a religious festival. See C. Manucci, "Emigrants", pp. 260–61.

30. "Although the Pentecostal and Catholic churches in Eastville condemned birth control and sterilization, and the Catholic women admitted that this was sinful, they said they had no other choice." E. Padilla, *Up from Puerto Rico*, p. 111.

31. H.J. Gans (*The Urban Villagers*, p. 111) found that West Enders in Boston "are a religious people, and accept most of the moral norms and sacred symbols of the Catholic religion. They believe that the church ought to be the source and the defender of these norms, and expect it to practice what it preaches. At the same time, they observe that it is in reality a human institution that often fails to practice what it preaches. Thus, they identify with the religion, but not with the church, except when it functions as a moral agency."

32. G. Simmel in K.Wolff, *The Sociology of Georg Simmel*, p. 416.

33. R. Merton, *Social Theory and Social Structure*, p. 288.

34. As R.A. Nisbet put it, "Once we clearly know ... what the dominant reference groups are in his life, we are put in a better position for understanding and for predicting that individual's behaviour ... the groups or aggregates within which a person may be seen living or participating need not be the entities that exert the greatest amount of influence upon his day-to-day behaviour." See R. A. Nisbet, *The Social Bond*, p. 108.

35. As J. Lopreato has stated (*Peasants No More*, p. 91): "There is reason to believe that initially many an immigrant becomes demoralised and for some time oscillates between nostalgia for the old society and thwarted hopes for the new in an uncomfortable succession of ambivalent feelings." English immigrants, A. Richardson noted (see "The Assimilation of British Immigrants in Australia", p. 159), resisted change in the early stages of settlement. This, he thought, may have been caused by the immigrants' marginal position at that time—when they were physically in one country, but their thoughts and feelings in another. The assimilation process is then temporarily broken down. This sequence resembled that of most Trevisani in Australia.

36. J. Lopreato (*Peasants No More*, pp. 226–27) discussed the changes in ideology of Italian emigrants who returned " ... displaying the attributes of egalitarianism that they experienced in the host societies, the English speaking countries in particular". He also referred to Foerster who wrote early this century " ... that returned emigrants manifested a certain self-assurance, a challenging disposition, even a sort of vainglory, which contrasted sharply with their former servility". Elsewhere (see "How Would You Like to Be a Peasant?, p. 430), Lopreato recounted the story of a man who returned from Australia and who told him that, "In Australia you never have to wait very long in the office of a doctor. You have an appointment with him, and when it's time for you to go in, you go in. If you don't have an appointment, it is first come first served. Here it is first come last served, unless you come accompanied by a *commendatore*." (*Commendatore* is an honorific title.)

37. This is not unlike the reaction of many British migrants who returned to England. Appleyard wrote that an overwhelming majority of respondents in England said that their decision to return to Britain was not economic. While in Australia they had earned more and accumulated more capital. Over three-quarters stated that they hoped to re-settle in Australia. Most were disappointed with the environment when they returned. They quarrelled with their relatives and found that few things were as they had imagined them to be. They also realized how much they themselves had changed. See R. T. Appleyard, "Determinants of Returned Migration", pp. 365–68.

38. Friuli is part of the Veneto adjoining Treviso.

39. J. Heiss, "Sources of Satisfaction and Assimilation Among Italian Immigrants", pp. 165–77.

40. Italian statistics for 1950–68 show that for every 100 emigrants leaving 75 were returning. Statistics for 1959 show that about half of the Italian emigrants settle permanently abroad. (See K. B. Mayer, "International Migrations of European Workers", p. 3 and J. Lopreato, *Peasants No More*, p. 44.)

CONCLUSION
Treviso, Griffith and Sydney

My aims at the outset were to demonstrate the significance of socio-economic factors in the development of patterns of settlement of Trevisani in Australia. I also wished to show that adjustment to the new environment is easier if traditional institutions can be reconstituted or adapted.

We have now seen how the varying economic conditions in Australia at the time of the migrations led to different sequences in the process and attitudes to permanent residence in Griffith and Sydney. Furthermore, the environment in Griffith favoured adaptation and reconstruction of traditional institutions. This was not so in Sydney.

Table 28 summarizes the changes that occurred in Australia. It does not represent a single rural-urban continuum with pre-war Treviso at one end and Sydney at the other but presents a conspectus of the diverse lifestyles that Trevisani experienced. I said earlier that they came from the same socio-economic background. This was true only in part. The Trevisani in Griffith came before the war, those in Sydney after. As I indicated, Treviso before 1939 was not the same as after 1945. Although old values and customs still affected the society, gradual changes in the economy loosened their rigidity. With this qualification it is a fact that the two groups had a homogeneous background.

Leaving a peasant-type economy and the hardships that accompanied it, Trevisani became commercial farmers in Griffith. Home was on the farm, and there was no separation from work. Most owned their farms and thus achieved their ambition. As in Treviso, they enjoyed the relief from monotony that seasonal work-rhythm permitted.

Table 28. Summary: Treviso, Griffith, Sydney

	Pre-World War II Treviso	Post-World War II Treviso	Griffith	Sydney
The economy and occupational status	Peasant economy: no separation of work and home; small land-owners, tenants sharecroppers, and landless labourers	Gradual shift to industry and some commercial farming increased; separation of home and work; peasants became rural and urban proletariat	Commercial farming; no separation of home and work; self-employed, farmers: fluctuating income	Industry: separation of home and work; unskilled urban proletariat; employed, fixed wage
Household	Extended	Shift from extended to nuclear	Nuclear household but numerous relatives nearby	Nuclear household but few or no relatives
Husband/wife	Strict husband/wife role segregation	Husband/wife role segregation	Husband/wife role segregation	Husband/wife roles joint
Father/sons	Father and sons have same occupation; hierarchical relationship	Father and sons' occupations beginning to diverge; some loosening of parental authority	Father and sons have same occupation; relationship approximates partnership	Father and sons' occupation likely to diverge; father's status low in a socially mobile society
Education	Almost total lack of formal education	Increasing stress on education	Early settlers less handicapped by lack of education than migrants to Sydney	Handicapped by lack of education and English
Church	Strong influence	Lessening influence	Influence of church based on personal decision	Little influence
Social interaction	Primary groups; overlapping role-sets; fixed reference groups; rigid constraints and few alternatives	Decrease of primary and increase of secondary groups; less overlap of role-sets; additional reference groups; fewer constraints, greater alternatives	Mainly primary groups but also secondary networks; some overlap of role-sets; fairly fixed reference groups; greater constraints and fewer alternatives than in Sydney	Few primary groups; mainly secondary networks; little overlap of role-sets; several reference groups; fewer constraints and more alternatives than in Treviso or Griffith
Dispersed settlement	Dispersed settlement (no agrotowns)	Shift from dispersed to dense settlements; improved communications	Dispersed settlement on farms but easy communication	Dispersed settlement in metropolis and more difficult to communicate than Griffith
Migration	Seasonal migration of men aimed at bolstering the social structure and status quo	Seasonal migration that is conducive to social change	Migration to Griffith regarded by almost all as permanent	First migration regarded as temporary; second migration regarded as permanent

In Sydney Trevisani were employed in industry, and earnings depended on the length of time worked. They travelled backwards and forwards between home and the job. Hours were regular, and each week was the same as the last. Work and domestic relations were separated. They preferred the outdoors to a factory and missed the fields and seasonal changes.

I have not met anyone who, given a choice, would have elected to live in an extended family. People admitted that in certain circumstances, such as illness or death, the large body of relatives had advantages, but these did not outweigh the drawbacks. In Griffith, Trevisani felt they had the best of both worlds. They enjoyed privacy of a nuclear family household but had sufficient kin close at hand to help in emergencies. The result was an encouragement of conjugal role-segregation and the persistence of the traditional division of labour and male-female segregation in recreation similar to, but not as rigid as in old Treviso.

In Sydney, on the other hand, the nuclear family was isolated. Even when the members had relatives or friends, these either lived too far away or were at work and therefore could offer neither company nor help. The husband and wife thus drew closer to one another, their roles were joint, and the division of labour in the home was less well defined. Trevisani in Sydney liked the close conjugal relationship but missed the contacts with friendly relatives.

In Treviso, as in most rural communities, sons had to wait till their father died before gaining access to land. Adult men deferred to the male head of the household for many years, and the relationship was one of superordination-subordination. This contrasted sharply with conditions in Griffith where, as a result of the land tenure system young men ideally received farms early, and the bond between them and the parent resembled a partnership. They enjoyed being farmers. In Sydney, by contrast, no father wanted his son to be an unskilled labourer. All hoped that their offspring would become either white-collar workers or professionals. In these circumstances fathers and sons are less likely to have common interests.

Those who migrated to Griffith were not as handicapped by their lack of education as were the immigrants who went to Sydney and had to cope with the institutions of an industrial society. Those who settled on the land found themselves in a comparatively familiar environment. The all-pervasive church domination of old Treviso gave way to a far greater degree of freedom in Griffith. People could choose whether or not they would allow it to influence them. Although most Veneti attended mass on Sundays, some did not. Yet they frequented the Catholic clubs and attended church functions. In Sydney few went to church more than two or three times a year, and the priest held little sway with them. They disliked the unfamiliar Irish-Catholic services, and there were few Italian-speaking clergy. Although after the war the church in Treviso lost some of its hold on the people, the moral constraints it exerted and the ceremonial *feste* it offered were still of some importance. In Sydney the immigrants missed *feste* and rarely if ever turned to the church for help or guidance.

In old Treviso social interaction outside the extended family was restricted. Social and working life centred on the primary groups made up at one and the same time of relatives, friends, and workmates. Numerous constraints imposed by the extended household, the economy, the church and village society limited alternatives. In the close Trevisan community in Griffith the primary groups were important, yet in spite of a considerable overlap of role sets, there were many secondary networks and a greater degree of freedom of action and alternatives than in pre-war Treviso though less than in Sydney. In Sydney, Trevisani were scattered throughout the metropolis and thus operated in networks rather than groups and did not form a community. Compared with Sydney, where there was no specific concentration of Trevisani, and where distance and transport were a problem, in Griffith cars and telephones enabled people to communicate with ease.

Men who brought out a family or married in Griffith intended to settle permanently. Life back home was too harsh to contemplate a return, and in Griffith the opportunity to become self-employed on the land was a prospect offering much satisfaction; farming they understood and liked. In Sydney the immigrants were ill-equipped to cope with urban industrial life. At the same time, opportunities for work and a better life in Treviso were increasing, and the old impediments to overseas travel, such as time and expense, were lessening. These factors led couples who had married and set up a nuclear household in Sydney to take an ambivalent attitude to permanent settlement. People refrained from making a final decision until they had been back home and reassessed their prospects. Had conditions in Treviso been as unfavourable as they had been at the time of the main migration to Griffith, few would have even contemplated return. But post-war improvement of conditions, as well as the creation of new occupations and perspectives in northern Italy constantly challenged incentives to settle abroad for good. In Griffith nuclear families were permanent settlers from the start, in Sydney most were transients for the first few years.

Immigrants in a new country find it easier to settle if core institutions can be adapted or reconstituted to dovetail with new ones. They can make the transition from one environment to another with some reassurance of realising their goals. As we have seen, in Griffith it was easier to do so than in Sydney.

Conditions in Griffith created a community that was unlike any other Italian rural settlement. The same cannot be said of Sydney where daily life was much like that of Trevisani in any other modern industrial metropolis.

APPENDIX 1

Suggestions for further research

A wealth of comparative material on Italian family life awaits research. One aspect which I feel is well worth studying is the environment in which the traditional family system thrives, adapts, or disintegrates.

A number of possible studies come to mind—a comparison of Trevisan kinship in Griffith with that in a Queensland sugar-cane town, or differences in adaptation of northern and southern Italian families in rural and urban settings.

We could compare the child rearing methods, dietary, and work habits of Southerners and Northerners, relating these to their cultural backgrounds.

Many Trevisan women have boarders and mind the offspring of southern mothers who work in factories. In this way they can add to the family income while still staying home and looking after their own children. The cultural background of southern women does not permit them to have single male boarders. They are, therefore, more likely to work in factories and arrange for others to look after the children. What effects do the different methods of rearing have on Trevisan and southern children?

I also suspect that women who work in factories are more likely to use tinned, frozen, or precooked foods than women who stay home and continue preparing traditional dishes. If this is so, then we could argue that in this instance a conservative attitude to male–female relations that say Southerners exhibit, may be conducive to quicker adaptation in other spheres of action such as eating habits.

Another study that would be of great interest is a comparison of the family life of a homogeneous group of

Italians in two non-agricultural centres, such as Wollongong with a population of 150,000, and Queanbeyan with 12,500.

In Wollongong a large proportion of Italian workers are employed at the B.H.P. steelworks and at Transfield, the firm engaged in such enterprises as erecting power lines. The steelworks operate twenty-four hours a day, and men work eight-hour shifts plus overtime. It is therefore difficult to have a normal church congregation or any other regular form of social life. When men are on night shift they frequently do not see their children for a number of days. Again, those who work for Transfield may be away from home for weeks, sometimes months, and the wives are left alone with their children. According to a priest, few places exhibit such social maladjustment. He contrasted Griffith and Queanbeyan with Wollongong. Most Italians who work in Canberra, mainly in the building industry, live in Queanbeyan. Trevisani who have been there speak of the "good life": regular work hours, opportunity for overtime, a relatively small community, no transport problems, and a new well-frequented club.

Studies such as these may enable us to forecast the conditions most likely to create an environment that the immigrants would view as a place in which they could not only earn well but also live well.

APPENDIX 2

Methodology

The methodological problems facing an anthropologist working in an urban industrial setting are different from those in a primitive community or a small rural area, and of necessity the techniques of study require adjustment. When the work centres on a comparative analysis of a rural and an urban environment, this in itself creates difficulties. Although there is much overlap, the material gathered is not always wholly comparable. I used two approaches, one in Sydney, another in Griffith.

In Sydney my work entailed visiting several families scattered throughout a number of suburbs. Setting up residence in one would not have helped me to observe all my respondents. Instead, I spent either a part or whole of the day for a number of weeks with each participant in the network of the eight families I studied intensively.

A number of attributes helped me to establish rapport. To speak Italian was essential, and although I make grammatical errors, I am fluent and have no accent. Because I am married and have children, we were able to discuss household chores and the problems of bringing up a family. In addition, the fact that I was neither born in Australia nor am I a Catholic meant that the people could criticize freely both the country and the church in my presence without embarrassment.

As soon as I felt that the women were at ease with me I started dropping in without prearrangement, talking to them while they sewed and cooked, and helping them with the dishes or hanging out the washing. Occasionally I changed a nappy. I found that observing them as they shopped or visited the children's school, the hospital, or the bank was an invaluable source of information. I rarely took notes in their presence but wrote an account when I came home each evening. I tried to stick as closely as possible to the actual words and sentences they used. At the same time, I filled in a comprehensive "questionnaire", I did much of this when I came home in the evening, and before completing the study on each family I made sure that all the questions had been answered.[1] I was cautious to do as little of this as possible in front of them. Although a questionnaire is a valuable guide and source of information, my days and weeks with these women taught me how unreliable it can be. Many immigrants (as also non–immigrants) purposely give incorrect information to people they do not know.

I gathered a vast amount of material inadvertently for instance by opening a refrigerator door to take out food. Problems I never suspected or would not have thought to ask about cropped up simply by going with them into shops, hospitals, or banks. On our outings I tried to remain in the background and only advised when asked.

I cannot state exactly how often I visited each household. I frequently dropped in for a cup of coffee after spending the rest of the day with someone else. It took me about a year to complete the intensive study of eight households. I saw far less of the men than of the women and children, and with them I never established the same easy rapport. They came home after six in the evening, washed, had dinner, watched television, and went to bed early. They all worked on Saturdays, many also on Sundays. On a few occasions when I visited in the evening I felt I was intruding and that the men were irritated by my presence. I therefore had to curtail these after-hour calls to a minimum. I did, however, go to church with a number of families at Christmas and Easter and attended several parties. I came to know a couple of the men reasonably well when they were home on worker's compensation.

I spent three one-month periods in Griffith during the winter, autumn, and summer, and also made a number of visits over long weekends. With the help of the local consul, a member of parliament, and a priest, I established contact quickly. Apart from two weekends, which I spent with my family in a motel, I always lived with one or other of four Trevisan families. Three of these were farmers, and the fourth a blacksmith who lived in the centre of town.

In contrast to the situation in Sydney, my rapport with the men in Griffith was just as good as with the women, probably because their work was on the farm or around the house. They came in for morning and afternoon tea as well as for lunch. Again, unlike Sydney, the agricultural cycle entailed different routines at different times of the year, and for this reason I spaced my visits to coincide with the changes in the work and social patterns.

Although I lived with four families, I visited many of their friends and was accepted as a surrogate relative. One woman referred to me as her new daughter. I joined in all the social outings such as debutante balls, parties, weddings, and christenings. I attended church each Sunday, and one Christmas went to five masses. The nature and size of the community and the good rapport I had established with the men as well as the women, made it very easy for me to take part.

In December, 1968 I visited Treviso briefly. I met close relatives of my respondents, conveyed their greetings and presented them with gifts and photographs from Sydney. One of my respondents who was visiting her family met me. She took me to her parents-in-law, with whom she was living for the duration of her stay, as well as to her own parents and siblings. Both families still lived in extended households. I called on Don Erasmo Pilla to whom I had been introduced earlier that year when he was in Australia seeing former parishioners. He arranged with a driver to take me from village to village meeting relatives of people I knew.

Although I was unable to meet anyone other than my respondents more than once, the experience of seeing the houses, households, and scattered villages afforded me additional understanding of the background from which Trevisan immigrants came.

In 1974 I again visited Treviso for a short time. I describe the meeting with one of my Sydney respondents who resettled in Treviso in "Postscript: 1974" (see pages 199–202).

NOTES

1. See appendix 5 for the outline of information sought during fieldwork. Although it is set out like a questionnaire, in fact it was used more informally than the traditional sociological questionnaire.

APPENDIX 3

Studies of Italians in Australia

Australian studies of Italian rural communities

Although studies of Italian agricultural communities in Western Australia (Gamba, 1949), Queensland (Hempel, 1959), and Victoria (Phillips, 1970), concentrated on problems different from those I looked at in Griffith, they offered some comparable and contrasting material.[1]

Western Australia

Before and after World War I the majority of Italians who settled in this state came from the south. In 1949 most were either agriculturalists or fishermen who aimed to own their farms or boats. People from the same region tended to cluster together, although, as Gamba discovered, there was no community spirit. The eldest son inherited the bulk of the property but was expected to give his brothers an interest or a portion of the estate and to look after his mother and unmarried sisters.

Queensland

The first group of Italians were recruited at the end of last century to replace South Sea island labour. By 1920 chain migrations from Piemonte and Lombardia established Italian settlements along a thin stretch of about 240 kilometres of the north coast suitable for growing sugar cane. Like the Italians in Griffith, these people consolidated their position during the depression years. Many had saved up enough to buy or clear farming land that no longer attracted Australians. Sugar demanded heavy labour but required smaller financial outlay and less mechanization than dairying, wheat growing, or mixed farming. As elsewhere, the ambition was to become a property owner. Men enlarged their holdings as much as possible—the larger they were, the more economically could they be run. Owners were, therefore, reluctant to subdivide. Although boys were encouraged to follow in their father's footsteps, many went to Brisbane, learned a trade or profession and did not return. The eldest son generally inherited the property but was expected to support his mother and unmarried sisters.

In Queensland the church was not a focal point, and no Italian institution or association was strong enough to keep the settlers together. The only substitute for the old community life was market day, when people met in the local town.

Victoria
The latest rural study of Italians is of those in the Ovens Valley, a tobacco growing area about 80 kilometres long located about 240 kilometres north-east of Melbourne. The first settlers in the 1920s established chains that brought many to the region. Sharefarming, availability of land, and the absence of restrictions on tobacco producers offered the sharers an opportunity to become farm-owners utilizing family labour intensively. About half the population came from the Veneto, the rest from Calabria.

The proximity of the Ovens Valley to Melbourne offered people the choice of local and metropolitan values. "In the local value system, inheritance of farms and family businesses was an important factor. It was expected that farmers' sons would spend all their lives on the family farm ... However, even farm owners who had bought property with this intention remained aware of the possibilities of metropolitan careers for their children. Sometimes the farm was destined to pass to one son, while others were educated for metropolitan careers."[2] Some farmers willed the property to all the sons jointly, some divided it, and some bought additional land to provide for younger sons not trained for another occupation.[3] Cases are recorded of a son and a son-in-law becoming joint heirs, a situation unthinkable in Griffith. At all times the father-son relationship was hierarchical. Thus although some fathers, to avoid probate, went through the technicalities of relinquishing legal control during their lifetime, they expected to retain the management.

In the Ovens Valley neither the Australian nor the Italian population was homogeneous; indeed, there were considerable differences in social status within and between the ethnic groups. Italians found life in the valley rather dull, and many suffered from isolation. Only about one-third of Phillips' sample frequented the one Italian club, and only 37 per cent of Italian-born informants belonged to any voluntary organization. Men used the church grounds as a social centre before and after mass on Sunday—certainly there was none of the active social life of Griffith.

Australian studies of urban Italians

As with the rural studies on Italian communities in Australia, so the urban studies do not directly pertain to problems discussed here relating to a small group of new immigrants.[4] Jones's was an area study of Italians in the Melbourne suburb of Carlton (1962), Petrolias's a general comparative discussion of Italians and Greeks in Melbourne (1959), and Borrie's about Italians in general (1954).

The Sting of Change, a recent work by Cronin (1970), is the only one whose aim in part coincided with mine. Like her, I hoped to show a process of change by explaining how the particular economic conditions, ambitions, expectations, and opportunities in Italy and in Australia affected the immigrants. She looked at Sicilians in Sicily and Sydney. Her respondents in Sydney, however, came from different parts of Sicily, some were unskilled and some professionals, their ages at emigration ranged from 13 to 56 years, and the time spent in Australia varied from 1 to 57 years. I could only compare my sample of Trevisani with her unskilled workers who had been in Australia a relatively short time.

Unlike Trevisani, most Sicilians had relatives on arrival in

Sydney. Many of the men came here before they married, but Cronin did not mention whether their savings, as among Trevisani, were crucial for the down-payment on a house. "One of the highest forms of praise, and one of the most frequent, is 'they bought a house two years after they came' ... [even Australians] marvel that immigrants can arrive with nothing tangible, not even skills or the language, and save enough money to make a large down-payment on a house, one, two, or three years after arriving."[5]

Until they paid for the house most young Sicilian women worked in factories and left their young children with Italian or Australian neighbours. Jones also mentioned that a significantly high proportion of southern Italian wives in Carlton were in the work force. He noted that more southern than northern households had unrelated boarders, but, he added, it was not statistically significant. Unfortunately Jones did not state whether single men tended to board with Northerners and married couples with Southerners.

He found that less than one-sixth of the northern wives but more than one-third of southern women were in the labour force, a fact he explained by pointing out that most northern wives married successful Italian migrants on arrival in Australia or by proxy beforehand. This contrasted with southern wives, a high proportion of whom already had children before the husband's emigration and therefore had heavier financial burdens on arrival here.[6]

This explanation may be applicable in some cases, but probably the real reason for the difference lies in the somewhat different cultural norms of north and south. While Trevisane frequently added to the family income by washing, ironing, and cooking for unmarried male boarders, it would appear that the cultural background of southern Italian women precluded this as a means to additional earnings.[7]

In two important fields, children's education and coping with the institutions of industrial society, Trevisani and Sicilians exhibited similar difficulties. Cronin commented on the frequent failure of second-generation children to advance occupationally. She attributed this to a "non-studious atmosphere" and to the fact that parents did not understand what studying entailed.[8] This problem may also occur among many second-generation Trevisani. The handicaps that some of her respondents suffered in dealing with banks, health insurance, and so on were similar to those I witnessed.[9]

Like the Trevisan respondents, few Sicilians belonged to associations or clubs, but the reasons may have differed. The group I studied were saving hard and were relatively isolated nuclear units. Sicilians on the other hand, may have had a sufficient number of relatives and friends to satisfy their need for social contact.

NOTES

1. Research by Bromley (see "The Italians of Port Pirie") in South Australia was concerned with a fishing community where the women could not help the men with their work. It is, therefore, not strictly in line with the other works.
2. D. Phillips, "Italians and Australians in the Ovens Valley Area", p. 183.
3. Ibid., p. 321.
4. The best known studies of Italian urban immigrants were all concerned with Italian communities in America and concentrated on second and subsequent generations. R. Firth's work on kinship in London discussed Italians from diverse regions and strata (see *Two Studies of Kinship in London*).
   For the American studies see I. L. Child, *Italian or American: The Second Generation in Conflict*; W. F. Whyte, *Street Corner Society*; H.J. Gans, *Urban Villagers*; and N. Glazer and D. Moynihan, *Beyond the Melting Pot*.
5. C. Cronin, *The Sting of Change: Sicilians in Sicily and Australia*, p. 163.
6. F. Jones, "The Italian Population of Carlton", pp. 308–10.
7. It is of interest to note that landladies with boarders are not included in the workforce. See my section on "The wife's work and earnings". In the section on "The new environment" I also pointed out that most Trevisan couples, immediately after marriage rented rooms from or boarded with southern families.
8. C. Cronin, *The Sting of Change*, p. 239.
9. As Cronin points out (ibid., p. 211): "A certain amount of book-keeping is necessary plus an elementary ability to write cheques and oversee financial papers ... In Australia, however, this chore becomes

much more complicated ... Even caring for the monthly child endowment cheque is rather complicated with legal papers to be filed at the beginning ... going to the local post office to get the cheque, and then cashing or depositing the money."

APPENDIX 4

Albert Jaime Grassby

To most immigrants in Australia, Al Grassby is a household name. For this reason I would like to include here a brief account of his career from about 1970, when I completed my field work, to the time of his appointment as Commissioner for Community Relations in 1975. The information for this section comes from my personal knowledge, from direct communication with Mr. Grassby, and from people who worked, or are still working closely with him.

As mentioned earlier, Grassby was born in Brisbane of Irish-Spanish background, and settled in Griffith as a young man in his twenties in 1950. In 1962 he married Ellnor Louez, a Griffith girl, also of Irish-Spanish descent, who is as flamboyant as he is, and who shares his enthusiasm for his work. His active interest in, and work with immigrants dates back to the time of his arrival in Griffith, fifteen years before he entered politics.

In 1965 he was elected to the state parliament as Labor member for the electorate of Murrumbidgee. In 1969 he switched to federal politics, and at the elections that year, defeated the sitting Country Party member for the electorate of Riverina with a swing of 16.8 per cent.[1] At the following elections in December 1972 the Labor Party gained office and Grassby became the ninth Australian minister for immigration. In this capacity he was able to initiate and guide legislation and reforms that had concerned him for a number of years.

One of the first reforms introduced at the instigation of Grassby was new selection procedures for immigrants. From 31 January 1973 onwards, all applicants were to be assessed on individual merits regardless of race or origin as had previously been the case. Subsequently, the old procedures relating to the granting of Australian citizenship were also eliminated. These had entailed a one, three, five, or fifteen year wait, depending on the race and place of birth of the applicant. Henceforth the period was to be three years irrespective of the applicant's racial or ethnic background. On 28 May 1973, legislation was announced amending the Aliens' Act of 1947–66, which had required aliens to notify the government annually of their address, occupation, and marital status. This was no longer necessary.

Grassby introduced legislation to repeal section 64 of the Migration Act of 1958–66 which discriminated against certain categories of Aboriginal Australians, requiring them to seek special government permission when wishing to leave the country. In introducing the measure in the House of Representatives on 28 February 1973, Mr. Grassby said,

> The action of the Government in making the repeal of these discriminatory provisions one of its first legislative acts is a token of our determination to banish racial discrimination within our community ... This repeal is also a recognition that such restrictive provisions on the national statute book constitute an affront to the Aboriginal people of the nation now emerging to new dignity and progress. It will also at long last enable us to ratify the International Convention on the Elimination of All Forms of Racial Discrimination".

Apart from altering or introducing new legislation, Grassby initiated services to assist newcomers. These included an adult migrant education programme offering full-time ten-week English courses during which immigrants were paid a living allowance; an emergency telephone interpreting service which began operations on 19 February 1973; migrant education centres in capital cities; and training courses for multi-lingual welfare officers. Forty-eight multi-lingual welfare officers were appointed to deal with problems encountered by new settlers. Grassby was also instrumental in persuading Cabinet to allocate $2 million to erect emergency classrooms for immigrant children. In May 1973, with the assistance of the Canberra College of Advanced Education, a new scheme was initiated to help migrant women study English. The technique used was based on a one-to-one home tutoring scheme, developed overseas but adapted to Australian requirements. Australian women who volunteered to help with this programme learned simple language techniques as well as something about the new settlers' background before visiting their homes.

During 1973 major changes were introduced affecting travellers entering Australia. The first was to abolish discrimination against Maoris. Until February of that year coloured New Zealanders needed travel documents which white New Zealanders did not. A further change was introduced in July 1973. Known as "The Easy Visa System", formalities which had previously caused long delays in the issuing of tourist visas were eliminated. These could now be arranged in Australian consular and embassy offices immediately. Abuses occurred however, which resulted in the need for modifications.

During his ministry, Grassby came under pressure from private industry to introduce into Australia the "*Gastarbeiter*" or guest-worker system that was operating in Europe. He led the opposition to this in Caucus and in the Cabinet and was widely supported in his stand to reject a system of migration which he described as "importing people like bottles and throwing them away when they are empty".

Another initiative taken during Grassby's ministry was the change in rules concerning overseas students, the majority of whom were Chinese from Malaysia or Hong Kong. Until 1973 students had to leave Australia at the end of their studies. The new rules permitted these students to remain after graduation if they found work that utilized their skills and qualifications.

Following a double dissolution of parliament, elections were held on 18 May 1974. The Labor Party retained government, but Grassby lost his seat. Later that year he was appointed special consultant to the Australian government on community relations.

In that capacity one of his main tasks was to co-operate

with the then attorney-general, Senator Lionel Murphy, in rewriting the Racial Discrimination Act which had been introduced into parliament in 1973, to enable Australia to ratify the United Nations Declaration against all forms of racial discrimination. The bill was passed and became law in June 1975.

Also in June 1975, Radio Ethnic Australia was launched. The motivation behind this, set out in Grassby's report to Prime Minister Whitlam, was based on experience with an ethnic radio programme, known as "The Continental Music Hour", which he first launched in the Murrumbidgee Irrigation Area in 1952. This programme still goes to air each week, and Grassby is a frequent contributor.

In October 1975 Grassby was appointed Australia's first Commissioner for Community Relations for a period of seven years. One of his first tasks in this capacity was to organize an education conference held in Sydney in March 1976. The object of this conference was to discuss the introduction of a second language into primary schools for the benefit of all children. This is designed, as he put it, " ... to give life and meaning to the concept and reality of a multi-cultural Australia".

The philosophy that guided Grassby during his ministry and that now guides him as commissioner could be summarized in his own words delivered in August 1973,

> Our prime task at this point in our history must be to encourage practical forms of social interaction in our community. This implies the creation of a truly just society in which all components can enjoy freedom to make their own distinctive contribution to the family of the nation. In the interests of Australians of the year 2000 we need to appreciate, embrace, and preserve all those diverse elements which find a place in the nation today.

Grassby and the May 1974 elections

Like many people prognosticating the results of the elections of May 1974, I expected the Australian Labor Party to lose some country seats, but not Grassby's Riverina.

During the days leading up to election day, Grassby had

been subjected to a barrage of abuse organized largely by groups outside the electorate who were upset by Grassby's immigration policies. The main campaign against Grassby was conducted by the Immigration Control Association (I.C.A.) whose national president is Robert Clark of Crows Nest, Sydney. The I.C.A. was supported by the White Australia League. A spate of newspaper advertisements and leaflets appeared in the electorate in the vein of "If you want an Asian (or an African) for a neighbour vote Labor".[2] Apart from accusing him of abolishing the White Australia Policy and "opening the gates" to coloured immigrants, Grassby was subjected to personal threats and abusive phone calls. Yet, in spite of all this, when talking to people in Griffith a week later, few had imagined that Grassby would lose his seat.

I flew to Griffith a week after the elections. Mrs. Grassby, who had borne the brunt of many of the abusive and threatening phone calls, was ill in hospital. Griffith, it seemed to me, was in a state of shock. Even people who admitted voting against the Labor Party said they had not expected to "topple Al". What had happened?

A number said they voted Country Party because of Labor's rural policies; they were against Labor, not against Grassby.

> The Labor Party is against the farmer. Look how they took away the superphosphate subsidy and what about the juice? All canned fruit juice had to have a percentage of real juice—this was great for us, we could sell more oranges and fruit to the canneries. But once Labor did away with that, it meant a real loss, so why should we vote Labor? But Al—that's different. We're all for Al, and we think it's a good thing he won't be Minister for Immigration any more. We want him to be in Griffith more and look after us here.

This man believed that Grassby would no longer be a minister but would still be in parliament as member for the Riverina. He was stunned when told that Grassby was now out of parliament. He was not the only one to believe that one could vote against the A.L.P. and still retain Grassby. Another fellow also told me, "We just wanted to stop him being Immigration Minister so he'd spend more time in the electorate, but we didn't think that'd finish him in parliament". Yet another said, "We just wanted to give Whitlam a kick in the pants, never Al." One person who voted for the Country Party said, "I always vote Country Party because of my family, but had I thought that Al'd lose I'd have voted for the A.L.P. If he were Country Party, he'd have a seat for life."

One Labor supporter, after talking at length about Labor's actions over the juice and superphosphate subsidy, gave the following additional explanations why people had been angry. The reasons given are indicative of the personal nature of Grassby's support in the electorate: "Not long ago, he [Grassby] attended a wedding at Narrandera and only got to the A.L.P. party in Griffith at eleven o'clock and a lot of the people were annoyed ... ; he spent too much time with the hoytepalloy when he should have been con-centrating more on the A.L.P. people who support him ... ; Veneti think he goes to too many Calabrese functions ... ; one fellow didn't vote for Al because when Al visited the hospital one day he talked to two patients in the ward, but not to him."

A family I knew well said they liked Grassby very much and were deeply sorry for him, but they felt threatened by the A.L.P. They, also, wished he belonged to the Country Party instead of being Labor. Nevertheless, they were stun-ned by the results. They knew nothing about the Country Party candidate who had won the seat. "That just shows that people voted along party lines this time, it wasn't against Al," one of the young men in that family insisted.

Most Calabresi were beside themselves with grief. A cons-tant stream of gifts of flowers, wine, cakes and fruit was ar-riving at the Grassby home. I saw one man with tears in his eyes, beating his chest and swearing at "those hypocrite bastards who didn't vote for the best friend they ever had".

Figures from the Australian Electoral Office indicated that although the actual numbers had dropped compared with the previous elections, Grassby still had a majority in the four subdivisions of Griffith, Hay, Leeton, and Narrandera. He had lost in the remaining seven subdivisions of the electorate. Malcolm Mackerras, commenting on the Riverina after the 1969 elections said, "Mr. Grassby enjoys an enormous personal vote and Riverina might best be described as safe for Al Grassby, otherwise fairly safe Country Party."[3]

In 1974, however, it would seem that Grassby's liberal immigration policies combined with Labor's rural policies, were sufficient to erode much of that personal vote, to the amazement of the electors themselves.

NOTES

1. M. Mackerras, *Australian General Elections*, p. 78.
2. For an account of the campaign against Grassby see J. Warburton, "Racism in the Riverina", *Issue* 4, no. 13 (June 1974).
3. M. Mackerras, *Australian General Elections*, p. 78.

APPENDIX 5

Outline of information sought during fieldwork

SYNOPSIS

A. Background information
B. Courtship, marriage, children
C. Work
D. Language
E. Social participation
F. Organization of familial activities
G. Children
H. Decision making
I. Division of labour: husband/wife
J. Family: ideology
K. Standard of living, income, expenditure, savings
L. Attitude to Australia

A. BACKGROUND

1. Year of birth, place?
2. Last permanent residence in Italy?
3. What age when left school, how many years' schooling?
4. History of family, genealogy. Did they own, rent, *mezzadria*, or landless?
5. Occupation of father, history of parents?
6. How many siblings, what do they do, where do they live, how much contact?
7. When did you leave Italy, arrive here?
8. In how many places have you lived?
9. What made you/your husband decide to come?
10. Who sponsored you, who paid for passage/or assisted?
11. Have you relatives in Australia, where, how many?
12. Name your husband's relatives, your relatives?

13. When did they come, what do they do?
14. Did they assist you, do you assist them?

B. COURTSHIP, MARRIAGE, CHILDREN

1. Where did you meet, who introduced you?
2. Describe your courtship?
3. Where were you married, what kind of wedding, who attended, what year?
4. Did you come to Australia together. If not, with whom did you live, for how long, when did you come here?
5. How many children, Name, sex, year of birth, would you/your husband like more?

C. WORK

1. What kind of work did you/your husband do in Italy?
2. Did you like this work, would you have preferred other work?
3. Was it acceptable for a single/married girl to work?
4. What kind of work was acceptable, what kind was not?
5. What did men think about married women working?
6. What did your father/mother think about single/married women working?
7. Have you/your husband had many different kinds of work in Australia?
8. If working, are you satisfied with your work, your pay?
9. Do you get on with your employer, what nationality is he?
10. What nationality are most of the workers there, what language do you speak there?
11. If you could, would you change your job, why?

The working wife

12. In which way do you think does a wife's working affect her relationship with her husband, with her children?
13. Do you think it is alright for a wife to work?
14. Does your husband approve?
15. Would you have worked in Italy?

16. What would people have said?
17. What do they say here?
18. Do you think that some household tasks do not get done because you work?
19. Does your husband help, would he help if you were not working?

The working husband

20. Husband's job, place of work, permanent or temporary?
21. Ideas about job compared with past and future jobs?
22. Does he have additional jobs?
23. How does he get on with his employer, does he have friends at work, how did he get the job?
24. Nationality of employer, work mates, what language does he speak at work?
25. When does he leave in the morning, come home at night?
26. How many jobs has he had in Australia, length of time at each, place, kind of work, reasons for change?

D. LANGUAGE

1. English speaking/reading standard?
2. Have you ever attended English classes, or listen to radio classes, for how long, would you like to attend classes, what stops you?

Exposure to mass communication

3. Do you/your husband read any newspapers or magazines, what sort, Italian or English, do you have any regular paper or magazine sent or delivered to your home?
4. How much time do you spend listening to radio, T.V., which stations?
5. What kind of programmes do you like best, why?
6. Are you interested in the news?

7. Would you like a programme in Italian, e.g. language classes, news etc.?
8. Do you think English classes on T.V. would be a good idea?
9. Would you like a teacher to come to your street and teach a group of you say 4 or 5 of you one evening a week, in one of the homes?
10. What would be the best way of learning English?
11. What is the biggest difficulty?
12. How well can she read/write Italian, attitude to putting pen to paper?
13. Where does information re e.g. compensation, wills, pensions, insurances etc., come from?
14. How confused is it?
15. How much information comes from reliable sources, from media, from people?

E. *SOCIAL PARTICIPATION [RELATIVES AND OTHERS]*

1. What type of contact, how often, when, where?
2. Do you help each other in crises: e.g. care of children, help with housework, borrowing, lending?
3. Who gets together for weddings, christenings, funerals, birthdays, holidays? How often do you write letters to them, telephone them?
4. Who are your *compare/comare*, how often do you see them, where, when?
5. Do you have friends here, where do they come from, are any of them Australians?
6. Where do they live?
7. Do you work with them, visit them, spend your leisure time with them?
8. Do you have anything to do with neighbours, are any of them your friends, what nationality are they?
9. How do you get on with Australian neighbours?
10. Do you go to any migrant, Australian or any other club? How often do you/your husband go, whom do you go with?

11. How often do you/your husband go to church, when did you last go, which one?
12. What do you/your husband do in your free time?
13. Have you ever had a holiday in Australia, would you like to, what would you do?
14. Do you ever go on a picnic, beach, pictures, Luna Park, etc. who with?
15. Do you think the family should spend their recreation together, do you think husband and wife should spend it separately or together?
16. How did people spend their recreation in your home?
17. In which way is it different here, which do you prefer?
18. How do you feel about using public transport?
19. Fear/lack of fear in moving around the city—spatial mobility.
20. Do you have any Australian contacts other than neighbours or work?

F. ORGANIZATION OF FAMILIAL ACTIVITIES

1. Routine: yearly, weekly, daily.
2. Give a typical week/s activities.
3. How does this kind of routine differ from what it would have been in Italy?

G. CHILDREN

1. Who helps you after you have had a baby?
2. Do you breast feed them, for how long?
3. When do you start to potty your children?
4. Do you take them to a baby health centre?
5. Who is stricter with the children you or your husband?
6. How much time do you spend with the children, what sort of things do you do with them. Do you ever help them with homework?
7. As above—for husband.
8. Do you/your husband ever punish them, for what, how?
9. Do you think Australians are too strict/lenient/just right with children?

10. For how long do you want your children to go to school?
11. What would you like them to be or to do when they leave school?
12. Do you think they are better off in Australia, have better opportunities than in Italy?
13. What school do they go to, private/public, why?
14. In which room do they do their homework?
15. Do you ever go to your children's school, talk to their teacher, join the mothers' club, attend P. & C. meetings?
16. Do you like your children to do sport, what sort, where, how often?
17. Do the children speak dialect, Italian, do they attend any Italian classes?
18. What do they speak better: dialect, Italian, English?
19. Do you ever have trouble understanding each other?
20. Do you ask your children to interpret for you sometimes, when?
21. How do you choose godparents, do you choose friends, relatives *paesani*, why? Does their wealth, status, matter?

H. DECISION MAKING

1. Since you have been in Australia, do you think there have been changes in your relationship with your husband as far as decision making is concerned? Who used to make more decisions in Italy, in which sphere of activities? Who makes decisions here, in which sphere?
2. Do you think the decision making process should be different if you worked/did not work?
3. How is it in Italy?
4. Would other people, say parents, have influenced you or your husband in Italy when making decisions?

I. DIVISION OF LABOUR: HUSBAND–WIFE

Housework

1. Which tasks do you think a husband should do, a wife should do?
2. Would you have thought differently in Italy? (Cooking, breakfast, lunch, dinner, snacks, lay table, wash up, cleaning, vacuum cleaning, shopping, laundry, ironing, cleaning shoes, locking up at night, getting up in the morning, repair things in the house, gardening, painting, getting up for the children at night, feeding them?)
3. What additional jobs does your husband do, or do you think he should do when you are sick?
4. Who goes to the bank, lawyer, real estate agent, etc.?
5. Do you have a driving licence, would you if you had a car?

J. FAMILY: IDEOLOGY

1. What are the most important differences between family life here and in Italy?
2. Are the husband and wife closer to each other in Australia/Italy, why?
3. Would you say that your family is typical of other Italian migrant families in Australia?
4. What are the most important things that keep a family united?
5. What things make family unity difficult?
6. Do you think you can overcome these difficulties, how?

K. STANDARD OF LIVING, INCOME, EXPENDITURE, SAVINGS

1. House: type of dwelling, structure, number of rooms etc.
2. How long have you been here?
3. How many other places have you lived in since you married?

4. How did you get your present dwelling?
5. How much do you spend weekly on house improvements?
6. How much did it cost, how much deposit, where did you get the deposit, if renting, how much rent do you pay?
7. How many people living here apart from nuclear family (i.e., paying or non-paying, give sex, age, nationality, relationship to you).
8. Have you a car, year, model, did you buy it new, do you use it for work, pleasure?
9. Household machinery: vacuum cleaner, refrigerator, washing machine, radio, T.V., tape recorder, fan, mixmaster, blender, coffee grinder, floor polisher, telephone, sewing machine etc.?
10. How much do you spend on hire purchase?
11. Weekly income: husband's wages, overtime, wife's earnings, other income.
12. Weekly expenditure: total household expenses: food, clothing, entertainment, fares, drinks, smokes, education, medical, remittances to Italy, helping relatives/friends, rent, hire purchase, insurance, Medical Benefits, Hospital Funds, etc.
13. Savings: How much do you save together, separately?
14. Do you have joint/separate accounts?
15. Who spends money on what? Who gives money to whom, how much?
16. Are you better or worse off than you would have been in Italy?
17. What would you do if you had more money?
18. What would you need to live comfortably?
19. What would you do if you won the Opera Lottery?
20. Attitude to debts?

L. ATTITUDE TO AUSTRALIA

1. What do you like about Australia, Australians?
2. What do you dislike about Australia, Australians?
3. What do you miss most of all in Australia?

4. Do you think that your social position in Australia is better/worse than in Italy?
5. Are you naturalized, do you intend to become naturalized?
6. How do you feel about it, how does your husband, friends, feel about it?
7. Who decided to become/not become naturalized?
8. Would you like to go back home for holidays/for good, would your husband?
9. Do you/your husband belong to a union?
10. General criticisms about institutions.
11. What do you think of other Italians in Australia?
12. Is the church important for you, in which way? What differences are there between the church at home and here? Which do you prefer?

APPENDIX 6

Griffith: additional voluntary associations

PARENTS' AND CITIZENS' ASSOCIATIONS

Beelbangera P. & C. Association
Bilbul P. & C. Association
Binya P. & C. Association
Catholic High School P. & C. Association
Egansford P. & C. Association
Griffith East P. & C. Association
Griffith Primary School Ladies Auxiliary
Hanwood P. & C. Association
High School Ladies Auxiliary
Griffith Infants' School Mothers' Club
Lake Wyangan P. & C. Association
Myall Park P. & C. Association
North Griffith P. & C. Association
Pre-school Kindergarten
St. Brendan's P. & F. Association
St. Mary's Mothers' Club
St. Patrick's P. & F. Organization
Tabitta P. & C. Association
Tharbogang P. & C. Association
Tharbogang Mothers' Club
Warrawidgee P. & C. Association
Widgelli P. & C. Association
Wumbulbal P. & C. Association
Yoogali P. & C. Association

YOUTH CLUBS

Griffith Group Council of Rural Youth Clubs
Lake Wyangan Rural Youth Club

Boy Scouts Association
Girl Guides
1st Youth Scout Group
Second Griffith Cubs and Sea Scouts

OTHER ORGANIZATIONS

Griffith Amateur Dramatic Society
Griffith Amateur Swimming & Life Saving Club
Griffith Jaycees
Griffith District Band
Girls Basketball Assocation
Marching Girls Association
Griffith & District Pony Club
M.I.A. Cat Club
Griffith Rowing Club
Griffith Sailing Club
Benerembah Pony Club

COUNTRY WOMEN'S ORGANIZATIONS

Arcoon
Benerembah
Coleambally
Griffith
Hanwood
Tabitta
Warrawidgee
Widgelli-Wumbulgal

CHURCH ORGANIZATIONS

Baptist Ladies Fellowship
C.W.S.G.
Methodist Evening Guild
Lutheran Ladies Guild
Methodist Ladies' Church Aid
Presbyterian Women's Association (day branch)
Presbyterian Women's Association (evening branch)
Protestant Friendly Society of Australasia

Salvation Army
Seventh Day Adventist Church
Church of St. Alban the Martyr
St. James
Young Anglicans

ORGANIZATIONS USING BANNA AVENUE KIOSK

Aborigine Advancement Organisation
Aid Retarded Persons, N.S.W.
Apex Club of Griffith
Ambulance Service
Association of Civilian Widows
Far West Children's Health Scheme
Griffith District Hospital Auxiliary
Griffith Jaycees
Legacy Contact Group
Lions Club of Griffith Ladies Auxiliary
Nurses Social Club
Griffith Old People's Welfare Association
Police Citizens Boys' Club
Red Cross Society
Returned Sailors, Soldiers & Airmen's Imperial League of
   Australia
Rotary Club of Griffith
Royal Blind Society of N.S.W.
Senior Citizens Club of Griffith
Save the Children Fund
Smith Family Ladies Auxiliary
Soroptimist Club of Griffith
Sub-normal Children's Welfare Association
Sunshine Club of Griffith
Sunshine Club of Yoogali
Total & Permanently Disabled Soldiers Social & Welfare
   Club
War Memorial Hostel
Women's Friendship Club
Warrawidgee Rural Youth
Hanwood Rural Youth Club

Griffith Rebekah Lodge
Griffith & District Spastic Centre Council
Children's Medical Research Foundation
Griffith Amateur Musical Revue Company
Griffith Agricultural Society Show Committee
Yenda Hospital Auxiliary

BIBLIOGRAPHY

Alberoni, F. "Aspects of Internal Migration Related to Other Types of Italian Migration". In *Readings in the Sociology of Migration*, edited by C. J. Jansen. New York: Pergamon Press, 1970.

Appleyard, R. T. "Determinants of Return Migration". *Economic Record* 38, no. 83 (1963).

Banfield, E. C. *The Moral Basis of a Backward Society*. New York: Free Press, 1965.

Bonutto, O. *A Migrant's Story*. Brisbane: H. Pole and Co., 1963.

Borrie, W. D. *Italians and Germans in Australia*. Melbourne: Cheshire, 1954.

Bosi, P. *Farewell Australia*. Sydney: Karunda, 1972.

Bott, E. *Family and Social Network*. London: Tavistock, 1957.

Bromley, J. E. "The Italians of Port Pirie". M.A. thesis. Canberra: Australian National University, 1955.

Child, I. L. *Italian or American: The Second Generation in Conflict*. New York: Russell and Russell, 1970.

Cohen, P. S. *Modern Social Theory*. London: Heinemann, 1968.

Coser, L. A. *The Function of Social Conflict*. London: Routledge and Kegan Paul, 1968.

Cronin, C. *The Sting of Change: Sicilians in Sicily and Australia*. Chicago: University of Chicago Press, 1970.

Department of National Development. *Atlas of Australian Resources: Immigration*. 2nd ed. Canberra: Australian Government Printer, 1970.

Eisenstadt, S. N. *The Absorption of Immigrants*. London: Routledge and Kegan Paul, 1954.

Enciclopedia Italiana di Scienza, Lettere, ed Arti. Roma, 1937.

Firth, R. *Two Studies of Kinship in London*. London: Athlone Press, 1956.

———. *Elements of Social Organization*. London: Watts and Co., 1961.

Fofi, G. "Immigrants to Turin". In *Readings in the Sociology of Migration*, edited by C. J. Jansen. New York: Pergamon Press, 1970.

Foster, G. M. "Interpersonal Relations in Peasant Society". *Human Organization* 19, no. 4 (1960–61).

———. "What Is a Peasant?". In *Peasant Society: A Reader*, edited by J. Potter, M. Diaz and G. Foster. Boston: Little Brown, 1967.

Friedl, E. "The Role of Kinship in the Transmission of National Culture to Rural Villages in Mainland Greece". *American Anthropologist* 61 (1959): 30–38.

————. "Lagging Emulation in Post-Peasant Society". *American Anthropologist* 66, no. 3 (June 1964).

————. *Vasilika: A Village in Modern Greece*. New York: Holt, Rinehart and Winston, 1967.

Gamba, C. "The Italian Immigration to Western Australia". M.A. thesis. Perth: University of Western Australia, 1949.

Gans, H. J. *The Urban Villagers*. New York: Free Press, 1966.

Glazer, N., and Moynihan, P. *Beyond the Melting Pot*. Cambridge, Mass.: M.I.T. Press, 1964.

Goffman, E. *The Presentation of Self in Everyday Life*. New York: Doubleday Anchor Books, 1959.

Gordon, M. M. *Assimilation in American Life*. New York: Oxford University Press, 1964.

Handlin, O. *The Uprooted*. New York: Grosset and Dunlap, 1951.

Heiss, J. "Sources of Satisfaction and Assimilation among Italian Immigrants". *Human Relations* 19, no. 2 (1966)

Hempel, J. A. "Italians in Queensland". Unpublished report. Canberra: Australian National University, 1959.

Henderson, R. F. *People in Poverty*. Melbourne: Institute of Applied Economic and Social Research, 1970.

Janowitz, M., ed. *W. I. Thomas, on Social Organization and Social Personality*. Chicago: University of Chicago Press, 1969.

Jayawardena, C. "Ideology and Conflict in Lower Class Communities". *Comparative Studies in Society and History* 10, no. 4 (July 1968).

Jones, F. L. "The Italian Population of Carlton". Ph.D. thesis. Canberra: Australian National University, 1962.

Langford-Smith, T. "Landforms, Land Settlement and Irrigation on the Murrumbidgee". Ph.D. thesis. Canberra: Australian National University, 1958.

————. *Water and Land*. Canberra: Australian National University Press, 1966.

Lewis, O. "Some of My Best Friends Are Peasants". *Human Organization* 19, no. 4 (1960–61).

Lopreato, J. "How Would You Like to Be a Peasant?" In *Peasant Society: A Reader*, edited by J. Potter, M. Diaz and G. Foster. Boston: Little Brown, 1967.

————. *Peasants No More*. San Francisco: Chandler Publishing Co., 1967.

Lutz, V. *Italy: A Study in Economic Development*. Oxford: Oxford University Press, 1962.

Macdonald, J. S. "Italy's Rural Social Structure and Emigration". *Occidente* 12 (1956).

————. "Migration from Italy to Australia". Ph.D. thesis. Canberra: Australian National University, 1958.

————. "Migration Versus Non-Migration: Regional Migration Differentials in Rural Italy". In *Proceedings of the International Population Conference, New York, 1961*. Brussels: IUSSP, 1961.

———. "Institutional Economics and Rural Development: Two Italian Cases". *Human Organization* 23 (1964).

———. "Migration from Italy to Australia: Conflict between Manifest Functions of Bureaucracy Versus Latent Functions of Informal Networks". *Journal of Social History* 3, no. 3 (Spring, 1970).

Mackerras, M. *Australian General Elections.* Sydney: Angus and Robertson, 1972.

Mammarella, G. *Italy after Fascism: 1943–65.* Notre Dame, Ind.: University of Notre Dame Press, 1966.

Manucci, C. "Emigrants in the Upper Milanese Area". In *Readings in the Sociology of Migration*, edited by C. J. Jansen. New York: Pergamon Press, 1970.

Martin, J. I. *Refugee Settlers.* Canberra: Australian National University Press, 1965.

———. "Migration and Social Pluralism". In *How Many Australians?*, edited by Australian Institute of Political Science. Sydney: Angus and Robertson, 1971.

Mayer, K. B. "International Migrations of European Workers". *New Community* 1, no. 3 (Spring, 1972).

Merton, R.K. *Social Theory and Social Structure.* New York: Free Press, 1968.

Miner, H. *St. Denis: A French Canadian Parish.* Chicago: University of Chicago Press, 1963.

Mintz, S. W., and Wolf, E. R. "An Analysis of Ritual Co-Parenthood". In *Peasant Society: A Reader*, edited by J. Potter, M. Diaz and G. Foster. Boston: Little Brown, 1967.

Nagata, J. A.; Rayfield J. R.; and Ferraris M. "English Language Classes for Immigrant Women with Pre-School Children". Research report. Toronto: York University, 1970.

Nisbet, R. A. *The Social Bond.* New York: Alfred A. Knopf, 1970.

Oxley, H. G. *Mateship in Local Organization.* St. Lucia: University of Queensland Press, 1974.

Padilla, E. *Up from Puerto Rico.* New York: Columbia University Press, 1964.

Patterson, S. *Dark Strangers.* Harmondsworth, Mddx: Penguin Books, 1965.

Pertolias, J. A. "Post-War Greek and Italian Migrants in Melbourne". Ph.D. thesis. Melbourne: University of Melbourne, 1959.

Phillips, D. "Italians and Australians in the Ovens Valley Area". Ph.D. thesis. Canberra: Australian National University, 1970.

Pitkin, D. S. "Land Tenure and Family Organization in an Italian Village". *Human Organization* 18, no. 4 (1959–60).

Price, C. A. "Italian Population of Griffith". Unpublished report. Canberra: Australian National University, 1955.

———. *Southern Europeans in Australia.* Melbourne: Oxford University Press, 1963.

———. *The Method and Statistics of Southern Europeans in Australia*. Canberra: Australian National University Press, 1963.

Provincia di Treviso. *Dati Sommari Sui Comuni Della Privincia di Treviso, Officio Studi*. Treviso, 1968.

Redfield, R. *Peasant Society and Culture*. Chicago: University of Chicago Press, 1961.

Richardson, A. "The Assimilation of British Immigrants in Australia". *Human Relations* 10 (1957).

Silverman, S. "The Life Crisis as a Clue to Social Functions". *Anthropological Quarterly* 40, no. 3 (July 1967).

———. "Agricultural Organization, Social Structure, and Values in Italy: Amoral Familism Reconsidered". *American Anthropologist* 70 (1968).

———. "Land Reform and the Creation of Cultural Traditions". Paper presented to the American Anthropologist Association, November 1969.

Smolicz, J. J., and Wiseman, R. "European Migrants and Their Children". *Quarterly Review of Australian Education*, June and September, 1971.

Tully, J. "Experiences in Integrating Italian Farmers into an Extension Programme and into the Farming Community of the M.I.A.". In *The Study of Immigrants in Australia*, edited by C.A. Price. Canberra: Australian National University Press, 1960.

Warburton, J. "Racism in the Riverina". *Issue* 4, no. 13 (June 1974).

Whyte, W.F. *A Street Corner Society*. Chicago: University of Chicago Press, 1969.

Wild, R. *Bradstow*. Sydney: Angus and Robertson, 1974.

Wolf, E. R. *Peasants*. Englewood Cliffs, N. J.: Prentice-Hall, 1966.

Wolff, K., trans. *The Sociology of Georg Simmel*. London: Free Press of Glencoe, 1964.

Zubrzycki, J. *Settlers of the Latrobe Valley*. Canberra: Australian National University Press, 1964.

INDEX